D1765043

WITHDRAWN

LIVERPOOL JOHN MOORES UNIVERSITY
Aldham Robarts L.R.C.
TEL 0151 231 3701/3634

LIVERPOOL JMU LIBRARY

3 1111 01287 8318

Palgrave Studies in European Union Politics

Edited by: **Michelle Egan**, American University, USA; **Neill Nugent**, Manchester Metropolitan University, UK; **William Paterson**, University of Birmingham, UK.

Editorial Board: Christopher Hill, Cambridge University, UK; Simon Hix, London School of Economics, UK; Mark Pollack, Temple University, USA; Kalypso Nicolaïdis, Oxford University, UK; Morten Egeberg, University of Oslo, Norway; Amy Verdun, University of Victoria, Canada; Claudio M. Radaelli, University of Exeter, UK; Frank Schimmelfennig, Swiss Federal Institute of Technology, Switzerland.

Palgrave Macmillan is delighted to announce the launch of a new book series on the European Union. Following on the sustained success of the acclaimed *European Union Series*, which essentially publishes research-based textbooks, *Palgrave Studies in European Union Politics* will publish research-driven monographs.

The remit of the series is broadly defined, both in terms of subject and academic discipline. All topics of significance concerning the nature and operation of the European Union potentially fall within the scope of the series. The series is multidisciplinary, to reflect the growing importance of the EU as a political and social phenomenon. We welcome submissions from the areas of political studies, international relations, political economy, public and social policy, and sociology.

Titles include:

Ian Bache and Andrew Jordan (*editors*)
THE EUROPEANIZATION OF BRITISH POLITICS

Derek Beach and Colette Mazzucelli (*editors*)
LEADERSHIP IN THE BIG BANGS OF EUROPEAN INTEGRATION

Morten Egebery (*editor*)
MULTILEVEL UNION ADMINISTRATION .
The Transformation of Executive Politics in Europe

Stefan Gänzle and Allen G. Sens (*editors*)
THE CHANGING POLITICS OF EUROPEAN SECURITY
Europe Alone?

Isabelle Garzon
REFORMING THE COMMON AGRICULTURAL POLICY
History of a Paradigm Change

Heather Grabbe
THE EU'S TRANSFORMATIVE POWER

Katie Verlin Laatikainen and Karen E. Smith (*editors*)
THE EUROPEAN UNION AND THE UNITED NATIONS

Esra LaGro and Knud Erik Jørgensen (*editors*)
TURKEY AND THE EUROPEAN UNION
Prospects for a Difficult Encounter

Paul G. Lewis and Zdenka Mansfeldová (*editors*)
THE EUROPEAN UNION AND PARTY POLITICS IN CENTRAL AND
EASTERN EUROPE

Hartmut Mayer and Henri Vogt (*editors*)
A RESPONSIBLE EUROPE?
Ethical Foundations of EU External Affairs

Lauren M. McLaren
IDENTITY, INTERESTS AND ATTITUDES TO EUROPEAN INTEGRATION

Christoph O. Meyer, Ingo Linsenmann and Wolfgang Wessels (*editors*)
ECONOMIC GOVERNMENT OF THE EU
A Balance Sheet of New Modes of Policy Coordination

Frank Schimmelfennig, Stefan Engert and Heiko Knobel
INTERNATIONAL SOCIALIZATION IN EUROPE
European Organizations, Political Conditionality and Democratic Change

Justus Schönlau
DRAFTING THE EU CHARTER
Rights, Legitimacy and Process

Palgrave Studies in European Union Politics
Series Standing Order ISBN 1-4039-9511-7 (hardback)
ISBN 1-4039-9512-5 (paperback)

You can receive future titles in this series as they are published by placing a standing order. Please contact your bookseller or, in case of difficulty, write to us at the address below with your name and address, the title of the series and one of the ISBNs quoted above.

Customer Services Department, Macmillan Distribution Ltd, Houndmills, Basingstoke, Hampshire RG21 6XS, England

Turkey and the European Union

Prospects for a Difficult Encounter

Edited by

Esra LaGro
Jean Monnet Professor for EU Enlargement and Governance
Istanbul Doğuş University, Turkey

and

Knud Erik Jørgensen
Jean Monnet Professor in EU Politics
University of Aarhus, Denmark

palgrave
macmillan

Editorial matter, selection, Introduction and Conclusion © Esra LaGro
and Knud Erik Jørgensen 2007
All remaining chapters © contributors 2007

All rights reserved. No reproduction, copy or transmission of this
publication may be made without written permission.

No paragraph of this publication may be reproduced, copied or transmitted
save with written permission or in accordance with the provisions of the
Copyright, Designs and Patents Act 1988, or under the terms of any licence
permitting limited copying issued by the Copyright Licensing Agency, 90
Tottenham Court Road, London W1T 4LP.

Any person who does any unauthorized act in relation to this publication
may be liable to criminal prosecution and civil claims for damages.

The authors have asserted their rights to be identified as the authors
of this work in accordance with the Copyright, Designs and
Patents Act 1988.

First published 2007 by
PALGRAVE MACMILLAN
Houndmills, Basingstoke, Hampshire RG21 6XS and
175 Fifth Avenue, New York, N.Y. 10010
Companies and representatives throughout the world

PALGRAVE MACMILLAN is the global academic imprint of the Palgrave
Macmillan division of St. Martin's Press, LLC and of Palgrave Macmillan Ltd.
Macmillan® is a registered trademark in the United States, United Kingdom
and other countries. Palgrave is a registered trademark in the European
Union and other countries.

ISBN 13: 978–0–230–01955–3
ISBN 10: 0–230–01955–2

This book is printed on paper suitable for recycling and made from fully
managed and sustained forest sources. Logging, pulping and manufacturing
processes are expected to conform to the environmental regulations of the
country of origin.

A catalogue record for this book is available from the British Library.

A catalogue record for this book available from the Library of Congress.

Printed and bound in Great Britain by
CPI Antony Rowe, Chippenham and Eastbourne

'La Vida es Sueño'

Contents

Preface

This book aims to provide a guide to the difficult encounter both Turkey and the European Union (EU) are facing. The idea of the book goes back to an international research project and three international conferences organized in Istanbul in 2003 and 2005, respectively. The EU research centre of Istanbul Doğuş University (the EUCU), directed by Esra LaGro, organized the first conference, entitled *EU Governance, Enlargement and Turkey*, in co-operation with a range of organizations within the framework of an international research project. The second international conference, *The EU for the World Leadership*, of which Esra LaGro was the main theme advisor, was organized by KalDer (the Turkish Society for Quality), representing the European Foundation for Quality Management (EFQM) in Turkey. More than four thousand people from across the world participated in the event that made an enormous contribution to the debate on the future of Europe and, significantly, the debate took place in the candidate country, Turkey. The third conference, the *International Jean Monnet Conference on Turkey's Accession Negotiations with the EU: Prospects for Political, Economic and Social Transformation* was organized in 2005 just before the start of the accession negotiations.

These events have been realized with the support of the EU Commission, Doğuş University; and with the co-operation of several institutions, including leading Turkish non-governmental organizations: the Republic of Turkey Prime Minister's General Secretariat for EU Affairs (ABGS); Turkish Society for Quality (KalDer); Turkish Industrialists' and Businessmen's Association (TUSIAD); Economic Development Foundation (IKV); Netherlands Institute for Academic Studies (NIAS); Netherlands Organization for Higher Education in Europe (NUFFIC); CIRP – International Interdisciplinary Research and Policy Platform; Economic and Foreign Policy Forum (EFPF – now known as EDAM – headed then by Dr Kemal Derviş, the current president of United Nations Development Programme (UNDP); former Vice-president of the World Bank; former Economics Minister, and later MP of the Republic of Turkey 2001–5); and with the participation of high-level experts from leading universities from all over Europe. The NGOs mentioned above deserve special thanks for the spirit of co-operation and teamwork they have shown during these processes, among which KalDer has been exceptional as its name suggests. Leading national media institutions such as TV8, CNN Turk, TRT, Milliyet, Hürriyet, Radikal and Sabah covered these events.

We would like to thank all contributors, partners and participants. Unfortunately, it is impossible to name them all. However, Esra LaGro especially wishes to thank the Rector of Doğuş University, Professor Dr A. Talha Dinibütün and the academic and administrative staff of the university for their support; as well as *H. E. the former Minister of Foreign Affairs the late and much respected Mr İsmail Cem for his invaluable contribution in 2003,* and Ambassador Murat Sungar, former Secretary General for EU Affairs of the Prime Minister's Office, who provided valuable insights concerning Turkey's accession process throughout the conference in 2005. Special thanks are also due to Ambassador Pulat Yüksel Tacar who has provided valuable intellectual insights and support at all the events mentioned above. She also wishes to thank Dr Kemal Derviş for his support and encouragement. She had the privilege of attending a number of events with him during 2004–5 in Europe and was able to witness personally the contributions of Dr Derviş to the EU process of Turkey; moreover, she has also benefited greatly from his outstanding knowledge on issues pertaining to Turkey and the EU and beyond. Finally, she would like to thank the two keynote speakers at the KalDer conference for their invaluable intellectual contribution to the debate: Lord Professor Dr William Wallace (LSE); and H. E. the former Prime Minister of New Zealand and former Head of the World Trade Organization, Mr Mike Moore.

The international high-level group of experts, opinion leaders, policy-makers, businessmen, journalists, diplomats, members of academia from around the world, and the participants of these conferences provided most valuable insights, ideas and contributions. We are grateful to all of them individually although we are unable to list their names here. The editors would like to thank the contributors to this volume for their input, and their flexibility. We would also like to thank the editors at Palgrave for their encouragement and support during the production of this book. Furthermore, we extend our thanks to Ms Ulla Veronica Willner, Mr Jesper Madsen-Østerbye and Ms Volga Çağlayangil for their valuable work during the final preparation of the manuscript. Finally, we would like to thank our families for their support during the preparation of this book, and their understanding for the time we have stolen from them.

We believe that the volume will be a very useful source of information for those who have an interest in understanding the difficult path Turkey will take towards full EU membership in the years to come. We explore the encounter in its economic, political and socio-cultural dimensions, but the process will undoubtedly require further exploration in the future.

ESRA LAGRO   KNUD ERIK JØRGENSEN

Notes on the Contributors

Kenneth Dyson is a Research Professor at Cardiff University European School, UK; author and editor of several books on Europe and the European Union. His research expertise covers the politics and policies of the European Union, comparative political economy, and German politics and policies, and his main research area in recent years has been the politics of the euro. Currently he is working on issues in European economic governance. Some of his recent publications and co-edited books are *The Road to Maastricht: Negotiating Economic and Monetary Union* (Oxford University Press, 1999); *The Politics of the Euro-Zone: Stability or Breakdown?* (Oxford University Press, 2000); *European States and the Euro: Europeanization, Variation and Convergence* (Oxford University Press, 2002); and *Germany, Europe and Politics of Constraint* (Oxford University Press, 2003); *The Politics of German Economic Reform: Global, Rhineland or Hybrid Capitalism?* (Routledge, 2005).

Senem Aydın Düzgit is a PhD candidate in Political Science at the Free University of Brussels (VUB), and an Associate Research Fellow at the Centre for European Policy Studies (CEPS) in Brussels, Belgium. Her main research interests include EU enlargement, politics of identity, and democratization in Turkey and in Europe, and she has co-authored several articles on these topics. She is a contributor to Michael Emerson (ed.), *Democratisation in the European Neighbourhood* (CEPS Publications, Brussels, 2005).

Özgür Ünal Eriş is a Lecturer in the Department of EU Studies at Istanbul Bahçeşehir University, Turkey. She lectures on EU institutions and treaties, external relations of the EU, and theories of European integration. Her current research interests are soft security threats on the European continent, the European neighbourhood policy, and the external relations of the EU. She is the author of several articles on European security, and Turkey–EU relations. She has also hosted television programme on Turkey–EU relations on TRT 2, and has been involved in several projects designed by Turkish NGOs.

Knud Erik Jørgensen is Jean Monnet Professor in the Department of Political Science at the University of Aarhus, Denmark. He is the author, editor or co-editor of ten books, and has contributed chapters to numerous edited volumes and published articles in journals such as the *Journal of European Public Policy*, *European Journal of International Relations*, *Governance*, *Journal of Common Market Studies* and *Cooperation and Conflict*. He is currently preparing a monograph on European foreign policy and a new textbook on International Relations Theory.

Erol Katırcıoğlu is Professor of Industrial Economics and Head of Economics Department at Istanbul Bilgi University, Turkey, as well as being a columnist of the Turkish daily newspaper *Radikal* since 1996. He was the economics adviser to Vice-Premier İnönü during the 49th Government, and was involved in the preparation of the *Law on the Protection of Competition* in Turkey. His research interests include cartels, small and medium-size enterprises, competition and industrial policy in Turkey, and he has authored several publications on these issues.

E. Fuat Keyman is Professor of International Relations at Koç University in Istanbul, Turkey. He is the director of the Koç University Centre for Research on Globalization and Democratic Governance (GLODEM) and a member of the co-ordination committee of the Centre for Research on Economy and Foreign Policy (EDAM). He works on democratization, globalization, international relations, civil society, Turkish politics, and Turkey–EU relations. His recent books include *Remaking Turkey: Globalization, Alternative Modernities and Democracy* (Oxford Lexington Books, 2006); *State Problems in Turkey* (Bilgi University Publications, 2006); *Citizenship in a Global World: European Questions and Turkish Experiences* (Routledge, 2005); *Changing World, Tranforming Turkey* (Bilgi University Publications, 2005); *Turkey and Radical Democracy* (Alfa, 2001); and *Globalization, State, Identity/ Difference: Towards a Critical Social Theory of International Relations* (Humanities Press, 1997).

Levent Kırval is Jean Monnet Lecturer in the Department of International Relations at Istanbul Doğuş University, Turkey. His research interests include Turkish and Comparative Politics, European integration, cultural convergence, identity and legitimacy formation in the EU, and Turkey–EU relations. He lectures on the history of European integration, and contemporary political ideologies.

Nedret Kuran-Burçoğlu is Professor of European Studies at Istanbul Yeditepe University, Turkey. She is the author and editor of several books on European culture, and Turkish identity/image in Europe. Some of her recent books are *Multiculturalism, Identity and Otherness* (ed.) (Boğaziçi University Press, 1997); *The Image of the Turk in Europe* (ed.)

(ISIS Press, 2000); *Representations of the Other/s in the Mediterranean World and Their Impact on the Region* (ed.) (ISIS Press, 2005); *Die Wandlungen des Türkenbildes in Europa vom 11. Jahrhundert bis zur heutigen Zeit. Eine kritische Perspektive* (Spur Varlag, 2005). She is also the President of CIRP-International Interdisciplinary Research and Policy Platform.

Esra LaGro is Jean Monnet Professor for EU Enlargement and Economic Governance at Istanbul Doğuş University, Turkey; head of the EUCU; member of the Department of International Relations; also a founder member of the International Masters Programme on European Studies (IMPREST). She is the CIRP Co-ordinator, and Director of CIRP European Studies Programme, as well as being a member of other international scientific organizations, and leading NGOs in Turkey. In addition to her academic work and civil society involvement, she works as an EU consultant. She is holder of several international awards for European studies, and is the author of several articles with a comparative and interdisciplinary approach on Turkey–EU economic and political relations, European politics, EU governance and policies, and EU enlargement. She is the editor of *The EU for the World Leadership: Towards New Global Governance?* (KalDer, 2004).

An Schrijvers is a PhD candidate in the Department of Political Science at Ghent University, Belgium. She is specializing in European politics and EU enlargement, and the EU accession process of Poland.

Menno Spiering is Director of the MA Programme on European Studies at Amsterdam University, the Netherlands. He is the author or editor of several books on national identity and Europe, and is executive editor of the *European Studies* journal. His recent publications include *Ideas of Europe since 1914: The Legacy of the First World War* (Palgrave, 2002); *Euroscepticism* (Rodopi, 2004).

Pulat Yüksel Tacar is a retired Ambassador, former Vice-President of UNESCO National Committee; former Turkish Ambassador to the EU; author of award-winning books on politics and governance in Turkey, as well as an expert on Turkey–EU relations He has published several articles on governance, minorities, and cultural and political issues. His books include *Cultural Rights, Implementations around the World and a Model Suggestion for Turkey* (Gündoğan, 1996); *Financing Politics* (Doruk, 1997); *Terror and Democracy* (Bilgi, 1999).

Introduction: Prospects for a Difficult Encounter

Esra LaGro and Knud Erik Jørgensen

Each successive enlargement of the European Union (EU) signifies a turning point in the history of European integration. While each enlargement accelerates debates on deepening versus widening, specific policy issues, budgetary concerns and the EU politics of conditionality, it is significant that the political context of successive enlargements is highly informative concerning the future of the EU. The 2004 enlargement, with its ten new member states, amounts to a historical dream come true – that is, the unification of Europe. The recent accession of Bulgaria and Romania added to this unification process, and will possibly be followed by one or more of the newly independent states of the former Yugoslavia. However, the ideal of a united Europe aside, the political power play and shifting policy paradigms of the EU member states seem to be moving up on the EU's political agenda.

With all this in mind, the start of accession negotiations with Turkey – an associate member of the EU since 1963 – only adds to already existing political tensions among EU member states. Debates about Turkish membership abound, but it is unclear how much of this controversy originates from the country itself, and how much stems from the EU's own domestic political problems, including the its current identity crisis. The policy paradigm shift and the new power equilibrium to be constructed between core and peripheral member states will be crucially important for the final outcome of the accession negotiations. Until this outcome has been concluded, we shall all be witnesses as the process unfolds. This book has been written in order to address the key issues of this difficult encounter, which will hold up the agenda of both the EU and Turkey for at least the next decade – not allowing for any unexpected major external events or shocks.

1

Political, economic and cultural dimensions

The process of EU enlargement and the future of EU – Turkey relations include an array of issues that can be categorized as political, cultural and economic. A brief overview of these issues will be presented below, in line with the chapter structure of the book.

The political dimension relates to the general political background of the accession negotiations, a background that will be shaped by the well-known Copenhagen criteria on the rule of law, human rights, democracy or, in general terms, good governance. While the notion of *Europeanization* sometimes creates negative connotations, the interpretation of this concept as an ongoing transformation process, both for the individual EU member states and for Turkey, provides new insights to the accession process. These aspects undoubtedly relate to the political dynamics of the EU as well as to the effects of each enlargement wave on individual EU member states. The political culture of both parties is also a significant element in this context. Turkey has undergone a set of reforms in recent years, basically since the launch of the National Programme, and has fulfilled most of the requirements that constitute the Copenhagen criteria. However, it is striking that while the speed of the democratization process is increasing in Turkey, new demands from the EU and its member states seem to be increasing exponentially – in a way that often raises questions in the mind of careful neutral observers *vis-à-vis* the EU itself. While the EU is learning-by-doing through its experiences stemming from past enlargements, it is also trying to shape its new paradigms and define its future identity. The impact of this politically agonizing process still remains to be seen, also with reference to Turkey. The start of accession negotiations in October 2005 is believed to give further momentum to the democratization and transformation of Turkey, with the risk that the process will trigger widespread Euro-scepticism in Turkish society, as recent opinion polls already indicate.

Concerning the economic dimension, the accession negotiations entail both hopes and anxieties for both sides. The Turkish people lean towards perceiving the EU as a symbol of welfare. Expectations reflect this image and are related to the knowledge deficit in Turkey concerning the EU. However, the public does not ask how this welfare level can be reached with mechanisms of a free market economy, a means that often contradicts the development objectives, the current infrastructural problems, and the crisis prone nature of the Turkish economy. Moreover, the Turkish public does not have a clear idea of the costs involved in adopting the Union's *acquis*. The EU, on the other hand, does not want to include a large, middle income developing country such as Turkey, at least not before it has digested the economic effects of the 2004 enlargement. Since the budgetary worries will be on the agenda of the EU for the foreseeable future, this is hardly a surprising position. What perhaps represents a glimmer of hope for the EU is that Turkey's young and dynamic population might prove to be important during the coming decades, not least when seen in the context of the ageing population of the EU.

The socio-cultural dimension is also important and should not be underestimated. It is also characterized by both hopes and anxieties regarding the difficult encounter. Any successful outcome of the encounter depends on the ways in which culture, religion and identity will play a part, and consequently will reflect on Turkey. This depends on a range of internal and external factors. In this context, one of the key questions is how the EU will be (re-)defining its own socio-cultural identity. Domestic politics in the EU member states is an important part of the game, and could easily influence the outcomes at the EU level in a negative way. This aspect is likely to create more problems in the future, but it could also lead to greater integration. The dynamics of Turkish identity transformation is the other unknown parameter. The adoption of the *acquis* and the full implementation of the Copenhagen criteria will further generate a massive modernization process, comparable to Kemal Atatürk's revolution during the 1920s. As any such large-scale process produces challenges along the socio-cultural dimension, there are problems ahead.

EU–Turkey relations 1959–2007: a brief overview

Turkey's EU adventure has always been complicated. Given this fact, the aim of this section is to provide an overview of the process that began as early as 1959, when Turkey applied for the first time to the European Economic Community (EEC) for an association agreement, shortly after Greece's application. The rationale of this application was twofold: both political and economic. The political rationale resulted from one of the main priorities of Turkish foreign policy at the time: to be a member of all Western institutions (such as the membership of NATO and the Council of Europe), while the economic rationale was to be part of an economic integration scheme in the making, which might turn out to be important for Turkey's international economic relations, depending, obviously, on the future success of the EEC.

Turkey submitted its application to the EEC in July 1959 and received a positive response in September of that year. This short response period, taking into account the summer break in between, indicates that the Turkish application was favoured by the EEC. The applications of both Turkey and Greece seem to have generated a kind of self-assurance and were a source of pride in the EEC, in the sense that other countries perceived the endeavour of the EEC member states as positive and potentially successful.[1] A closer look at the Ankara and Athens association agreements demonstrates that the EEC initially treated both countries equally. Further evidence is provided by the fact that the agreements were almost identical in content and were signed in the same year. On the other hand, the implementation of the agreements has been characterized by significant differences.

The negotiations of the Ankara (association) agreement took three years and nine months. The two delegations met ten times and spent seventy-seven days in negotiation before the agreement was eventually signed on 12 September 1963.[2] It is important to mention the content of the Ankara agreement and its legal status in the present context, not least in order to provide food for thought concerning the current state of affairs. The Ankara agreement is both a European Community and an international legal document, since it was also signed by the six individual member states. It based the association partnership on the principle of equality. The agreement foresaw economic integration, the free movement of workers, and the strengthening of social ties between the parties. Its aim was full Turkish membership eventually, and had thus a political content as much as an economic one. Some six years after the Ankara agreement came into force, Turkey also signed an Additional Protocol, legally an integral part of the Ankara agreement, containing the conditions of transition periods and methodology of the provisions 10–21 of the Ankara agreement. The foundations of the customs union – envisaged to be established between Turkey and the EEC, and which eventually came into force from January 1996 – can be found in the first part of the Additional Protocol, specifically in articles 7–21.

About the time when the Additional Protocol was signed, Turkey was for the first time criticized concerning human rights issues. For Turkey, 1975 was generally a difficult year, as a series of assassinations of Turkish diplomats by Armenian terrorist groups was carried out, and continued extensively until the Orly airport incident.[3] During the same period, Turkey's neighbour Greece applied for full membership in 1976 and became a full member in 1981. Turkey, on the other hand, was preoccupied with terrorist attacks and economic difficulties. In 1977, for the first time, the International Monetary Fund (IMF) was involved in solving the economic difficulties, and a standby agreement was concluded the following year. Turkey's economic difficulties continued, and a radical economic programme – in line with the neo-liberal economic trend of the time – was announced on 24 January 1980, thus opening the Turkish economy further to the world economy. However, the subsequent improvements on the economic front were overshadowed by dramatic developments on the Turkish domestic political scene. A military government replaced civil governance for a few years, but following peaceful general elections the military eventually handed power to a civilian government. During this period, the EC and other international institutions criticized Turkey extensively for its human rights record.

If the Ankara agreement's clause on the free movement of workers had been implemented, 1986 could have been an important year for both the EC and Turkey,[4] but it was not. This prompted the Turkish government to apply formally for full membership in 1987. The application was rejected two years later, and Turkey was instead offered the option of a customs union. Because such an option was already included in the Ankara agreement, the offer was not big news for Turkey. Subsequently, the Maastricht Treaty, establishing the European Union, was signed in 1991 and the post-Cold War developments took pace. Two important issues related to Turkey and the EU played a role during the following years. First, a technical co-operation agreement was signed between the two parties towards establishing a customs union. Furthermore, the EU decided at its Lisbon meeting to expand relations with Turkey. Finally, the Copenhagen criteria era began and provided future accession processes with a new key.

In 1995, both parties approved the customs union, which came into force in January 1996.[5] During the same month, the Kardak crisis between Turkey and Greece occurred, and the already very modest financial assistance resulting from the customs union agreement was blocked by Greece. Subsequently, Turkey–EU political relations began to fade, reaching their nadir in 1997, a completely disappointing year for Turkey. First, Christian Democrat party leaders declared that Europe was essentially a Christian club, a 'civilizational project' and 'there was no place for a country like Turkey' in the EU.[6] Ever since then, this discourse has been among the main debates in some of the EU member states. Islam has consistently been one of the key arguments against Turkey's full membership. However, Turkey is a secular state, as emphasized in its constitution, where the majority of the population has Islam as their faith. Hence, it is not a religion-based state. This important fact seems constantly to be overlooked in debates on Turkish membership. Furthermore, the European Commission report, *Agenda 2000* – issued in July 1997 – declared that Turkey was far from being a candidate state, but it recommended keeping the country anchored to the EU.[7] Finally, the European Council meeting in December 1997 decided not to include Turkey as a candidate country. This was unacceptable to Turkey, and the government decided to freeze political dialogue with the EU – a policy that was upheld decisively until 1999, when candidacy status was affirmed. In the meantime, the European Commission prepared a 'European Strategy for Turkey'. This was seen as a positive move, but insufficient to provide a platform for improving relations.[8] At the Helsinki Summit in December 1999, the candidacy of Turkey was finally accepted. This was welcomed by Turkey, but with certain reservations.

Subsequently, the accession process followed standard operating procedures, and an Accession Partnership Strategy was provided for Turkey. This was, in turn, transformed into a National Programme by the government and later approved by the Turkish Parliament. Since 1997, Turkey's progress has been monitored and the European Commission has prepared annual reports. However, the discussions concerning the starting date of accession negotiations have been somewhat paradoxical. First, Turkey was given a date in 2002, not for opening negotiations but for talks on setting the date for the negotiations. Then, in 2004, with explicit preconditions, Turkey was given a possible date for negotiations to begin. Finally, the negotiation process started on 3 October 2005, with the initial screening of the EU *acquis*. In June 2006, accession negotiations began; the Science and Research chapter was opened and provisionally closed. This has been followed by the EU Commission *Regular Report* on Turkey's progress and a recommendation in November 2006 to suspend negotiations partially due to the Cyprus issue. In December 2006, the EU Council of Ministers suspended the negotiation of eight out of thirty-five chapters, simultaneously discussing the future enlargement strategy of the EU and its integration capacity. At the time of writing, the negotiation process continues.

Between 2003 and 2006, a range of debates about Turkey's relations with the EU was launched.[9] These debates cover a wide spectrum, from political and economic to socio-cultural concerns, especially on the part of the individual EU member states. Reflections on these discussions and the fate of the relationship constitute the essence of this book, aiming to provide readers with a comprehensive overview. It is clear to most people that the debates are far from over: on the contrary, they are about to start.

Whither Turkey's accession?

Whether Turkey can accede to the EU or not is obviously a difficult issue. Yet, this very question is the main question of this book. Therefore, several chapters have been commissioned in order to scrutinize the political, economic and cultural aspects of Turkey's accession to the EU.

The first four chapters of the book address significant political issues relevant to Turkey's accession process. Chapter 1 provides an analysis of the politics of the accession negotiations both in general and with specific reference to Turkey. The content of this chapter is very much related to the highly political nature of the negotiations. The conditions pertaining to the question of Cyprus and other issues indicate this clearly. This chapter also serves as a background of Chapter 2, which addresses the significant issues to be tackled during the accession negotiations by referring to past experiences in this context, especially the Polish experience. In Chapter 3, the Europeanization of Turkey is assessed and specific issues are raised concerning the pros and cons of the Turkish accession process. Chapter 4 addresses an important issue area – namely, human rights – and the democratization process in Turkey, which also constitutes one of the main pillars of the Copenhagen criteria and the EU's politics of conditionality.

Chapters 5 and 6 explore the political choices and policy priorities Turkey has to make *vis-à-vis* the economic dimension of the accession process. In this context, the authors discuss the possibility of the Lisbon criteria becoming a future part of the EU's politics of conditionality; the pros and cons of economic governance; the costs of compliance, and the issue of catching up with the EU while simultaneously responding to the globalization process. The reflections in this part of the book emphasize the importance of a sound industrial policy together with increased societal participation and democracy. Hence, it should be a political priority in line with the needs of Turkey, and the negotiation process as well as aiming at sustaining stability, competitiveness and legitimacy in the country.[10]

The next group of chapters concerns the socio-cultural issues inherent in the accession process. In this context, Chapter 7 addresses the socio-cultural dimension of the accession negotiations with specific reference to the governance of multiculturalism and the policy priorities to be decided in this context. The chapter also addresses the differences and similarities in the political culture of specific EU member states and Turkey concerning policy priorities. Chapter 8 emphasizes the importance of national identity, and the image of the Turks as Europe's 'other'. Consequently, the chapter tries to answer why Turks historically have been Europe's 'other' and to what extent this can be transcended. Chapter 9 addresses the issue of Euro-scepticism – that is, one of the crucial features of the accession process. The discontent of the citizens of Europe regarding the EU manifests itself clearly in public surveys as well as in the French and Dutch referenda on the Constitutional Treaty, and in the debate concerning the future of Europe. The issue is bound to be used effectively in national politics. Thus the chapter is an important contribution to ongoing debates on national and European identity. Chapter 10 explores the identity issue with reference to political culture. Finally, Chapter 11 is a discussion of the compatibility of the EU's Neighbourhood Policy and contemporary Turkish foreign policy. The chapter also addresses the issue of a so-called privileged partnership – that is, the scenario in which Turkey is offered a substitute for full membership.

It will be obvious after reading the diverse accounts in this volume, that the prospect of full Turkish membership of the EU is highly controversial. We believe that the book provides a comprehensive yet detailed assessment of this difficult encounter between Turkey and the EU. It is designed to help readers make up their own minds concerning Turkey's accession process. However, it is imperative to note that the questions concerning the prospect of Turkish full membership are more or less the same, but the answers are changing and evolving in line with the changing developments in both EU member states, in the EU as such, and in Turkey. These changing answers constitute the focus of this book, with a view to providing food for thought for readers.

Notes

1. For a detailed account, see Saraçoğlu (1992).
2. The original text of the agreement is in French: *Agreement Establishing an Association between the European Economic Community and Turkey (EEC–Turkey Association Agreement)* (1963) Official Journal No. 217 of 29.12.1964). For further information on the legal dimensions of Turkey–EU relations, see the website of the Republic of Turkey Prime Minister's Secretariat General for EU Affairs, where it is also possible to access records of all the decisions of the Association Council: http://www.abgs.gov.tr/en/. See also official web site of the European Union http://ec.europa.eu/enlargement/turkey/key_documents_en.htm.

3. 'As a result of the bombing of a Turkish airline counter at Orly Airport in Paris in 1983, eight were killed and 55 wounded among which there were also French citizens', *New York Times*, 9 October 1983.

4. Article 12 of the Ankara Agreement, and the Additional Protocol Section II Articles 36–40 can be further consulted concerning references to the free movement of workers. In this context, Article 36 of the Additional Protocol is significant, since it also defines the time envisaged.

5. *Decision of the EC–Turkey Association Council on Implementing the Final Phase of the Customs Union*, No. 1/95, 22.12.1995 (96/142/EC).

6. On this debate, see newspaper articles by the former German Chancellor, Helmut Kohl (*Guardian*, 7 March 1997), and by the former French President, Valéry Giscard d'Estaing (*Le Monde*, 8 November 2002). See also *Reuters*, 4 March 1997; *Financial Times*, 5 March 1997.

7. EU Commission (2000) *Agenda 2000 – Vol. I: For a stronger and wider Union; Vol. II: The challenge of enlargement*, COM/97/2000 final, Vol.I/Vol.II.

8. *European Strategy for Turkey: Communication from the Commission to the Council*, COM (98) 124 final, 04.03.1998.

9. There is an enormous literature on various aspects of the Turkey–EU debate, especially covering the years 2003–5. Obviously, it is both impossible and pointless to list them all. However, for a balanced overview of the debates concerning Turkey and EU relations, readers are advised to consult the following publications: Barysch, 2005; Barysch *et al.*, 2005; Derviş *et al.*, 2005; EU Commission, 2004; Everts, 2004; Grabbe, 2004; Hubel, 2004; Hughes, 2004; Independent Commission on Turkey, 2004; Kramer, 2004; LaGro, 2004; Lejour *et al.*, 2004; Maes, 2004; Tocci and Evin, 2004. See also Centre for European Policy Studies (CEPS) papers published online in 2005, and similar Centre for European Reform (CER) publications on Turkey.

10. During the screening process of the Enterprise and Industrial Policy Chapter on 4–5 May 2006, Turkey was asked whether industrial policy is a political priority for Turkey. The answer was affirmative (see screening documents accessible through http://www.abgs.gov.tr/indexen.html)

References

Barysch, K. (2005) *The Economics of Turkish Accession*, London: Centre for European Reform.

Barysch, K., Everts, S. and Grabbe, H. (2005) *Why Europe Should Embrace Turkey*, London: Centre for European Reform.

Derviş, K., Emerson, M., Gros, D. and Ülgen, S. (2005) *The European Transformation of Modern Turkey*, Brussels: CEPS; and Istanbul: Economics and Foreign Policy Forum.

EU Commission (2006) *Turkey 2006 Progress Report*, [COM (2006) 649 final] SEC (2006) 1390 Brussels, 8.11.2006.

EU Commission (2004) *Issues Arising from Turkey's Membership Perspective*, Commission Staff Document, SEC (2004) 1202, Brussels, 06.10.2004.

EU Commission (2000) *Agenda 2000 – Vol. I: For a stronger and wider Union; Vol. II: The challenge of enlargement* COM/97/2000 final, Vol. I/Vol. II.

EU Commission (1998) *European Strategy for Turkey: Communication from the Commission to the Council*, COM (98) 124 final, 04.03.1998.

Everts, S. (2004) *An Asset but not a Model: Turkey, the EU and the Wider Middle East*, London: Centre for European Reform.

Grabbe, H. (2004) *When Negotiations Begin: the Next Phase in EU-Turkey relations*, London: Centre for European Reform.

Hubel, H. (2004) 'The EU's Three-level Games in Dealing with Neighbours', *European Foreign Affairs Review*, vol. 9, pp. 347–62.

Hughes, K (2004) *The Political Dynamics of Turkish Accession to the EU: A European Success Story or the EU's Most Contested Enlargement?*, Stockholm: Swedish Institute for European Policy Studies, December.

Independent Commission on Turkey (2004) *Turkey in Europe: More Than a Promise?*, Report of the Independent Commission on Turkey, Brussels.

Kramer, H. (2004) 'The European Commission's Report on Turkey: An Intelligent Guide', *SWP Comments 33*, Berlin: German Institute for International and Security Affairs.

LaGro, E. (ed.) (2004) *The EU for the World Leadership: Towards New Global Governance?* Istanbul: Turkish Society for Quality Publication Series.

Lejour, A. M., de Mooij, R. A. and Capel, C. H. (2004) *Assessing the Economic Implications of Turkish Accession to the EU*, The Hague: Netherlands Bureau for Economic Policy Analysis (CBP), Document No. 56.

Maes, E. (ed.) (2004) *Turkey and the EU: Looking Beyond Prejudice*, Proceedings of the International Symposium organized by Maastricht School of Management, 4–5 April, Maastricht.

Saraçoğlu, T. (1992) *Türkiye Avrupa Ekonomik Topluluğu: Anlaşmalar*, Istanbul: Akbank Ekonomi Yayınları.

Tocci, N. and Evin, A. (eds) (2004) *Towards Accession Negotiations: Turkey's Domestic and Foreign Policy Challenges Ahead*, Florence: European University Institute Robert Schuman Centre for Advanced Studies.

1
The Politics of Accession Negotiations

Knud Erik Jørgensen

The process of EU enlargement has never been a straightforward affair. Whereas every single instance of EU enlargement has followed a path of application, accession negotiations, ratification and membership, some applications have been rejected without much ado (Morocco) and others have been rejected twice, as in the case of the United Kingdom. Some accession negotiations have been concluded successfully, only to be rejected during the process of ratification (Norway). One partial breakaway has also occurred – Greenland leaving the EC (but not Denmark) in 1986. Sometimes political reasoning has trumped economic logic – for example in the cases of Greece, Spain, Portugal and, more recently, Central and East European applicants. No matter which sequence applies, analysts widely agree that enlargement processes are made up of politics and law, administrative systems, socio-economic interests, grand bargains, phases of adjustment and EU self-reform. By contrast, cultural factors seem not to have played a significant role in any previous accession. In debates on relations between the EU and Turkey generally, and the 1987 Turkish application for EU membership specifically, cultural factors figure prominently among master variables, sometimes almost by default, constituting the seemingly most relevant or powerful explanatory factor. Thus, on the one hand, we have more than a dozen previous accessions that were 'culture-free', but on the other, in the case of Turkey's potential accession, the 'cultural factor' has been introduced as a key nodal point in public and political discourse. This is truly puzzling. Are we perhaps witnessing an example of 'culturalizing' affairs that are anything but cultural?

Heinz Kramer emphasizes that the issue of accession 'is highly complex, multi-faceted and not easy to handle' (Kramer, 2004, p. 1). In the following, an attempt will be made in handling the issue analytically by means of two distinctions and a delimitation. Against this background, the prime aim of this chapter is to analyse the *politics* of accession negotiations, but throughout the chapter the distinction between politics and culture will play an important structural role. Furthermore, it is useful to make a distinction between the politics of accession negotiation in a narrow, and a wider sense. The first sphere comprises accession negotiations in a narrow sense – that is, the actors directly involved, the procedures for their interaction and the institutional framework providing an environment for their negotiations. The second sphere focuses on accession negotiations in a broader sense – that is, the sphere includes political and economic actors in society who have direct interests in the outcome of negotiations. In a certain sense they constitute the political *hinterland* of negotiators. The third category focuses on public debates on Turkish membership of the EU, public opinion, general images and widespread conceptions of Europe and Turkey. Ever since the 2002 Copenhagen summit reconfirmed the accession perspective, this third sphere has been heavily politicized. Referenda have been promised in Austria and France, and debates on the Constitutional Treaty have been mixed with debates on Turkish membership. The relationship between these three spheres determines the politics of accession negotiations.

Finally, regarding the politics of accession negotiations, a delimitation will be made so that the period in focus will last from the opening of negotiations (3 October 2005) until a treaty of accession has been signed. Obviously, it is not possible to analyse future events and developments but the likely framework for political action can be outlined. Hence, I will not include the politics of the follow-on ratification process, a phase that will be influenced by the outcome of the accession but is likely also to display its own specific political dynamics. In this fashion, the outcome of the accession negotiations will not only cast a shadow into the future but the negotiations will also be conducted in the shadow of the future.

From a long-term perspective, negotiations will be among the key factors determining economic, political and legal developments in Turkey – and in the EU – during the next twenty-five years. Thus, some observers expect negotiations to last eight to ten years, to be followed by a long transition period of ten to twenty years. Such a scenario is not unlikely, in part because long transitions are known from previous accessions. In short, to the degree to which social engineering is possible, the first three decades of the twenty-first century are already on the drawing board as part of the pre-accession strategy. During this time span, not only Turkey but also the EU is likely to change significantly, in part as a consequence of the Turkish accession perspective.

The politics of accession negotiations: take one

Every single previous enlargement of the European Union (EU) has prompted debates on issues such as applicants' qualifications, the need for EU self-reform, the impact of specific policies such as the common agricultural policy or regional policy, and the appropriate or prudent balance between widening and deepening. These issues have been described in a rich literature on EU enlargement (Schimmelfennig and Sedelmeier, 2005). However, it is also worthwhile noting that every enlargement has been accompanied by a fairly brief but distinct and seemingly powerful emergence of the so-called *acquis communautaire* (Jørgensen, forthcoming 2008). Turkey's application is no exception. A careful reading of official documents related to Turkey's accession reveals no predominant cultural content, and no cultural encounter between Turkey and the European Union.[1] Instead, issues being addressed include such things as the *acquis communautaire* and the Copenhagen political criteria. According to the former European Commissioner, Günter Verheugen, speaking at Boğaziçi University in 2000, the accession process includes three dimensions: political, economic and legal. As mentioned earlier, many of the documents related to the pre-accession strategy refer to the *acquis*. When browsing the 523-page *Turkish National Programme for the Adoption of the Acquis*, we learn that it is divided into three main sections: criteria (subdivided into political and economic) and capacities (subdivided into administrative and 'undertaking membership obligations') and, third, 'global financial assessment of the reforms'. Among issues such as the death penalty, cosmetics, toys, plant health, statistics, air quality and many, many more issues, we find, on pages 389–92, 'culture and audio-visual policy'. In other words, whereas the list of Turkish laws and regulations that need to be changed in order to comply with the *acquis* is very long, the list of cultural aspects hardly exists.

Second, from a certain perspective it makes no sense to talk about the politics of accession negotiations. First, because negotiations are highly technical, and truly political matters do not find their way on to the agenda of the talks. Rather, talks will focus on, for example, the future distribution of milk quotas and standards related to radio frequencies or trucks. Furthermore, because it is not negotiations among equals, characterized by give and take, and aimed at reaching some consensus. On the contrary, there is a highly asymmetrical relationship between a 'wannabe' or 'demandeur' and an exclusive club having strict rules for membership. It is therefore easy to predict that the possibility of negotiation will be very limited. According to recent assessments, some 95 per cent of the issues on the agenda are beyond the scope of genuine negotiations (Grabbe, 2004, p. 2). Also, Kramer is explicit on this point:

> the Union and its member states are faced with the difficult task of bringing home to Turkey's politicians, media, and public the very unpleasant reality that accession negotiations are not a level playing field. Accession to the EU does not mean the negotiated merger of the Union with the respective candidate, but a process of mostly one-sided adaptation to the EU by a state accepting the EU's demands for accession. (Kramer, 2004, p. 7)

As it will be seen in the next section, this point can be overstated with a view to playing down the processes of mutual adjustment. But even mutual adjustment is not necessarily a *negotiated* mutual adjustment. In general, it follows from this proposition that the politics of accession negotiations consists in determining where and when there is room for manoeuvre – that is, within which chapters the temporary measures should be aimed at, when, and for how long in force? But then again, it is the EU – the presidency in close collaboration with the Commission – determining when to open and when to (provisionally) close chapters for negotiations. Thus it is worthwhile to keep an eye on the planned sequence of future presidencies (see Figure 1.1). In brief,

Germany, 2007–1
Portugal, 2007–2
Slovenia 2008–1

France, 2008–2
Czech Republic, 2009–1
Sweden, 2009–2

Spain, 2010–1
Belgium, 2010–2
Hungary, 2011–1

Poland, 2011–2
Denmark, 2012–1
Cyprus, 2012–2

Figure 1.1   Rotating presidencies 2007–12 (as of 2006)[2]

the kind of politics at play are to a large extent the politics of tactical manoeuvre. Since room for manoeuvre is so limited, the term 'accession negotiations' is a rather unhelpful euphemism that creates an image of real negotiations and is subsequently a prime source of predictable future frustration.

If institutionalist approaches to the study of politics have any merit, then the politics of the framework for negotiations should have our attention; – that is, we should explore the institutional set up for negotiations – institutions (in a broad sense), the machinery and the road map, including inbuilt roadblocks that can be activated. Unlike the fifth enlargement, the EU need not contemplate whether negotiations should be concluded by means of a regatta approach or by some other common approach. On the contrary, a country-by-country approach has been adopted and no common entry time has been suggested. Negotiations with other candidate countries (Croatia) or potential candidate countries (the Ukraine, Bosnia-Herzegovina, Montenegro, Albania, Serbia, Macedonia) seem not to have had an impact on the conduct of negotiations with Turkey.[3] As in the case of previous accession rounds, a pre-accession strategy has been in place for some time, and has been instrumental in shaping expectations among those closely involved. In this fashion, the pre-accession strategy will structure the accession negotiations, in part by introducing the thirty-five chapters of the *acquis* (mirrored in the *Turkish National Programme for the Adoption of the Acquis*). In the Commission's recommendation to open negotiations, a three-pillar approach has been suggested. The first pillar focuses on the Copenhagen political criteria, an accession partnership framework and an annual Commission review of implementation. The second pillar concerns the accession negotiations as such, conducted within an intergovernmental conference. So-called benchmarks will be specified by the Council – that is, preconditions for closing individual chapters of the *acquis*. The Commission has attempted to shape expectations by pointing to a need for special arrangements concerning the CAP, structural policies, and the free movement of workers. The Commission also points out that the EU's budget for 2014–21 needs to be in place before negotiations can be concluded. In this context, it is useful to note that the budget covering 2007–13 was concluded in December 2005, a year before it was applicable. The third pillar focuses on inter-society dialogues on issues such as culture, religion, migration, minorities and terrorism. According to the EU Presidency Conclusions, the European Council at its meeting in December 2004 'invited the Commission to present to the Council a proposal for a framework for negotiations with Turkey, on the basis set out in paragraph 23. It requested the Council to agree on that framework with a view to opening negotiations on 3 October 2005' (Presidency Conclusions, Brussels, 16–17 December 2004).[4]

Two kinds of actors will be involved in the intergovernmental conference: Turkey's chief negotiator – currently Mr Ali Babacan – and his experts, as well as the EU permanent representatives representing Council ministers. In addition, the European Commission (DG Enlargement) is closely involved and the European Parliament is also involved. The General Secretariat of the Council provides a secretariat for the accession intergovernmental conference. No matter how precise the framework for negotiations is, the first phase of negotiations is the screening of existing Turkish legislation, and that has already been completed.

Finally, the politics of accession negotiations will be determined by attitudes on both sides. Relatively recently, the EU has concluded negotiations with ten states. This fifth enlargement was in terms of population (some 60 million combined) of a size that is fairly similar to Turkey. However, it will not necessarily be easier to negotiate with negotiators representing a single state. Furthermore, while Central and East European states have been reinvented after the Cold War, Turkish state institutions are well established and relatively efficient. Such well-established administrative cultures may induce Turkish negotiators to believe that they are in a stronger position than in fact they are. It may also take a longer time for the adaptation of the *acquis* to 'sink through' the institutions.

Box 1.1   An illustrative example of non-adoption

Concerning the chapter of the acquis on fisheries, the Commission 2003 Report points out that: 'No progress has been made with regard to resource management, inspection and control, structural actions, market policy, state aids and international fisheries agreements.' Is the situation described more positively in the subsequent report one year eater? Not really. In the 2004 report, the Commission points out that: 'Since the last Regular report, Turkey has made no substantial progress concerning the alignment of its regulation with the *acquis* ... No progress can be reported with regard to resource and fleet management, inspection and control, structural actions and state aid' (EU Commission, 2004, p. 99).

The relatively slow (voluntary) adoption of the *acquis* suggests that negotiators believe that most issues are up for discussion, applicable for special arrangements, or that the EU is not serious in demanding compliance with the *acquis*.[5] During the first phase of negotiations, the European Commission has screened Turkey's adoption of the *acquis*, going through the 80,000–95,000 pages, and provision after provision. The present outcome of the screening indicates a considerable gap between the EU's *acquis* and Turkey's present legislation. The size of the gap is a helpful measuring rod for assessing how long it will take to conclude all thirty-five chapters. On the other hand, achievements so far have been impressive in terms of Turkish domestic reforms. Indeed, the pace and scope of these reforms have caused the accession of Turkey to rise the top of the European agenda. Only a few years ago, not many observers believed such developments would be possible.

In summary, it seems that contemporary relations between Turkey and the EU are anything else but 'cultural'. Not much in the accession negotiations invite the exploration of cultural issues. Of course, it is common knowledge that Turkey and the EU have previously engaged in cultural encounters continuing the old, seemingly endless, story about Turkey 'and' or 'in' Europe. Politicians, diplomats and media people on both sides have employed representations of the other that clearly define the relationship foremost as 'cultural'. Some politicians have been inclined to reject Turkey's application with reference to Article 237 of the Treaty of Rome – that is, that any 'European state' may submit a request to accede. From their perspective, the boundaries of Europe should be drawn at the Bosphorus. The European Council effectively rejected such an option in 1999, stating in the conclusions of the Helsinki Summit that 'Turkey is a candidate state destined to join the Union on the basis of the same criteria as applied to the other candidate states' (Presidency Conclusions, December 1999). Seemingly, relations between the EU and Turkey have been free from the burden of culture since 1999. If issues at stake in the context of Turkish membership of the EU are political, economic or legal, then why employ the entire apparatus of a cultural explanation? What is the value of bringing culture back in?

One possible answer is that cultural aspects may be important in a different sense, not least if we focus on phenomena such as administrative cultures, cultures of national security (Katzenstein, 1996) or political culture (see Chapter 11 in this volume). The accession process is likely to have an impact on all three spheres of culture. Indeed, the entire idea of fulfilling the Copenhagen political criteria and adopting the *acquis* is to *change* administrative cultures in Turkey. Furthermore, part of the essence of the common foreign and security policy (CFSP) and European Security and Defence Policy (ESDP) is to leave certain traditional conceptions of national security behind. Finally, a key variable is the degree to which Turkish negotiators have become familiar with the specific political culture of EU institutions and EU member states.

The politics of accession negotiations: take two

The handling of this sphere of second-tier negotiations is crucially important for a successful outcome. According to the Czech Republic's former chief EU negotiator, Pavel Telicka, 'Accession negotiations are 80 per cent in your own country, 15 per cent in the EU member-states and only 5 per cent in Brussels' (Grabbe, 2004, p. 5). This Czech experience is far from unique and is in fact the rule rather than the exception. In order to describe the politics of accession negotiations in this second, broader meaning, five illustrative aspects have been selected.

The politics of two-level games

Most chapters of the *acquis* will have a direct impact on the interests of numerous NGOs, interest groups and individual companies. Turkish negotiators will therefore face both diplomatic challenges and domestic actors, thus being involved in a classic two-level game (Putnam, 1988; see also Evans *et al.*, 1993).[6] In other words, while the chapters and the contents of the *acquis* are fairly well-known, it is less often taken into consideration that behind most chapters we find a complex setting of policy communities – that is, policy networks of interest groups, NGOs, businesses, politicians and so on (see Peterson, 2004). These policy networks and collective actors have strong vested interests in the standards, rules and norms of given chapters. Negotiators will know about these interests – or will be informed informally about them – and hence will not be a free agent in a closed-circuit system of accession negotiations. This observation is valid for both Turkish and EU negotiators. Negotiators on both sides will therefore have to be very patient, capable of listening but also most skilful in explaining – presenting reasons for action, and justifying or legitimizing positions and decisions taken. In the future, vested interests will be challenged and well-established channels of influence will be redefined. The management of expectations is a crucially important aspect of the accession process, in part because the process is not bound to produce winners only.

The politics of temporary measures

The treaty of accession with country X can serve as an illustrative example of transition periods, derogations and so on. It should be noted that Turkey is not alone in wishing for transition periods. It also applies to the EU. Akçakoca, *et al.* (2004) identify a number of sectors in which Turkish players are not fully competitive – for example, 'livestock, dairy and cereals' as well as 'banking and insurance'. Some chapters include provisions that will be extremely costly to implement in the short run, such as provisions on certain environmental standards. In such cases it would make sense for Turkish negotiators to plead for the acceptance of transition periods or other temporary measures. Other chapters include provisions on state subsidies, competition rules and mutual market access. It is predictable that actors in Turkish society will suggest – softly or less – to negotiators that they go for the adoption of (temporary) protective measures, particularly in sectors where these actors are less competitive. In some cases it will be very difficult to deliver such measures, and in other cases it will be downright impossible, not least because the EU negotiators also will have EU 'domestic' actors closely monitoring events.

The politics of sovereignty

Several authors (Caporaso, 1996; Sørensen, 1997, 2001; Cooper, 1996, 2002) employ a typology of state types – modern, postmodern and postcolonial – in order to conceptualize the contemporary diversity of statehood in different parts of the world. When using such taxonomy, where should we place Turkey? It is common knowledge that Turkey has never been a colonial state, thus logically cannot qualify as a postcolonial state, and it can hardly be regarded as a postmodern state either. Hence the country seems to belong to the category of *modern* states. Indeed, this category suits dominant political conceptions of the Turkish Republic extremely well. Ever since its was created in 1923, being *modern* has been among the country's prime political endeavours. It has quite simply been the official state identity, even if the self-image of being *also* the successor state to the Ottoman Empire adds flavour to Turkish conceptions of modernity (for Ottoman legacies 'alive and kicking', see Jung, 2001). By extension of this observation, and in the context of Turkey's possible accession to the EU, two particularly relevant questions arise. First, does Turkey really want to change from being a modern state to become (merely) a member state of the European Union – that is, becoming a postmodern European state? In other words, is Turkey prepared to redefine or reinvent itself, to transform itself from being a nation-state into a member state; accepting that accession negotiations is a strong instrument of Europeanization (see Glenn, 2004; see also Chapter 4 of this volume) Clearly, this implies leaving something behind that key political and sometimes military, actors have fought very hard for.[7] Therefore, the second question is what, in this context, is Turkey?

The politics of foreign policy

Chapter 27 of the *acquis* concerns Common Foreign and Security Policy (CFSP) and ESDP issues.[8] Within this context, at least three dangers lurk. The first is to underestimate fatally the significance of CFSP and ESDP – to believe that accession will have no impact on Turkish foreign policy, or that the CFSP is nothing but declaratory politics. Certainly, there is plenty of evidence to support such an approach to Chapter 27; for example, the EU's handling of the conflict in Bosnia, non-preparedness to take responsibility of operation Albania, and the EU's absence in the political process leading to the war in Iraq. In general, many would find it comfortable to generalize such findings – that the CFSP is foremost a declaratory action and not worthy of the attention of men of real action. The problem is that there is also plenty of evidence supporting the proposition that the CFSP/ESDP *does* matter, that together they make a difference, and that Turkish foreign policy on certain issues will have to change in order for Turkey to comply with the CFSP. The second danger is to believe that the event of accession negotiations presents a particularly good opportunity to leave Turkish fingerprints on the priorities of the CFSP and ESDP. On the one hand, all member states concentrate on their traditional foreign policy areas. To have such areas is considered appropriate, indeed a fact of life, and is often a source of inspiration for EU foreign policy in the making. Thus, soon after Spain and Portugal joined the EC in the late 1980s, the EC foreign policy (EPC) got a stronger Latin-American dimension. When Finland and Sweden joined in the mid-1990s, the EU's northern dimension was launched soon afterwards and since Central and East European states have joined, the eastern dimension has been strengthened. In short, the CFSP and ESDP reflect member states' interests and concerns. In theoretical terms, we are talking about a process of collective identity and preference formation (Wendt, 1994). In the case of Turkish foreign policy, there is a clear overlap between the EU's newly launched New Neighbourhood Policy (NNP) and Turkish areas of concentration. A comprehensive foreign policy analysis would point to numerous examples of shared EU and

Turkish areas of concentration, but also to a range of contentious issues. At this point there is no need to elaborate further on this issue, because all these policy issues (as well as the CFSP machinery) are not up for negotiation during the accession talks.

Concerning the third danger, the European Commission has pointed out that Turkey to some degree has aligned herself with EU positions; that Turkey is relatively less alignment-prepared than other applicant countries and that a number of problem-loaded issues remain.[9] Furthermore, the EU and Turkey have been on collision course on specific issues, such as the planned second EU–Organization of Islamic Conferences (OIC) Summit in Istanbul (October 2004). When reading the EU Commission's Regular Reports on Turkey, it is difficult not to get the impression that alignment on foreign policy issues is not really that important for Turkey, and that CFSP and ESDP commitments do not really matter. Perhaps Turkey's foreign-policy-makers believe it will be possible to negotiate special arrangements – for example, with reference to Turkey's key concerns. The logic of the CFSP rules is that individual concerns are sometimes elevated to become shared EU concerns. At other times, partners may conclude that concerns are legitimate or understandable, and therefore provide passive support. However, sometimes understanding is not forthcoming, and some of Turkey's key concerns belong to this latter option. If this description of attitudes about the CFSP, of beliefs and ideas about foreign policy are correct, it will be very difficult to reach a conclusion concerning Chapter 27 of the *acquis*.

The politics of mutual adjustment

The terms of accession are often presented as a 'take-it-or-leave-it' option and, they are just that – a fairly accurate description of the state of affairs. None the less, it is also a misleading notion, because every single enlargement has been a process of mutual adjustment (see Chapter 4 of this volume). It is highly unlikely that Turkey's accession will constitute an exception to this rule. However, the point is that EU decision-makers do not believe it is for Turkey or Turkish negotiators to determine how, when and to what degree the EU should or should not adjust itself. Rather, the impact of Turkey's possible accession will automatically force the EU decision-makers to contemplate possible avenues of adjustment. In other words, the EU that Turkey might eventually join will not be the EU we know today – and the Turkey that might eventually join the EU will not be the Turkey we know today. Thus, when thinking about the politics of mutual adjustment, we are talking futures.

The politics of accession negotiations: take three

Denmark's former chief EU negotiator, Poul Skytte Christoffersen, emphasizes that negotiations with Turkey have to be conducted on the basis of a shared aim of arriving at a successful outcome, defined as Turkey's accession. In this view, there are two preconditions: first, that Turkey fulfils all criteria for membership; and, second, that current EU member states are under on obligation to create public support for Turkish membership (*DJØF-Bladet*, 15 April 2005, p. 30). The point is, once again, that negotiations should not be regarded as a narrow diplomatic game, – they are part of a broader picture. The third sphere focuses on public discourse on Turkish membership, general images and widespread conceptions of Europe and of Turkey.

On the one hand, public discourse and opinion can be regarded as an obstacle, created intentionally to function as a barrier of last resort against Turkish membership. But public opinion can also, on the other hand, be regarded as a fact of life – the result of non-intentional political action. The two claims are not mutually exclusive. This third sphere has increasingly been politicized. Referenda on Turkish membership have been announced in Austria and France, and the issue of Turkish membership has to some degree influenced debates within the EU on the Constitutional Treaty.[10]

This third perspective on the politics of accession negotiations can be sub-divided into three aspects, called 'upgrade', 'under the varnish' and 'autonomous fields', respectively. The first school of thought claims that talking about EU–Turkish relations as a cultural encounter is unnecessarily diplomatic. Instead, the relationship should be viewed as an example of clashing civilizations. The second school of thought argues that culture may not figure prominently or explicitly in Turkey's accession strategy, yet just underneath the thin layers of technical, political and legal varnish, the deep layer of culture lures, and as long as this remains unrecognized, it is bound to cause endless problems. The third school of thought argues that relations between Turkey and the EU cannot be a cultural encounter, because a common culture is absent on the EU side. What we find in Europe is not a European culture but many national cultures, occasionally sharing some features but often not sharing much, and thus leading to a continent characterized by cultural diversity.

Upgrade, please

Istanbul is, seemingly, a perfect symbol of 'cultural encounters'. After all, an endless number of guidebooks point out that Istanbul is where

Europe meets Asia. An equally intriguing image points to Turkey as a borderland between Europe and the Middle East. Both conceptions push Turkey beyond the boundaries of Europe, and indeed are based on a distinction between Europe and Turkey. On the other hand, the Ottoman Empire was in Europe; during the latter half of the nineteenth century being perceived as 'the Sick Man of Europe'. A 'sick man' for sure, but, significantly, *of* Europe. Similarly, a dominant image of Turkey is that of a democracy, based on the rule of law, strictly secular, with a French-inspired constitution and a Swiss-inspired penal code. In short, Turkey is a 'European state', enjoying the right to apply for membership of the EU. In other words, if we are looking for a symbolic venue for *political* Europe meeting Asia, we should be looking at cities such as Kars, Van or Urfa. To the degree that a cultural encounter can be observed in Istanbul, it is the dramatic encounter between urban and rural cultures.

But then, this first perspective is more demanding, because relations between Europe and Turkey should not be regarded merely as a cultural encounter. Rather, they should be viewed as an encounter between civilizations. One version of this perspective suggests that such encounters cause deep and enduring conflict; see Samuel Huntington's (1993) notion of a clash of civilizations. While Huntington's book does not need our attention in the present context, its reception does, since many people seem to share his ideas. When Russians explain why they are fighting in Chechnya, some point out that they, on behalf of Europe, are fighting the forces of Islam. When Serbs were fighting the governmental forces of Bosnia or the Albanian minority in Kosovo, their line of reasoning was pretty similar. When representatives of West European parties argue why Turkey should not be allowed to join the EU, they point out that Europe does not, cannot or should not include states in which Islam is the pre-eminent religion. In other words, Europe and Turkey belong to different civilizations.

This line of reasoning is in some way a continuation of a discourse that was particularly strong in the nineteenth century. Every standard textbook on relations between Europe and the Ottoman Empire point out that it was hotly debated whether the Ottoman Empire met the standard of civilization (Gong, 1984; Neumann, 1999). Reluctantly, the conclusion was reached that the Ottoman Empire could join the international society of states, provided that it complied with the rules and principles that guided relations between states in international society.

In general, a significant part of public discourse is constituted by such images, which in turn underlie the formation of public opinion.

Orientalism has been in place for centuries, long before the EU was created.[11] In comparison with the task of explaining to the public why Turkey should be allowed to join the EU, the task of conducting accession negotiations is a relatively straightforward affair. Often diplomats are not very good at public relations.

Under the varnish

The essence of this position is that many issues can be presented in more than one way – for example, as political, legal, economic or cultural. Such issues belong to the essentially contested features of social and political life, having a presence in several representations, serving different functions. For example, what are human rights if their political, legal and cultural dimensions are not combined? They are part of the values and principles that the EU claims to employ in its conduct of foreign policy, and some Turkish actors quote human rights as one of the reasons they support Turkish accession. Some Turkish ways of life will be challenged significantly by accession (for better or worse). The EU also knows that some technical issues are considered cultural. Thus, in the context of World Trade Organization (WTO) negotiations, the EU has argued strongly that films, at least some films, are not just commodities being produced for a market. They are 'culture'. Perhaps, 'culture' has been a hidden, unrecognized dimension that has influenced all previous instances of Enlargement. Perhaps, we can explain certain difficulties experienced during the construction of Europe by pointing to British, Irish, Danish or Greek cultural characteristics.

Autonomous fields

Some claim that culture is culture, politics is politics and social technology is nothing but that. Hence it is acknowledged that culture exists, yet it does not and should not interfere with politics. Former Enlargement Commissioner, Günther Verheugen, does not attempt to hide or dismiss cultural aspects. He begins a speech by pointing out that 'Istanbul is one of the most cosmopolitan cities in the world, a crossroad of cultures and civilisations with a glorious past and no doubt a dynamic future.' Furthermore, he addresses the 'culture of fear' issue, pointing out that 'some people fear the country will lose its cultural and linguistic identity. I want to reassure you that cultural diversity is the very heart and soul of Europe – a heritage we cherish and preserve at all costs' (Verheugen, 2000). In other words, he claims to be cherishing and preserving cultural diversity and, in his view, the reform process flowing from Turkey's pre-accession strategy does not interfere in cultural affairs. Key players will be aware of this non-linkage, but outside the confines of the technically highly competent epistemic community, such knowledge is limited.

Conclusion

Though accession negotiations will take place in the shadow of considerable uncertainty, their politics is very simple: to make possible a transfer from A (the opening of negotiations) to B (a signed treaty of accession). In the case of the ten Central and Eastern European accession states, this process took between three and five years.[12] Having reached B, then follows the exercise of getting from B to C – that is, to get through the no less important ratification process. Accession negotiations began on 3 October 2005. However, this does not change the fact that Turkish membership of the EU remains nothing more than a possibility. Turkey has been deemed sufficiently qualified to open negotiations, but to qualify for membership is something fairly different and much more demanding.

This chapter has argued that the politics of accession negotiations is constituted by three separate yet intimately linked 'games': the accession negotiations as such; the broader framework of negotiation positions and domestic politics; and the wider game of general images, public opinion and contending conceptions of Europe. The conduct of accession negotiations in the narrow sense is an elite affair, involving highly skilled diplomats and experts. Negotiations will not be a case of negotiation across cultures (see Cohen, 1997) but a rather dull process, focusing on political, economic and legal dimensions. Relations between diplomacy and domestic politics (the second game) also involve politicians and representatives of interest groups and NGOs. The third game is likely to be the most difficult and, apart from groupings mentioned so far, this game will also include journalists, academics and many others.

Notes

1. A simple search on the European Commission's website (http//www.europa.eu) reveals that the key word 'Turkey' generates a list of some 5,000 documents.
2. Provided that the Treaty on European Constitution will eventually be ratified in all member states, group presidencies will be introduced by 2007. Each group presidency will serve for 18 months and will comprise one large and two smaller member states. In case the Constitutional Treaty is not ratified, the sequence above and the traditional six-month term will apply.

3. Accession treaties with Bulgaria and Romania, respectively, have been signed and they have become full members as of January 2007. This will thus not interfere directly with Turkey's accession negotiations. On the other hand, the two new member states might contribute to accession fatigue.
4. The Commissions recommendations have largely been followed by the European Council; see Turkey in the 2004 Brussels European Council Presidency Conclusions, http://www.mfa.gov.tr (accessed 20 April 2005).
5. Concerning the Customs Union, observers have noted a similar reluctance to comply with obligations.
6. It could be argued that a three-level game model more accurately describe the parallel levels of Turkish domestic politics, bilateral relations with EU member states and negotiations with the European Commission (on three-level games, see Patterson, 1997). However, in the present context, the aim is not to analyse the games themselves but to point to the presence of more than one level.
7. Obviously, accession would also imply giving up political visions of becoming pre-modern.
8. For overviews of the CFSP, see Smith (2003) and Smith (2004).
9. In several Commission Regular Reports on Turkey.
10. According to a Eurobarometer survey, 11 per cent of respondents state the prospect of Turkish membership as a reason for voting 'no' to the Constitution.
11. According to an intriguing article by Makdisi (2002), Orientalism is not an exclusive Western European feature, but can also be identified in the Ottoman Empire. He explicates his view in the following fashion, 'By Ottoman Orientalism, I mean a complex of Ottoman attitudes produced by a nineteenth-century age of Ottoman reform that implicitly and explicitly acknowledged the West to be the home of progress and the East, writ large, to be a *present* theatre of backwardness (italics in original)' (p. 770).
12. First opening in 1998/9 and the treaty was signed in Athens in April 2003.

References

Akçakoca, A., Cameron, F. and Rhein, E. (2004) *Turkey – Ready for the EU?*, CEPS Isssue Paper, No. 16, Brussels: CEPS.

Caporaso, J. (1996) 'The European Union and Forms of State: Westphalian, Regulatory or Post-Modern', *Journal of Common Market Studies*, vol. 34, no. 1, pp. 29–53.

Cohen, R. (1997) *Negotiating Across Cultures. International Communication in an Interdependent World*, Washington DC: United States Institute of Peace Press.

Cooper, R. (1996) *The Post-Modern State and the World Order*, London: Demos.

Cooper, R. (2002) *The Breaking of Nations*, London: Atlantic Books.

Discussion (2005) *Does 'Muslim' Turkey belong to 'Christian' Europe?*, The Pew Forum on Religion and Public Life, http://www.pewforum.org/events/prit. php?EventID=66 (accessed 15 April 2005).

DJØF-Bladet (2005), 15 April.

European Commission (2003) Report COM (2003) 676 Final.

European Commission (2004) *2004 Regular Report on Turkey's Progress towards Accession*, COM (2004) 656 final.

EU Council (1999) *Presidency Conclusions*, Helsinki, 10/11 December 1999. http://europa.eu (accessed 17 July 2006)

EU Council (2004) *Presidency Conclusions*, Brussels, 16/17 December 2004. http://europa.eu (accessed 17 July 2006)

Evans, P. B., Jacobson, H. and Putnam, R. (1993) *Double-Edged Diplomacy: International Bargaining and Domestic Politics*, Berkeley, Calif.: University of California Press.

Glenn, J. K. (2004) 'From nation-states to member states: accession negotiations as an instrument of Europeanization', *Comparative European Politics*, vol. 2, pp. 3–28.

Gong, G. (1984) *The Standard of 'Civilisation' in International Society*, Oxford: Clarendon Press.

Grabbe, H. (2004) *When Negotiations Begin: The Next Phase in EU–Turkey Relations*, London Centre for European Reform Essays.

Huntington, S. (1993) 'The Clash of Civilisations?', *Foreign Affairs*, vol. 72, pp. 22–49.

Jung, D. (2001) *Turkey at the Crossroads: Ottoman Legacies and a Greater Middle East*, London: Zed Books.

Jørgensen, K. E. (2008) 'The Acquis Communautaire: A Cornerstone of the European Edifice?, unpublished.

Katzenstein, P. (ed.) (1996) *The Culture of National Security*, New York: Columbia University Press.

Kochenov, D. (2005) 'EU Enlargement Law: History and Recent Developments: Treaty – Costum Concubinage', *European Integration Online Papers* http://www.eiop.or.at/eio 14.4.2005.

Kramer, H. (2004) Whither Turkey's EU Accession? Perspectives and Problems after December 2004, *AICGS Advisor*, September 30, http://www.aicgs.org/c/kramer_turkey.shtml (accessed 17 April 2005).

Makdisi, U. (2002) 'Ottoman Orientalism', *American Historical Review*, vol. 107, no. 3 pp. 769–96.

Neumann, I. B. (1999) *Uses of the Other: 'The East' in European Identity Formation*, Minneapolis: Minnesota University Press.

Patterson, L. A. (1997) 'Agricultural policy Reform in the EC: A Three Level Game Analysis', *International Organization*, vol. 51, pp. 135–65.

Peterson, J. (2004) 'Policy Networks', in Antje Wiener and Thomas Diez (eds), *European Integration Theory*, Oxford University Press.

Putnam, R. D. (1988) reprinted in Evans *et al.* (1993) 'Diplomacy and Domestic Politics: The Logic of Two-Level Games', *International Organization*, vol. 42, Summer, pp. 427–6.

Schimmelfennig, F. and Sedelmeier, U. (eds) (2005) *The Politics of European Union Enlargement: Theoretical Approaches*, London: Routledge.

Smith, K. E. (2003) *European Union Foreign Policy in a Changing World*, Cambridge: Polity Press.

Smith, M. E. (2004) *Europe's Foreign and Security Policy. The Institutionalization of Cooperation*, Cambridge University Press.

Sørensen, G. (1997) 'An Analysis of Contemporary Statehood: Consequences for Conflict and Cooperation', *Review of International Studies*, vol. 23, no. 3, pp. 253–69.

Sørensen, G. (2001) *Changes in Statehood. The Transformation of International Relations*, Basingstoke: Palgrave.

Turkish National Programme for the Adoption of the Acquis, Ankara.

Verheugen, G. (2000) Speech by Commissioner Verheugen, Bogazici University, Turkey on 'The Enlargement Process and Turkey's Place in this Process', 9 March 2000; http://europa.eu (accessed 17 July 2006).

Wendt, A. (1994) Collective Identity Formation and the International State, *American Political Science Review*, vol. 88, pp. 384–96.

2
What Can Turkey Learn From Previous Accession Negotiations?

An Schrijvers

The European constellation Turkey currently encounters is, without any doubt, different from the context in which Central and Eastern European countries entered. After all, the Union draws lessons from past experiences and adapts – when necessary – procedures and rules. Preliminary analyses have already pointed to the impact of the previous enlargement on the accession process of Bulgaria and Romania, who entered the EU in January 2007 (Phinnemore, 2004). Despite several statements by the EU that the political principles underpinning the accession negotiations will remain the same for all countries, this does not seem to be the case. The EU has become more demanding in general. This change is explained by the fact that the political imperative for the EU to enlarge is much weaker after the Cold War division in Europe was removed. Suffering from a pronounced enlargement fatigue, the EU will handle future accessions – including the Turkish one – with more reluctance than before. Furthermore, Turkey's road to Europe will not only depend on the European context (the EU rules and procedures), but will also be conditioned by Turkish domestic conditions. After all, the final responsibility for accession does not lie with the EU, but with the national government, and its capability of dealing with the EU. As will be demonstrated in this chapter, the same was true for Poland. Not only the external conditions imposed by the EU, but also – and perhaps even more – the domestic conditions, determine the accession process of a given country, and its consequences.

On 1 May 2004, the EU took a historical step and reunited the continent. Apart from Malta and Cyprus, eight former communist countries of Central and Eastern Europe (CEEC) officially entered the EU after a successful accession process that had begun fifteen years earlier.[1] In order to draw lessons from these previous negotiations for Turkey, this

29

chapter identifies some of the key dynamics of the accession negotiations with CEEC countries.[2] In particular, the Polish case will provide
illustrative examples, as this country, among all CEEC countries, is the
one most similar to Turkey, not only in terms of size and population,
but also in areas such as the level of democratisation, and the role of
agriculture and religion in society. As the chapter will demonstrate, the
latter aspects can be significant, by providing the breeding ground for
some unintended side effects of accession to the EU.

The chapter consists of two parts. The first part addresses the nature
of the accession negotiation context in which Poland and the other
CEECs found themselves. Seen through the eyes of candidate states,
including Turkey, the larger institutional context of the negotiations
makes up the *external* dimension of the process. Here, different theoretical perspectives and insights will be used, although the focus lies on
rational choice approaches. The second part focuses on the *internal*
dimension of the accession process – that is, it examines how domestic
actors deal with the external context, including the strategy that the
country's representatives adopt in the negotiations. While drawing on
recent studies of Europeanization, the analysis points to some largely
unintended consequences of the accession procedure on Polish polity
and politics. The chapter argues that similar consequences are likely to
come into play in Turkish politics.[3] It is evident that the two dimensions are highly interdependent. External EU pressures can cause or
affect domestic tensions, which, in turn, can influence the country's
relations with the EU. It is precisely the link between these two dimensions that makes EU accession so special and so difficult to handle for
candidate states.

The external dimension of EU accession negotiations

Seen from a widespread Turkish point of view, the CEECs were offered
the perspective of EU membership fairly quickly. However, in the
opinion of the Polish political elite, the response of the EU (at that
time still the EC – European Community) to the historical events of
1989 was reluctant. After half a century of exclusion from the West,
Poland had expected much more than merely technical assistance (the
PHARE programme – Pologne, Hongrie Assistance à la Reconstruction
Economique) and association agreements, the more because the former
GDR (German Democratic Republic) was welcomed in the EC as early
as 1991. Because of disagreement among the then twelve (and later
fifteen) member states, it took the EC/EU four years before it could

officially respond to the membership aspirations of the CEECs. This was done in December 1993 at the Intergovernmental Conference (IGC) in Copenhagen, with the formulation of the accession criteria. Although the criteria were not new in a strict sense, and had evolved over time based on previous experiences, the EU for the first time formalized the accession procedure. In this fashion, a kind of common EU enlargement policy, based on strictly objective criteria, was established. Turkey will experience the EU policy of accession conditionality. The policy mainly follows a 'strategy of reinforcement by reward', not by punishment (Schimmelfennig *et al.*, 2003, pp. 496–7). Under this strategy, the EU gives the reward (membership) if the target government complies with the conditions, but it withholds the reward, though does not punish by inflicting extra costs), if the government fails to do so. The instrument of conditionality, also used in EU foreign policy towards third countries was meant to redirect the domestic and external policy of the CEECs and to stimulate them to undertake the necessary reforms. It characterized the whole accession process from the start, association agreements and pre-accession support included (Dimitrova, 2002, p. 175).[4] Compared to earlier EU enlargement rounds (for example, with Spain) the EU applied a much stronger conditionality towards the CEECs, a tendency likely to be continued in the future (Smith, 2003).[5]

The principle of conditionality is highly interconnected with the principles of bilateralism and differentiation (Smith, 2005, p. 352). In this regard, the EU accession governance differs to a great extent from the multi-level governance model of the EU in daily use (Dimitrova, 2002, pp. 174–5). In the governance of accession negotiations, only a limited number of actors are directly involved, such as the Commission, the Council (the ministries of foreign affairs of the member states) and the government of the candidate state. The European Parliament and non-governmental organisations (NGOs), which can be effective in the daily decision-making procedures of the EU, are barely present in the process. The same is true for the parliament of the given candidate country. Accession consists predominantly of a bilateral intergovernmental negotiation between the applicant state and the EU, in which the Commission plays the part of mediator. In the previous enlargement, this bilateral character rendered it difficult for the CEECs to present a common front to the EU. On the other hand, it maintained the principle that each country was treated separately on its own merits. This is called the principle of differentiation (Avery, 2003, p. 5). By handling accession in this way, the EU, in theory, passes all the responsibility for becoming a member to the candidate country: 'The path to accession is one taken by individual countries, not groups of them' (Smith, 2005, p. 357). The faster and better a given country implements the EU rules, the more rapidly it becomes a member. In the previous enlargement, this generated strong competition among the candidate states. They all tried to close as many of the thirty-one negotiation chapters as fast as possible, which resulted in a kind of 'regatta'.[6]

Since the EU is not a unitary actor, negotiations with a candidate inevitably involve even more negotiations among the EU member states and institutions. Before a negotiation chapter can be opened, in addition to the government of the candidate state, the EU as a whole has to define its common position on the given chapter. This is a difficult process, because each accession entails an uneven distribution of costs and benefits among the member states, resulting in a division between 'drivers' and 'brakemen' (Schimmelfennig, 2001). In the past enlargement, some member states (for example, Germany) had strong interest in the accession of Poland. Others (such as Spain and Portugal) did not expect any benefits at all, and felt they would experience only disadvantages.[7] This is why they tried to delay the process by demanding extra payments, insisting on very strict adherence to some parts of the *acquis*, raising objections to closing chapters, or by connecting certain reform conditions primarily related to intra-EU policy with their approval to enlarge to the given country (Inotai, 2003, p. 96). These kinds of strategies led to much bargaining among the member states, often preceding or running parallel with the negotiations with the candidate country, and often complicating and delaying the process.[8] Another element making the EU enlargement a difficult operation to undertake, especially for the existing EU members, lies in the specific nature of accession, as explained by Avery (1995, pp. 2–3). Because accession does not concern traditional matters such as trade concessions, but touches on the EU's whole range of activities, policies and institutions, which are examined to see whether they pose a problem for the candidate state, it tends to be an occasion where the existing members are forced to face fundamental questions about what they want the EU to do, and how they want it to be done.

As the candidate state has to comply with the whole *acquis communautaire* and *politique,* one cannot speak of real negotiations. It is a misleading term. There is little to negotiate about, apart from the length and quantity of transition periods and the budget (Verheugen, 2000, p. 442). Newcomers have to comply with the EU system, 95 per cent of which is untouchable (Grabbe, 2004, p. 2). It was defined in the past, before accession, without any contribution from the candidate country. This is why Wiener (2002, p. 14) speaks of the 'static and past focused compliance rationale of the EU'. Engert *et al.* categorize this relationship as strongly 'asymmetrical, shaped by pre-determined and non-negotiable formal rules, and dominated by governmental, bureaucratic actors' (Engert *et al.*, 2001, p. 2). The fact that the candidate country did not contribute to the legislation means that parts of the *acquis* can be in strong contradiction to the country's primary needs and priorities. The past enlargement towards CEECs demonstrates that the EU Commission even meddles in affairs such as domestic management and politics, which are not covered by the *acquis* (Pridham, 2002, p. 960). By demanding more from future members than from present ones, the EU applies 'double standards', which the former will have to accept in order to show their commitment to membership. Recent research (Hughes *et al.*, 2004; Smith, 2003) has also pointed at the often contradictory and diffuse nature of EU conditionality. As the different EU actors involved do not always act univocally, ambivalent signals are often given. That is why Grabbe (2002a, p. 257) calls conditionality a 'blunt instrument'.

The candidate has much weaker negotiating powers than does the EU side.[9] Basic rational choice bargaining theory can explain this intrinsic feature of the accession process. As a prospective member has more to gain from membership and a greater desire to become a member, it is always in the underdog position, through which it is forced to make disproportionate concessions and carry nearly all the costs of accession on its own,[10] the EU side only marginally matching these costs. Whereas accession was a priority for Poland and the other CEECs, it was not for the EU member states. They prioritized deepening (Smith, 2003, p. 106) and were determined to minimize the costs of the operation by providing a limited financial package for the CEECs.[11] In this respect, Brücker *et al.* (2004) present the accession negotiations as a simple 'war of attrition' bargaining game. Although, in the long term accession benefits both sides of the process, adopting the *acquis* is costly for the applicants, particularly in the short term. Meanwhile, the EU prefers to absorb substantially reformed or 'fit' candidates. This is why, according to Brücker *et al.*, a kind of waiting game unfolds. In this game, the EU effectively applies several strategies, such as delegating the evaluation of applicants to a third objective party (the Commission); compensating the applicants for their reform efforts with assistance through which their benefits ultimately increase albeit minimally; and the strategy of postponing the most difficult chapters to the final negotiation phase in order to put more pressure on the candidates, which will eventually have to surrender (Pridham, 2001, pp. 61–2). In any case, whatever theoretical framework is applied on the accession negotiations, these are far from 'horizontal' between autonomous and equal parties (Engert *et al.*, 2001, p. 8). They do not constitute a process of reaching a mutually acceptable agreement, but rather serve the EU actors by explaining the rules and telling the candidate country paternalistically what it will have to do in order to receive the rewards of assistance and membership.

The candidate country can enhance its poor negotiation powers, though, by seeking allies among the major EU institutions involved; the Commission and the member states in the Council. When Polish officials realized that the formal sessions of the Accession Conferences in Brussels did not provide any chance for real negotiations, they started negotiating in the European capitals. In Berlin in particular they found an important ally (Avery, 2003, p. 6). Also the Directorate General for Enlargement (DG Enlargement) was quickly enlisted as an ally for the Polish case. Although it was regularly asked to defend the point of view of some member states, it also often acted in favour of the candidate countries, as it shared the goal of accession, whereas the member states and/or the other DGs did not do so all the time (Sedelmeier, 2000, 2002). In this sense, the theoretically bilateral accession negotiations became in practice multi-level.

DG Enlargement or the allied member states cannot, however, work miracles. Their margins are limited, as the objective procedure leaves little room for generous concessions. This was especially true in the previous enlargement, ensuring that the outcomes of the negotiations (the entry conditions) were more or less – besides some minor nation sensitive concessions – the same for all candidates. On the other hand, accession is not based on the fulfilment of criteria only (Smith, 2003, p. 130). Concerning the CEE region, the EU had a strong political imperative to enlarge in order to overcome the Cold War division. The CEECs more than once called upon this imperative to advance their case successfully. They often sent the promises quickly made by the EC/EU leaders at the beginning of the 1990s back as threats (Wiener, 2002). A similar strategy was adopted by the member states supportive of the process. In this sense, Schimmelfennig (2001) uses the terms 'rhetorical action' or 'the strategic use of norm-based arguments'. By referring to the Community's pan-European orientation and liberal constitutive values and norms the 'drivers' of enlargement were able to shame the 'brakemen' and 'entrap' them argumentatively in a firm EU commitment to Eastern enlargement. The kind of 'negative consensus' resulting from this had the consequence that the process could not be blocked in practice (Sedelmeier, 2000, p. 188). Apart from the imperative or negative consensus, path dependency also explains why the enlargement became irreversible. As the accession process moves on, mutual dependence grows and the process develops a dynamic of its own. Because of this, the CEECs, even before they received the official status of candidate state, were already rather certain of getting the EU ticket. Only the date and the conditional terms were still to be defined. Because of a similar dynamic, the principle of differentiation (entering one by one according to the respective progress made) resulted in the 'big bang' approach with ten countries. This has been important in accelerating the process, especially for Poland, which since 2000 has begun to lag behind. Based on the postulated objective criteria, the brakemen of enlargement could have vetoed the Polish entry, as each candidate is only considered to be ready when all member states declare this to be the case (Grabbe, 2002a, p. 264). Or they could postpone it to a later date.[12] But as Germany could not think of a first wave without Poland, it immediately started to promote strongly the more practical group approach (Tuschhoff, 2002, p. 30). The economic perspectives that Poland offered in terms of an export market could not be neglected, therefore additional pressure was put on the country to speed up EU compliance (Smith, 2003, p. 123ff). Despite successful Polish efforts to catch up with the other CEECs, it is nevertheless hard to deny that the group approach, the increasing time pressure resulting from it, and the political imperative, made the initially strict conditions erode in some way, to the benefit of laggard countries such as Poland. It demonstrates that, despite the intention of establishing an objective EU accession procedure, *subjectivity* and *politics* remain inherent features of the process.

What are the main lessons Turkey can draw concerning the external dimension of the accession process? Turkey may expect the EU side to be reluctant. The country's prospective accession will cause more disagreement between the different member states than between Turkey and the EU as a whole. Therefore, Turkey will have to seek allies among them. The country will also find an ally in DG Enlargement, through which the country's weak negotiation powers intrinsic to the highly asymmetrical accession process may be enhanced. Although some dynamics such as path dependency can go some way towards softening the stringent conditionality, possibilities for these will be limited. This will be the case especially for Turkey. Entering the EU on its own, it may not experience the competition and group dynamics, specific to the previous enlargement, keeping and accelerating the CEECs on the rails of compliance. Even as the process moves on and Turkey finds some strong advocates among the member states, it may well remain a very lengthy and difficult process, as the EU will be even more demanding than it was towards the CEECs. Strategies of returning the EU promises and earlier engagements (Turkish–EC Association Agreement of 1963) as threats will have no effect, at least as long as Turkey does not match the political criteria. One possibility for rhetorical action may lie in the argument that Turkish accession may lead to more stabilization in the Middle East, generating spill-over effects in neighbouring states. Also, the consolidation of Muslim minorities in many member states can be an asset, if properly used, to enhance the Turkish negotiation position. Probably the most convincing argument will be to confront the EU with its alleged, though not undisputed, identity of being a liberal democracy open to cultural and religious diversity. Nevertheless, it is still to be seen whether these strategies will be able to entrap the EU brakemen rhetorically and soften the asymmetry, as they are much weaker than the imperative of reuniting the continent after the Cold War. This means that Turkey in the end will be forced to make disproportionate and painful concessions, while carrying the major compliance costs on its own. In the EU 27 the financial discrepancy characterizing the latest enlargement is likely to be put even more sharply, as the new members in particular will be lukewarm towards sacrificing their small benefits.

The internal dimension of the EU accession process

The internal dimension has been crucially important for all accession states, and Turkey will be no exception to this general rule. In order to explore the nature of key aspects, the Polish experience will be analysed and compared to the Turkish case.

Although the take-it-or-leave-it situation presented by the EU's conditionality and intrinsic to the accession process, left little room to defend the national interest, the Polish government announced that it would adopt a tough strategy in the negotiations starting in March 1998. In terms of 'demanding the maximum in order to get at least something' (Bachmann, 2002, p. 203), they tried to withstand the pressures resulting from the external dimension before the domestic public eye. To illustrate this point, the Polish negotiation team asked for an eighteen year transition period on the sale of land to foreigners. Such a long period had never been demanded or granted before in EU enlargement history, nor had this been claimed by the other CEECs. Poland, being a potentially powerful EU member, also appealed often to the principles of 'solidarity' and 'equality' by defending full direct payments in the agricultural chapter and full accession rights for their labour force in the chapter on free movement of labour (Trzaskowski, 2002, p. 18). The EU, being in a stronger negotiation position, did not answer these requests, through which the already existing popular awareness of a de facto second-class membership ticket seemed to be confirmed.[13] Whereas many citizens had indeed expected high costs for joining the EU and were willing to pay them, the fact that they would not be subject to the same rules and have the same rights as the member states' citizens, was (and still is) difficult to digest.

The maximalist Polish negotiation strategy was not only a reaction to the highly asymmetrical external context, but also resulted from increasing domestic tensions. The unstable national political scene, with its endless coalition problems, subsequent minority governments and strong opposition forces urged the government to compensate for their weakness at home by playing it hard in Brussels. The pressure on the negotiators became especially high, when the country was, to a greater extent and earlier than was the case for the other CEECs, confronted by rising Euro-scepticism among its population. Two and a half years after the negotiations had started, these popular Euro-sceptical moods were reflected in the Polish parliament following the elections of 2001 (Szczerbiak, 2002). Two newly formed, extremely anti-European parties won a significant share of seats (20 per cent) in parliament, one being leftist-populist in nature, and the other a conservative rightist party. In addition, two soft Euro-sceptical parties won nearly 20 per cent of the parliamentary seats. This made up a total of 40 per cent of euro-sceptical or anti-European opposition seats in the Polish parliament. When the accession negotiations were nearing the end phase in mid-2002, and the most sensitive chapters still had to be discussed, the opposition forces used this occasion to polarize increasingly the domestic Europe debate. It is true that, by doing this, they gave the ruling government an extra asset in the negotiations, but then again they confronted the government with a tricky Janus-faced communication exercise. On the one hand, the presence of growing Euro-sceptical feelings among the domestic population and parties was used successfully 'as a threat' by the Polish negotiators to obtain extra concessions, but on the other, it nevertheless remained difficult for them to maintain credibility, since

LIVERPOOL JOHN MOORES UNIVERSITY
LEARNING SERVICES

the situation forced them to speak two languages. The Polish negotiators had to downplay the benefits of accession to the EU partners in order to enhance their position and achieve the best possible deal, but at the same time, and especially in the run-up to the accession referendum scheduled for June 2003, they had to overstate these benefits at home, especially to the Euro-sceptics among the domestic public, in order to sell the final deal and assure a positive outcome in the referendum.

Despite their commitment to 'hard' bargaining in order to maintain the trust of the Euro-sceptical segments of Polish society, the government position in the EU negotiations was weak in reality. This limited negotiation power intrinsic to the specific accession context was further weakened by the poor state and administrative capacities of the country after the collapse of communism. For the sake of managing the accession negotiations and the *acquis* compliance process, Poland established a central co-ordination unit (the method preferred by the Commission), but the decision-making structure remained unstable and was heavily constrained by the weak coalition governments. This often led to hastily prepared, badly argued and contradictory negotiation positions, even in chapters very sensitive to the Polish nation (Schrijvers, 2004). In order to avoid this after accession and ensure that the Polish administration fit for functioning within the EU multi-level governance system, the EU Commission put extra attention into creating effective administrative capacity. It began to emphasize civil service reform, but instead of stimulating the New Public Management (NPM) format, already introduced in many West European states, it confirmed the Polish government's preference for a traditional, hierarchically organized type of administration (Goetz, 2001, p. 1035), which remained to a large degree politicized because of communist legacies and practices (Dimitrova, 2002, p. 180). This means that, even after accession, Poland still has a rather fuzzy and inefficient EU policy co-ordination system, backed by often fragmented, deficient and politicized administration (Nowak-Far and Michonski, 2005). This hinders the development of an effective Polish EU policy, as it is self-evident that only a stable and well organized government, backed by a capable administrative apparatus, can be successful in the EU multi-level environment (Stawarska, 1999, p. 831). Developing institutions and effective procedures is difficult.

Making sure that the negotiation positions are legitimized through a broad deliberation process, is another issue in which all actors (governmental and non-governmental) are involved. In the rush for the EU membership the link with civil society was often lacking in Poland (Korkut, 2002). As the EU Commission more than once signalled, there were no effective information, co-ordination and deliberation channels. That is why the negotiations happened, especially in the beginning, completely behind closed doors. Even the parliament was not involved systematically. Only in March 2004, more than a year after finalizing the negotiations, a law was passed concerning the information and communication duty of the ministers to the parliament on EU-related policy.

Path-dependent elements such as the communist legacy of centralization and lack of democratic experience can partially explain this. The accession procedure is also responsible for this phenomenon. Besides the formal *acquis* conditionality, the EU directly or indirectly influences national political systems by evaluating them and formulating recommendations. Especially in institutional demands, where the *acquis* is rather thin, a great deal of 'informal conditionality' (Hughes *et al.*, 2004, p. 525) is exerted. It was the Commission which preferred to deal with one central Polish co-ordination unit for EU policy, as this would make the highly technical process easier to manage. Because of time pressure, a heavy workload and the highly technical nature of *acquis* implementation, the EU accession process led to a strengthening of the Polish executive to the disadvantage of the legislature and to the emergence of a 'core executive' (Zubek, 2001). Although the administration in general remained largely incompetent during the negotiations, centres of technocratic excellence and professionalism did emerge in the administrations of the main executive departments, which Goetz and Wollmann call 'islands of excellence' (2001, p. 882). These islands had (and still have) the nearly absolute monopoly on co-ordinating and defining Polish EU policy. In this respect Lippert *et al.* (2001, p. 1004) speak of the 'technocratization of governance', which happens at the expense of political actors, who are accountable to the electorate.

As a result of this evolution, the Polish parliament lost some of the significant controlling power it gained in the early 1990s. In order to wipe out the communist past, the new Polish Democratic Republic after 1989 introduced very powerful parliamentary structures. These have played a significant role in defining the transition policies, since the post-communist executive was weak at that time (Zubek, 2001). The EU accession, however, has reversed this tendency, by weakening the legislature to the benefit of the executive (Grabbe, 2001, p. 1017). Especially in the first years, this made the process an even more elite and executive-driven undertaking than was the case in the EU-15. In this way, the accession has further widened the gap between Polish state and citizenry, which was already large after half a century of communism. This is a unintended effect of EU accession, because it comes at the cost of participative democracy, the model the EU is committed to promote (Pridham, 2002, p. 954).

The Polish national executive did not only centralize its power in 'islands of excellence', but also strengthened the centre at the expense of the sub-national level. Although Poland immediately after 1989 undertook reforms to decentralize the country and empower the sub-national levels in order to erase the communist centralized past, the EU accession has reversed this process (Hughes *et al.*, 2004). The sub-national level was not involved at all. In this respect, Hughes *et al.* (2002) speak of a regional deficit. Because of inconsistent advice and ambivalent recommendations from the EU Commission concerning the management of pre-accession regional and post-accession structural aid, the EU accession has led to a re-centralization of the state structures, at least in the short term, which is another side-effect, contradictory to the model of regionalization the EU is committed to stimulating.

As EU accession had an impact on the Polish polity or mode of governance and decision-making,[14] it also affected the power relations and constellation between domestic political actors. Poland is one of the only CEECs in which the Europeanization process has had a large impact on the party system by reinforcing certain tendencies already existing during the transition (Grzymala-Busse and Innes, 2003). The bankruptcy of the communist state and the failed reforms of the 1980s left Poland with no choice but to liberalize and reform after 1989. This reform imperative, increasingly pressured by the international community, did not leave much room for inter-party debate. It constrained the available policy options heavily and held the political parties 'hostage' (Innes, 2001, p. 5). The strict EU conditions have further strengthened this to the maximum degree. The EU Commission favoured and underlined the need of an inter-party consensus on accession. This hindered any genuine debate and undermined the basic function of political parties. Parliamentarians were reduced to being puppets, passing at a very high speed the necessary bills and legislation in order to fulfil the EU criteria (Grabbe, 2001, p. 1016). This left little room for them to create a distinct profile. As all centre parties were united behind the goal of accession (as they had been previously towards transition) and had few opportunities for party competition, they tended to develop catch all strategies. This left a vacuum from which, in particular, extreme rightist or leftist parties could benefit by adopting an anti-EU position. These parties were less constrained, tapped the sceptical views among the population, and quickly gained support.[15] In Poland this happened more easily than in other CEEC countries, as the communist legacy had left this country with a very weak party system, with high levels of party fragmentation, fluidity and volatility among the voters, and a lack of firm party structures. The vulnerability of the system, with its subsequent party splits and mergers, was the ideal breeding ground for new anti-EU populist parties, which made the system even more unpredictable than it had already been.

Basically, these parties gained support in three segments of society. First, they could easily convince the quarter of the population who are farmers or live in the countryside, because they feared competition with the EU farmers.[16] Second, the conservative nationalistic Roman-Catholic segment, accounting for almost another fifth of the population, was also conducive to Euro-scepticism. They feared a loss of national sovereignty and culture, and were frightened of the 'decadent' West with its 'immoral' practices such as abortion, gay marriage and euthanasia. A third segment susceptible to a populist anti-EU vote, not only in Poland but also in the whole CEEC region, was found in the group of transition losers. Because of what Pridham (2001, p. 66) calls an 'exaggerated policy inter-linkage', EU accession became synonymous with and responsible for all the socially painful reforms of the previous decade, at least in the public perception. The scarce financial aid and concessions granted by the EU did little to take away the frustration felt among these segments.

Rulikova (2004) argues that the nature of popular Euro-scepticism in the candidate countries differs from the one existing in the old member states, in the sense that it does not concern opposition against the integration project as such, but results directly from the specific pre-accession context and how the public perceived it. Henderson (2002) points to the fact that the role of the Commission during the accession phase was generally overplayed in the national press, as its critical reports often became headline news. While it indeed had substantial influence over the accession process by preparing the initial opinions and regular progress reports, this focus of attention produced a false impression. The decision-making powers of member states' governments in the Council were constantly underplayed, thus creating the perception that EU membership would entail a greater loss of national sovereignty than is in fact the case. This is just one example of how the pre-accession context gave rise to increasing nationalistic feelings, resulting in popular Euro-scepticism. As has already been mentioned, some parties used the EU issue successfully – essentially being of a second order – for electoral gains, leading to an overrepresentation of Euro-sceptic voices in the Polish parliament.[17] These had an impact on the government's management of the accession negotiations by polarizing the domestic debate (Lewis, 2005). The agency of the Polish negotiators at the final Copenhagen IGC in December 2002,[18] and the dismissal of the Polish premier only one day after the official entry of Poland into the EU are illustrative examples in this respect.

The breeding ground for catch-all parties, for growing popular Euroscepticism, for the emergence of populist anti-EU parties in parliament, and for the destabilization of the government resulting from this, was already present in Poland during the transition period, which was characterized by weak party structures and a reform imperative excluding any debate. But, undeniably, the accession process strengthened these tendencies. Rather than leading to more consolidation of the political scene, it had the unintended effect of shaking it. This also had an impact on the Polish–EU relations and the accession process in general.

These examples of the impact of EU conditionality on domestic polity and politics, called 'the internal dimension of the process', have revealed how EU accession does not necessarily lead to better governance, more democracy, regionalization and stabilization. The interaction of domestic factors (such as communist legacies, actors' preferences and practices) and deficiencies in the EU conditionality (its diffuse and often contradictory nature) may lead, directly or indirectly, to unexpected effects. Instead of curing past legacies, EU accession can reinforce them, and rather than consolidating reform measures it can reverse them. While acceding to the EU, Turkey needs to be cautious of this, since it also seems to possess the conditions that make such developments probable. Its relatively large agrarian population and conservative Muslim elements in society make Turkey equally susceptible to Euro-sceptical tendencies, which may be translated successfully by domestic political parties into populism. Similarly, the increasing formal and informal EU pressures will probably tempt major Turkish actors to take in haste – and thus not always the best – decisions concerning effective and accountable institution building. This can possibly lead to a centralization of power and the emergence of a 'core executive' at the expense of the participative democracy. The relatively weaker Turkish administrative structures may not be able to cope with the *acquis* overload, leading to inconsistencies in the negotiations and shallow *acquis* implementation. This is why Turkey will have to establish a well-organized and legitimate EU co-ordination system, based on a competent administration and on effective channels of deliberation and information. Only then will the country have the capacity to negotiate successfully and legitimately within the EU multi-level environment. This currently seems to be the important problem to solve before Turkey is given its initial institutional negotiation structure.

Conclusion

The main lesson to draw from the 2004 enlargement is that accession processes are highly dynamic. They are not only determined by EU rules and procedures imposed on the candidate state, but also conditioned by the domestic context of the acceding state. As has been demonstrated in this chapter, it is precisely the interaction between the two dimensions that makes accession such a challenge. It is likely that Turkey's accession process will become even more complicated, as the country will be faced with an even more stringent external dimension than has been the case so far. In a complex interplay with certain domestic factors – present in Turkish and Polish societies alike – this can generate some negative effects on Turkish polity and politics.

The EU will continue to handle accession guided by the principles of conditionality, bilateralism and differentiation. It will put Turkey in a highly asymmetrical context, in which its intrinsically poor negotiation powers will be further limited. As the EU will impose an even stronger conditionality on the country, there will be little for Turkey to negotiate about. In order to alter this situation – if only minimally – Turkey will have to find allies among the major EU actors involved – that is, the Commission or member states. While using the internal divisions among them, Turkey will find advocates for its case, especially in DG Enlargement, which shares the goal of accession, where the others may not always do so. Nevertheless, the obtained confederates cannot perform miracles as they are heavily constrained by the formal accession procedure. While some dynamics of the process, such as path dependency, can erode this somewhat, and while Turkey can try to entrap the non-supportive EU actors strategically by referring to the role of its accession for the benefit of the Middle East region, it remains to be seen whether this will work as effectively as was the case in the previous enlargement (see also chapter 11 of this volume). The latter was significantly accelerated by competition dynamics resulting from the unique group approach, which Turkey, entering the EU on its own, will miss. This means that, while acceding the EU, Turkey will ultimately be pushed into the position of making even more painful concessions than was the case with Poland.

Although the Turkish government can adopt hard negotiation strategies to withstand the EU pressures in order to achieve the best deal possible, it will remain difficult to avoid the rise of Euro-sceptical feelings in society. As the accession negotiations advance and as the tough conditions become clearer, EU-negative feelings tend to increase, and political parties can use the emergence of popular Euro-scepticism strategically. As EU conditionality tends to constrain the possibilities of genuine intra-party debate and competition, the consensual Turkish parties may leave a vacuum, which can be filled by radical or populist parties. This can happen easily, especially when they succeed in reaching the segments of society directly affected (or feeling they are affected) by measures taken within the framework of accession. In this regard, the presence of an agrarian population and a group of orthodox nationalistic Muslims can be of significance in generating a shake-up of Turkish politics. The internal Turkish Europe debate may become polarized to such a degree that it will affect the government. It can do this both in a positive way by enhancing the government's negotiating position in Brussels, and in a negative way, by hindering the consolidation of the party system, limiting the possibilities of coalition formation and of stable government, causing delays of *acquis* implementation, and inconsistent and deficient positioning in the negotiations with the EU.

In order to avoid this, the Turkish government will have to establish a well functioning and accountable national EU-policy co-ordination structure, backed by a competent administration. Although the EU will stimulate institution building and administrative capacity during the process, these incentives may not necessarily lead to the intended results. Because of time pressure and *acquis* overload, the Turkish actors will not always be directed to the best and most legitimate policy options. As the past enlargements demonstrated, the application of diffuse EU conditionality can lead to a process of state (re-)centralization, rather than decentralization. This tends to empower the executive at the expense of the legislative and civil society, through which the process in the end will become a highly elite-driven one. It will be handled primarily by a small group of technocrats within the central executive, rather than by politicians accountable to the public, pushing the latter ever more to the adoption of anti-EU strategies. These potential effects on the Turkish polity, and by extension on Turkish politics, can result in EU accession coming at the cost of participatory democracy, regionalism and good governance – the models the EU is committed to promoting. Moreover it does not necessarily lead to the suppression of extremist tendencies in society, a hypothesis often heard among the Turkish elite. On the contrary, the process may reinforce these.

Notes

1. The countries are Hungary, Poland, Czech Republic, Slovakia, the three Baltic states (Latvia, Lithuania, Estonia), and Slovenia. The analysis does not concern the accession process of Malta or Cyprus.
2. The negotiations lasted between four and six years. Hungary, Poland, the Czech Republic, Slovenia and Estonia, together with Cyprus, began accession negotiations in March 1998, following the conclusion of the intergovernmental conference (IGC) in Luxembourg in 1997. Lithuania, Latvia and Slovakia – together with Malta, Bulgaria and Romania – were declared official candidate states by the IGC of Helsinki in 1999, and started the negotiations in 2000.
3. The impact of the EU accession process on Polish policy-making (changing content of specific policies due to EU-convergence), makes up a third area studied in the Europeanization literature. However, this aspect is beyond the scope of this chapter. The Europeanization literature predominantly uses sociological or historical institutionalism approaches.
4. Although the association agreements theoretically did not have the intention of including the CEECs in the EU, as was stated in the preamble to the agreement that they did in practice prepare the CEECs for membership. This is why Lippert *et al.* (2001) consider association negotiations to be the first phase in the accession process of CEEC.
5. Smith (2003) analyses the evolution of conditionality during time and explains why it has become more stringent in the CEECs accession, using a club approach.
6. Although the EU in this respect was accused of a divide-and-rule strategy, the applicants were just as insistent on the principle of differentiation (claiming its reinforcement on the Helsinki IGC in 1999), since they did not wish the progress of their accession to be linked to that of others (Friis and Murphy, 2000).
7. Breuss (2002) demonstrates in his analysis of the costs and benefits of enlargement that Germany, Austria and Italy would gain the most, while Spain, Portugal and Denmark would suffer the biggest losses. Baldwin *et al.* (1997) and Tuschhoff (2002) come to similar conclusions.
8. In some sensitive chapters like the one on the direct payments to farmers (the CAP), the EU member states could not reach a common position. In this case, only the Commission handed over a negotiation proposal to the candidate state.
9. According to Smith (2003, p. 108) the asymmetry between the two negotiation partners is even greater because of 'the pool of attraction' that is the EU. Engert et al. (2001, pp. 5–6) in this respect make notice of an ideational asymmetry in the past enlargement. Because of the collapse of the communist regime, in addition to superior material power, the West-European countries also possessed stronger normative power. The liberal democratic

Community norms, accepted by all major international organizations, formed the sole alternative to comply with for CEECs.

10. When it comes to economic relations, the CEECs were far more dependent on the EU market than the other way around (Schimmelfennig and Sedelmeier 2004, p. 665).

11. The EU member states agreed on the financial package at the IGC in December 2002 in Copenhagen. Here they decided to allocate even fewer sources to the accession of the ten new members, than the ceiling they had previously provided in Berlin 2001 for the accession of only six new members of the Luxemburg group.

12. Austria tried this in 2000 by putting forward the idea of a small enlargement with only the best and most advanced countries being Slovenia, Hungary and Czech Republic.

13. Schrijvers (2004, pp. 401–3) puts forward the thesis that the adopted Polish maximalist and defensive negotiation strategy may have done little to temper, but rather reinforced the popular feeling of second-class membership resulting from the asymmetrical pre-accession context.

14. With this change in polity what is meant is the power shift from the legislative to the executive, centralization of power in a 'core executive' consisting of 'islands of excellence', and centre–periphery relations.

15. Beichelt (2003) explains in more detail why Euro-scepticism is more common among radical rightist and leftist parties. The literature and analyses on party-based Euro-scepticism is rich. There exist two main conflicting theories. Authors such as Szczerbiak and Taggart (2000, 2003) see the phenomenon driven basically by electoral strategy. Others, such as Kopecky and Mudde (2002) explain it predominantly by referring to the party's identity and ideology. Researchers such as Batory and Sitter (2004), Beichelt (2003) and Bielasiak (2004) combine both.

16. See Batory and Sitter (2004) for the tendency toward Euro-scepticism among agrarian parties in both East and West Europe.

17. Most authors (Beichelt, 2003, Bielasiak, 2004, Henderson, 2002, Lewis, 2005) agree that the EU accession is a second-order issue in party politics of CEECs, cutting through the normal cleavage lines. It does not make up a cleavage in itself.

18. Reuters described this agency as "a cocktail of French arrogance, British euro-scepticism and Spanish impudence". (For an analysis of the Polish strategy on the IGC and its results, see Grabbe, 2002b).

References

Avery, G. (1995) 'The Commission's Perspective on the EFTA Accession Negotiations', Sussex European Institute (SEI) Working Paper, No. 12.

Avery, G. (2003) 'Lessons of the Accession Process', Paper presented for the 'Symposium on Enlargement and Governance in the New Europe', Marburg, 18–21 September 2003.

Bachmann, K. (2002) 'Reprezentacja interesów i negocjacje akcesyjne na przykładzie wybranych obszarów negocjacyjnych', in M. A. Cichocki (ed.), *Polska – Unia Europejska. W półdrogi. Wybrane Problemy*, Warsaw: Centrum Stosunków Międzynarodowych.

Baldwin, R. E., Francois, J. F. and Portes, R. (1997) 'The Costs and Benefits of Eastern Enlargement: The Impact on the EU and Central Europe', *Economic Policy*, vol. 12, no. 24, pp. 127–76.

Batory, A. and Sitter, N. (2004) 'Cleavages, Competition and Coalition-building: Agrarian Parties and the European Question in Western and East Central Europe', *European Journal of Political Research*, vol. 43, pp. 523–46.

Beichelt, T. (2003) 'Nationalism and Anti-EU Mobilization in Post Socialist Europe', Paper for the 'Eighth Biennial International Conference of the European Union Studies Association', March 27–29, Nashville, Tennessee.

Bielasiak, J. (2004) 'Party Systems and EU Accession: Euroscepticism in East Europe', Paper for the Conference on 'Public Opinion about the EU in Post-Communist Eastern Europe', Indiana University, Bloomington, Ind., April 2–3. 2004.

Breuss, F. (2002) 'Benefits and Dangers of EU Enlargement', *Empirica*, vol. 29, pp. 245–74.

Brücker, H., Schröder, P. J. H. and Weise, C. (2004) 'Doorkeepers and Gate-crashers: EU Enlargement and Negotiation Strategies', *European Integration*, vol. 26, no. 1, pp. 3–23.

Cichocki, M. A. (ed.) (2002) *Polska – Unia Europejska. W półdrogi. Wybrane Problemy*, Warsaw: Centrum Stosunków Międzynarodowych.

Cremona, M. (ed.) (2003) *The Enlargement of the European Union*, New York: Oxford University Press.

Dimitrova, A. (2002) 'Enlargement, Institution-Building and the EU's Administrative Capacity Requirement', *West European Politics*, vol. 25, no. 4, pp. 171–90.

Engert, S., Knobel, H. and Schimmelfennig, F. (2001) 'European Organizations and the Governance of Non-Member States. Domestic Conditions of Success', Paper prepared for the '4th IR Conference of the European Standing Group on International Relations', Canterbury 8–10 September 2001.

Friis, L. and Murphy, A. (2000) '"Turbo-Charged Negotiations": the EU and the Stability Pact for South Eastern Europe', *Journal of European Public Policy*, vol. 7, no. 5, pp. 767–86.

Goetz, K. H. (2001) 'Making Sense of Post-communist Central Administration: Modernization, Europeanization or Latinization?', *Journal of European Public Policy*, vol. 8, no. 6, pp. 1032–51.

Goetz, K. H. and Wollmann, H. (2001) 'Governmentalizing Central Executives in Post-communist Europe: a Four-Country Comparison', *Journal of European Public Policy*, vol. 8, no. 6, pp. 864–87.

Grabbe, H. (2001) 'How Does Europeanization Affect CEE Governance? Conditionality, Diffusion and Diversity', *Journal of European Public Policy*, vol. 8, no. 6, pp. 1013–31.

Grabbe, H. (2002a) 'European Union Conditionality and the Acquis Communautaire', *International Political Science Review*, vol. 23, no. 3, pp. 249–68.

Grabbe, H. (2002b) 'The Copenhagen Deal for Enlargement', Briefing Note, December 2002, London: CER, http://www.cer.org.uk.

Grabbe, H. (2004) 'When Negotiations Begin: The Next Phase in EU–Turkey Relations', London: CER Essays, Centre for European Reform, November.

Green Cowles, M. and Smith, M. (2000) *The State of the European Union. Risks, Reform, Resistance, and Revival*, New York: Oxford University Press.

Grzymała-Busse, A. and Innes, A. (2003) 'Great Expectations: The EU and Domestic Political Competition in East Central Europe', *East European Politics and Societies*, vol. 17, no. 1, pp. 64–73.

Henderson, K. (2002) 'Opposing Europe: Euroscepticism and Political Parties. Exceptionalism or Convergence? Euroscepticism and Party systems in Central and Eastern Europe', Paper for the ECPR Joint sessions of Workshops, Turin, 22–27 March.

Hughes, J., Sasse, G. and Gordon, C. (2002) 'Saying "Maybe" to the "Return To Europe". Elites and the Political Space for Euroscepticism in Central and Eastern Europe', *European Union Politics*, vol. 3, no. 3, pp. 327–55.

Hughes, J., Sasse, G. and Gordon, C. (2004) 'Conditionality and Compliance in the EU's Eastward Enlargement: Regional Policy and the Reform of Subnational Government', *Journal of Common Market Studies*, vol. 42, no. 3, pp. 523–51.

Innes, A. (2001) 'Party Competition in Post-Communist Europe: The Great Electoral Lottery', Centre for European Studies Central and Eastern Europe, Working Paper Series, 54, June.

Inotai, A. (2003) 'The 'Eastern Enlargements' of the European Union', in M. Cremona (ed.), *The Enlargement of the European Union*, New York: Oxford University Press.

Kopecky, P. and Mudde, C. (2002) 'The Two Sides of Euroscepticism. Party Positions on European Integration in East Central Europe', *European Union Politics*, vol. 3, no. 3, pp. 297–326.

Korkut, U. (2002) 'The European Union and the Accession Process in Hungary, Poland and Romania: Is There a Place for Social Dialogue?', *Perspectives on European Politics and Society*, vol. 3, no. 2, pp. 297–324.

Kułakowski, J., Stępniak, A. and Umiński, S. (eds) *Strategy of Poland's Membership in the European Union*, Warsaw: Urząd Komitetu Integracji Europejskiej.

Lewis, P. G. (2005) 'EU Enlargement and Party Systems in Central Europe', *Journal of Communist Studies and Transition Politics*, vol. 21, no. 2, pp. 171–199.

Lippert, B., Umbach, G. and Wessels, W. (2001) 'Europeanization of CEE Executives: EU Membership Negotiations as a Shaping Power', *Journal of European Public Policy*, vol. 8, pp. 980–1012.

Nowak-Far, A. and Michoński, A. (2005) 'Coordination of European Policy in Poland: The importance of Path Dependence and Increasing Returns for the Determination of European Viability', Paper for the 'European Union Studies Association's Ninth Biennial International Conference' Austin, Texas, 31 March–2 April.

Phinnemore, D. (2004) '"And not forgetting the rest ...": EU (25) and the Changing Dynamics of EU Enlargement', Paper for the Second Pan-European Conference Standing Group on EU Politics, Bologna, 24–26 June.

Pridham, G. (2001) 'EU Accession and Domestic Politics: Policy Consensus and Interactive Dynamics in Central and Eastern Europe', *Perspectives on European Politics and Society*, vol. 1, no. 1, pp. 49–74.

Pridham, G. (2002) 'EU Enlargement and Consolidating Democracy in Post-Communist States – Formality and Reality', *Journal of Common Market Studies*, vol. 40, no. 3, pp. 953–73.

Rulikova, M. (2004) 'The Influence of Pre-accession Status on Euroscepticism in EU Candidate Countries', *Perspectives on European Politics and Society*, vol. 5, no. 1, pp. 29–60.

Schimmelfennig, F. (2001) 'The Community Trap: Liberal Norms, Rhetorical Action, and the Eastern Enlargement of the European Union', *International Organization*, vol. 55, no. 1, pp. 47–80.

Schimmelfennig, F. and Sedelmeier, U. (2004). 'Governance by Conditionality: EU Rule Transfer to the Candidate Countries of Central and Eastern Europe', *Journal of European Public Policy*, vol. 11, no. 4, pp. 661–79.

Schimmelfennig, F., Engert, S. and Knobel, H. (2003) 'Costs, Commitments, and Compliance. The Impact of EU Democratic Conditionality on Latvia, Slovakia, and Turkey', *Journal of Common Market Studies*, vol. 41, no. 3, pp. 495–517.

Schrijvers, A. (2004) 'When Outsiders become Insiders. When 'oni' becomes 'my'. Poland as a Full Member of the EU in Need of a New Negotiation, Legitimization and Communication Strategy. A New EU discourse in Poland?', in J. Kułakowski, A. Stępniak, S. Umiński (eds.) *Strategy of Poland's Membership in the European Union*, Warsaw: Urząd Komitetu Integracji Europejskiej, pp. 381–414.

Sedelmeier, U. (2000) 'Eastern Enlargement: Risk, Rationality, and Role-Compliance', in M. Green Cowles and M. Smith, *The State of the European Union. Risks, Reform, Resistance, and Revival*, New York: Oxford University Press.

Sedelmeier, U. (2002) 'Sectoral Dynamics of EU Enlargement: Advocacy, Access and Alliances in a Composite Policy', *Journal of European Public Policy*, vol. 9, no. 4, pp. 627–49.

Smith, K. E. (2003) 'The Evolution and Application of EU Membership Conditionality', in M. Cremona (ed.), *The Enlargement of the European Union*, New York: Oxford University Press, pp. 105–39.

Smith, K. E. (2005) 'The EU and Central and Eastern Europe: The Absence of Interregionalism', *European Integration*, vol. 27, no. 3, pp. 347–64.

Stawarska, R. (1999) 'EU Enlargement from the Polish Perspective', *Journal of European Public Policy*, vol. 6, no. 5, pp. 822–38.

Szczerbiak, A. (2002) 'Poland's Unexpected Political Earthquake: The September 2001 Parliamentary Election', *Journal of Communist Studies and Transition Politics*, vol. 18, no. 3, pp. 41–76.

Szczerbiak, A and Taggart, P. (2000) 'Opposing Europe: Party Systems and Opposition to the Union, the Euro and Europeanization', Sussex European Institute Working Paper, No. 36.

Szczerbiak, A. and Taggart, P. (2003) 'Theorising Party-Based Euroscepticism: Problems of Definition, Measurement and Causality', Sussex European Institute Working Paper, No. 69.

Trzaskowski, R. (2002) 'From Candidate to Member State: Poland and the Future of the EU', Institute for Security Studies, Occasional Papers, No. 37, September, http://www.iss-eu.org.

Tuschhoff, C. (2002) 'The Politics of Finalizing EU Enlargement: Towards an Ever Looser Union?', AICGS Policy Paper, No. 19, Washington, DC: American Institute for Contemporary German Studies.

Verheugen, G. (2000) 'The Enlargement of the European Union', *European Foreign Affairs Review,* vol. 5, pp. 439–44.

Wiener, A. (2002) 'Finality vs. Enlargement. Constitutive Practices and Opposing Rationales in the Reconstruction of Europe', Paper prepared for Jean Monnet Working Papers, NYU, 20 September 2002, http://www.qub.qc.uk/ies/staff/wiener.html.

Zubek, R. (2001) 'A Core in Check: The Transformation of the Polish Core Executive', *Journal of European Public Policy*, vol. 8, no. 6, pp. 911–32.

3

Reinventing Europe? Turkey, European Union Accession and Europeanization

Kenneth Dyson

This chapter offers a critique of the prevailing view within 'old' European Union member states that EU enlargement is essentially a problem for the accession states. EU enlargement is not only a core project through which the EU has established its comparative international advantage in 'soft' power by means of the instrument of the conditionality attached to accession (Leonard, 2005). In addition, each enlargement round – 1973, 1981, 1986, 1995, 2004 and 2007/8 – has been a stimulus to reflect on the nature of the EU's identity, to reinvent what it does, how it sees itself and how 'older' member states relate to it. The 'big bang' enlargement to East Central Europe (and Cyprus and Malta) in May 2004 was a particularly dramatic example, underlining the acute adjustment problems among 'old' member states. Enlargement to the western Balkans, and especially to Turkey, further highlights the extent to which the EU is challenged to reinvent itself: whether by a continuing collective 'deepening', a 'rolling back' of collective EU action, or new forms of 'differentiated' integration (at the extreme a 'core' Europe, perhaps based on the euro area or a 'directorate' of large states). 'Deepening' and 'differentiation' have been the historic patterns, but continuity is not assured if a particular enlargement acts as a critical juncture in EU development.

'Accession' Europeanization prior to EU entry is problematic in two respects. It is not always clear what precisely compliance with the EU *acquis communautaire* requires from accession states (for example, in meeting environmental policy requirements, regulating freedom of movement or regionalizing government) (see Grabbe, 2003; Hughes *et al.*, 2005). More fundamentally, the history of enlargements from the first round in 1973 has shown that each enlargement is also a problem of painful adaptation for the existing EU member states and

.as raised often divisive questions about the EU's identity and EU 'deepening' in institutional and policy terms. For example, the debate between 1961 and 1973 regarding the UK's entry precipitated an internal debate between Gaullist and Atlanticist conceptions of the EU. Though Turkish entry raises similar questions in an acute and difficult form, there is nothing new in principle about how the process works. EU member states have learnt from painful experiences with past enlargements to be very conscious and protective of the EU's 'absorptive capacity'. For this reason, the strategic self-interests of an accession state reside in making a firm, unequivocal commitment not just to meeting entry conditions but also to the long-term political project of 'deepening' the EU. Seeking the first objective without the second would raise serious doubts about the credibility of Turkey as a potential member, and invite disruption of the accession process.

In developing the argument, this chapter addresses two questions: what is EU accession doing to Turkey, and what is Turkish accession (and the most recent waves of eastern enlargement) in the process of doing to the EU? This two-way perspective is important, because the EU is not a 'given' for compliance purposes: it is a changing and moving target, to which Turkey (and existing EU members) must adapt and ultimately contribute. The question 'Does Turkey fit into the EU?' must be set alongside the question: 'What are successive waves of accession doing to the traditional EU?' These are two sides of the same coin.

The clear 'no' votes in the 2005 referenda on the European Constitutional Treaty in France and the Netherlands – two 'founder' members – testify, in part at least, to the mounting sense that the traditional 'core' EU states are dealing with an EU that is no longer made in their image and set on their terms. How earlier waves of eastern enlargement affect the EU has profound implications for the adaptive pressures on Turkey and opportunities for Turkish influence.

The Europeanization of Turkey: what will EU accession do to Turkey, and how?

For Turkey, as for previous accession states, entry to the European Union is a historically novel, transforming experience, in that it is based not on the old European pattern of threat of external physical coercion by a 'big' power, but rather on voluntary compliance with a body of mutually constraining and independently enforced law. It involves the exercise of 'soft' power, even if it contains a large element of compliance with 'hard' law (rules with sanction mechanisms for their enforcement). In the sense that Turkey shares this experience with other earlier accession states, it is not alone or unique. Not least, Turkey can learn from the experiences of the first and second waves of eastern enlargement in 2004 and 2007/8.

The five central domestic challenges are related to political, institutional and policy domains and include the following. First, a firm domestic pre-commitment to a set of 'deep' political beliefs, which are outlined in the Copenhagen criteria of 1993 and further elaborated in the EU Charter of Fundamental Rights. They include stable institutions guaranteeing democracy, the rule of law, human rights and respect for the protection of minorities; the existence of a functioning market economy, as well as the capacity to cope with the competitive pressure and market forces within the Union; an ability to assume the obligations of membership, including adherence to the aims of political, economic and monetary union; and the Union's own capacity to absorb new members while maintaining the momentum of European integration. Domestic institutional arrangements, policies and practices must demonstrate compliance with these general beliefs for accession negotiations to be credible and brought to a clear conclusion. Without this 'deep' commitment of principle and practice on matters as wide-ranging as human rights, the rule of law, pluralism and tolerance, to open competitive markets and 'sound money and finances', membership should not be contemplated. This commitment extends to clear official support for an open debate about Turkish and European historical questions, including Armenia and the Kurds. 'Accession' Europeanization involves the domestic empowerment of actors who seek to root out authoritarian structures and practices in favour of a rights-centred and pluralistic political culture of open and tolerant debate. It works only to the extent that there is widespread public support for this type of political culture. In short, democratization cannot simply be imposed top-down via Europeanization (Vachudova, 2005).

Second, a domestic political consensus that informal or implicit conditionality requires a commitment to a Kantian conception of - international relations, with respect both to relations with other member states and to external relations. This Kantian value system includes a commitment to multilateralism, the primacy of law, the use of economic incentives, and social justice in organizing European and international relations – in short, a 'civilian power' perspective on international relations (Maull, 1992; Wendt, 1999). The associated policy of 'good neighbourliness' has to be applied to, and demonstrated in, relations that border on Turkey, including Armenia and Cyprus. 'Accession' Europeanization involves strong adaptive pressures on domestic security culture and military reforms.

Third, a domestic political acceptance of the implications of the underlying asymmetry of power in accession negotiations and consequent external incentives to adapt (Schimmelfennig and Sedelemeier, 2005). This asymmetry is unavoidable in that an accession state has to comply with an *acquis communautaire* that it had no part in agreeing. It becomes more visible with each successive wave of enlargement simply because the *acquis* has grown (for example, in justice and home affairs, the environment, the single European market, and European Monetary Union (EMU) since Spanish and Portuguese entries in 1986). The domestic legitimacy of this asymmetry can only derive from a shared belief among expert and political elites that the short-term costs of domestic transformation are overridden by the long-term benefits of EU entry – like access to a huge, rich and sophisticated market; locking in economic stability; support for regional and rural development through EU structural funds; environmental and infrastructural improvements; freedom of movement to live, study and work; and, more broadly the firmer anchoring of a set of fundamental rights. This legitimacy can be contested by domestic forces that place weight on symbolic issues such as loss of cultural identity and national sovereignty. Accordingly, 'accession' Europeanization tests vulnerability to traditional 'sovereignty' arguments and capacity for 'time-consistent' behaviour as well.

Fourth, sustained domestic political support for a protracted, difficult and painful process of domestic transformation in order to meet the EU requirements. This transformation embraces not just policies, but also – and more problematically – public institutions (including army, police, prosecution service and judiciary), and party and electoral politics. In the process vested interests are threatened, veto players are aroused, and domestic elites tested to use their political skills to negotiate complex reforms. EU accession involves two processes of Europeanization (Dyson and Goetz, 2003). Powerful 'top-down' pressures arise where clear EU policy and institutional templates highlight a 'misfit' with domestic rules and practices. The more specific and detailed the template, the greater the 'top-down' pressure and challenge to domestic politics (Green Cowles *et al.*, 2001). In addition, a more diffuse 'bottom-up' Europeanization occurs when domestic expert and political elites use European models – even where they are not enshrined in EU law – to justify and expedite domestic reforms. 'Accession'

Europeanization opens up new opportunities for domestic reformers, not least to anticipate the EU requirements. There is a strong 'top-down' element to accession Europeanization because of the 'condition-ality' requirements that are attached to membership and involve compliance with the *acquis*. Though varying in specificity and detail, they embrace competition, energy, telecommunications, environmental, health and safety, consumer protection, border control, monetary and fiscal policies, for example. 'Bottom-up' Europeanization characterizes the accession process in areas such as welfare state reform, employment policies, labour-market reforms and collective bargaining: especially those areas embraced by the Lisbon process of raising growth potential and the employment rate. In short, 'accession' Europeanization is a pervasive and at the same time differentiated process.

Fifth, given the timescale of the accession process, the scope and pace of EU-based domestic transformation raises the question of how to deal with threats from 'reform fatigue', from domestic veto players, and from national populists and 'hard' Euro-sceptics. Difficult domestic questions emerge about the political management of the time dimension of EU-related reforms: about their sequencing, timing and tempo, so that veto players and populists are not given incentives to mobilize fundamental opposition to the accession process. These problems of managing political time in 'accession' Europeanization speak in favour of a long period of negotiation.

In those policy sectors where there are 'derogations', the process of 'accession' Europeanization extends beyond the point of formal EU membership. These policies include Schengen policies on the freedom of movement of people, some aspects of agricultural and regional policies, and EMU – first accession to and membership of ERM II (the exchange-rate mechanism through which the currency is linked in a narrow band of fluctuation with the euro), and then entry into the Euro Area. Here 'accession' Europeanization continues after EU entry, with the EU institutions acting as 'gate-keepers' to full membership through continuing requirements to comply with conditionality. This shaping power exists in particular in relation to compliance with the so-called Maastricht convergence criteria, which cover inflation, budget deficit, public debt, exchange-rate stability and long-term interest rates (Dyson, 2002). Meeting these criteria involves difficult trade-offs between macroeconomic stabilization, industrial upgrading and social cohesion (Dyson, 2006).

What lessons can Turkey learn from the first wave of eastern enlargement (the entry of eight states, plus Cyprus and Malta, in 2004)?

Compliance with EU conditionality occasionally involves detailed and specific EU institutional models and policy prescriptions. More often, however, it involves various uncertainties. In the practice of accession negotiations some parts of the *acquis* prove to be more important than others: notably, issues such as external border controls and the treatment of minorities, like the Roma, rose up the agenda (Grabbe, 2003). Another source of uncertainty is whether accession states possess the basic administrative, judicial and police capacity to comply effectively (Schimmelfennig and Sedelmeier, 2005). This issue of domestic institutional capacity became sensitive in relation to Bulgaria and Romania, not just in health and safety or customs controls, but also more generally with respect to corruption in public life. Additionally, internal disagreements and variations of practice within the EU itself beg questions about just how far an accession state must go in compliance: for example, in reducing state subsidies to industry, in tax policy co-ordination, in social policy, in environmental policies, or in justice and home affairs. Another source of uncertainty stems from the question of 'whom to satisfy?' The potential EU veto player varies. The European Commission is the key player in the single market, the European Central Bank on EMU, the Council in justice and home affairs. Depending on the issue, different states are pivotal. In general political terms, because of entrenched domestic doubts and opposition, Austria, France and perhaps the Netherlands, are potential veto players for Turkey to satisfy. No less seriously, how EU member states might behave on particular issues can be difficult to predict, and is a matter of ongoing political intelligence. One can, however, expect that border controls and freedom of movement of labour are likely to be highly sensitive issues for Germany. Finally, the precise standard to be met can be unclear – for example, in environmental policy or state aid, even in meeting EU fiscal policy standards. Lurking in the background are the varying sensitivities and changing agendas of existing EU member states.

Failures of compliance by existing EU member states – for example, in state aid, in implementing single market rules, in fiscal policy rules, and in providing reliable and valid statistics, undermine the legitimacy and negotiating power of the EU and its capacity to exert 'soft' power. Compliance is relative for Turkey – to the standards set by traditional EU members and by first-wave accession states in 2004. However, the underlying realities of asymmetry of power in the accession process are a disincentive to a domestic accession strategy based on using charges of hypocrisy against existing member states. This strategy would invite accusations of Turkish complacency about what future membership entails. If accession is seen as a vital strategic interest of Turkey, the appropriate strategy is to highlight a relatively better Turkish performance in compliance. With respect to EMU, for example, this might involve making both economic forecasting and national statistical services completely independent of the Turkish government – with consequent credibility gains.

The relative character of compliance and the uncertainties attached to conditionality provide accession states with some room to manoeuvre. Clearly, this discretion varies across policy areas (it is more limited in telecommunications than energy, for example) and over time (more constrained with ERM II entry). The behaviour of 'first-wave' east central European accession states also reflected differences of domestic belief about whether and how to use their room for manoeuvre. Hungary was basically very accommodating; Poland was more assertive, notably over agriculture, the financial perspective, tax harmonization and voting rights in the Council. This difference can be explained at least in part by a Polish belief that it could count on not being vetoed by a large EU player because of its historical and cultural role, and its role as the largest eastern entrant. Such a belief does not have the similar credibility in the Turkish case. Here, the Austrians and French have created a 'gate-keeping' role on Turkish entry for themselves by pre-committing to referenda. This move reduces the room for manoeuvre of Turkey in accession negotiations.

The east central European accession process has been associated with substantial progress both in real and in nominal convergence with the EU (Dyson, 2006). Inward investment and trade have proved to be powerful motors of economic development, along with access to EU cohesion funds. Critically, as with previous enlargements, some parts of the so-called 'periphery' – such as Finland, Ireland and Spain earlier – have benefited more than others – like Greece and Portugal – and converged with the 'core'. At least in the short term, the perceived benefits of EU accession in Poland and elsewhere, not least in agriculture, have reduced opportunities for Euro-scepticism to flourish. A vanguard of 'first-wave' states led by the Baltic States, Slovenia, Cyprus and Malta (and more recently Slovakia) is targeting 2007/8 for entry into the Euro Area. Even before EU entry, Bulgaria has proved a pacesetter rather than a laggard in euro entry.

East central European accession is linked to increasing problems of centre–periphery relations within these states. Regional disparities reflect the geographic agglomeration effects of a single market and emerging currency union. The emerging centres are closely connected by transport and communications to the large, rich markets to the west – for example, the Prague region to Germany and the cross-national economic space that connects the automobile industry in Hungary, Poland and Slovakia. Turkey can expect a similar phenomenon around Istanbul and western Anatolia. The result is an internal geographic asymmetry of effects, with potentially long-term consequences, not least in inflaming Kurdish dissent. With EU entry eastern Anatolia poses increasing challenges for regional policy, including the construction of institutional capacity in this region to make effective use of pre-accession funding programmes.

Earlier experience of eastern enlargement has sensitized EU policy-makers to the importance both of supporting the development of executive, administrative and judicial capacity to comply with the *acquis* and of developing a vibrant civil society. The significance of institutional capacity and civil society was brought home to Turkey by the devastating earthquake of 1999 and what it revealed about state capacity, about civil society, and about how they relate to each other, not just in managing a crisis but more broadly in explaining its scale. For these reasons, priority has to be given to strengthening executive co-ordination and to administrative and judicial reforms at all levels. Not least, public policy has to focus on fostering the development and the role of non-governmental organizations (NGOs) in public policy. It also has to reflect on how to manage the tension between centralizing domestic preparations for EU accession, opening up a domestic 'democratic deficit', and building regional and social capacity through the active engagement of sub-national and societal actors in EU accession (Agh, 2004).

The 'first-' and 'second-wave' accession processes have demonstrated the growing importance of the European Parliament. It has sought to carve out an increased role, notably over Bulgarian and Romanian accession, where it has demanded more action to tackle corruption and to improve judicial capacity and independence. The sensitivities surrounding Turkish accession are likely to lead to an even stronger shaping influence from the European Parliament. Hence Turkish negotiation policy will have to pay even greater attention to the European Parliament than accession states in previous enlargement rounds.

Drawing lessons for Turkey is made difficult because its accession differs from east central European accession in three key ways: Islamic culture and religion; the absence of a post-communist transition experience; and population size. Islamic culture and religion functions as both an opportunity and a threat to the EU. To the extent that Turkey sees EU accession as a vital strategic interest, it is crucial for

Turkish policy and behaviour to demonstrate consistently that the EU has a historic opportunity to reinvent itself by developing a new world role as a bridge across traditional boundaries ('East meets West' in Europe). By showing in a practical way that globalization does not entail an inexorable 'clash of civilizations', the EU can reinforce its 'soft' power. In this way, a shared 'co-ordinative' discourse can be constructed to bind together Turkish and EU elites. In terms of a 'communicative' discourse aimed at Turkish public opinion, Turkish elites can stress that EU accession offers Turkey a historic opportunity to play a new shaping role in this process, and to escape what the novelist Orhan Pamuk (2005), writing of Istanbul, describes as a post-imperial melancholy and isolation. Conversely, many in the EU see Turkish accession in the context of threat from resurgent fundamentalism (not just Islamic) to the secular traditions of the Enlightenment. Ultimately, it is a matter of how elites and the public (and media) imagine Turkey in Europe. Turkish accession is, first and foremost a challenge to our imaginations to rethink collective European identity.

The absence of post-communist transition experience means that Turkey does not carry the legacy of the double historic shocks that shaped east central Europe: first, of externally imposed isolation and subjection as part of the Soviet bloc (1945–89), from which EU membership offers a final escape (hence the 'return to Europe' theme is highly compelling); and, second, of transition 'shock therapy' to liberal democracy and market economy after 1989. It might be argued that Turkey has also suffered isolation and subjection, but that this has been internal as well as external in source. If this is the case, then EU accession is another form of 'return to Europe': a historic leap, involving the re-branding of a new Republican Turkey that is no longer the 'sick man' but rather the 'rejuvenator' of Europe – young, energetic and cosmopolitan. 'Re-branding' alongside accession highlights a major challenge – that successful accession requires generational change in Turkey to make the process convincing. Generational change may prove to be a source of great domestic friction, not least as it accompanies changed narratives about Turkey.

Second, Turkey has not had the shock therapy and institutional rupture of east central Europe so close to EU accession. This means that the country has been spared the scale of shock endured by east central Europe. At the same time, as a consequence, Turkey lacks some of the flexibility of economic and political structures seen in much of east central Europe. On the other hand, it can draw on longer traditions of engagement with Western institutions and markets, at least to the extent that those who have been engaged in this way play leadership roles within Turkey. The big question is whether Republican institutional continuity, and continuity in domestic structures of economic governance, equate with capacity to adapt effectively to the challenges of the EU. Economic crisis (as in 2001) and the 1999 earthquake have been important in highlighting issues of executive and political capacity. A key question is whether Turkey can escape the long accession process without another, perhaps bigger, crisis that will shake confidence in its institutions and raise further questions about Turkish membership. This question touches *inter alia* on the stability of the banking and financial systems, and the prospects and implications of a resurfacing of the Kurdish conflicts.

The population size of Turkey (and demographic projection), combined with its low per capita GDP, makes it much harder for the EU to absorb than any previous single accession state. In institutional terms, Turkish entry has implications for voting rights in the Council and has the potential to re-open and sharpen conflicts between large and small states. Turkey's relative economic backwardness and size raise painful questions for net contributors to the EU budget and for states that lose out on eligibility for cohesion funds. This factor highlights the second theme of how EU enlargement is changing the EU.

Before moving on to the second question, it is helpful to put 'accession' Europeanization into perspective by asking what EU membership has done to traditional members such as France and Germany (Dyson and Goetz, 2003). They differ in that they have been exposed to its effects from the outset in all EU policy projects. EU membership is part of their 'genetic code'. This role as founding members has produced a traditional pattern of accommodation rather than resistance to the EU. Nevertheless, research on Europeanization shows that, even there, the effects of European integration have been very differential (Heritier, 2001; Knill and Lehmkuhl, 2002). Public policies and expert elites have been affected the most by EU membership. In contrast, domestic political elites have been driven by a preference for reconciling the benefits of the EU with their paramount strategic interest in party competition for national office and winning national elections. This interest has not created a political incentive to pay close attention to European issues. Hence, increasingly, Europeanized policies and expert elites co-exist with weakly Europeanized public institutions (such as national parliaments) and politics (parties and elections). This phenomenon highlights the central problem of European integration: its technocratic bias and the lack of deep engagement by political elites and the public (and the media) (Majone, 2005).

How is enlargement affecting the EU?

Despite the asymmetry of power and conditionality involved in accession negotiations, successive waves of enlargement are changing the EU itself and how its traditional member states relate to it. New questions are emerging such as 'whose EU is it?' and 'What kind of EU?' – for example, whether it will be characterized by more 'differential' integration, perhaps even the emergence of a 'core' Europe; or what kind of social model, if any, it represents. The emergence of attempts to co-ordinate the 'big' three – the UK, France and Germany – in foreign and security policy are seen as indicative of a potential for a core Europe. Similarly, EU policy-makers debate the relative claims of the 'Anglo-Saxon', Mediterranean, Nordic and Rhineland models of capitalism as the basis for constructing the EU social model (Sapir, 2005).

While these are not answered definitively in the European Constitutional Treaty, some answers about the nature of European identity are ruled out and some are included. It is not a Christian, let alone a Roman Catholic Europe, though it respects Christian (and other) principles. Fundamentally it is a pluralist community that tolerates and encourages diversity (and insists that diversity of beliefs, opinions and practices be respected) within a broad framework of Enlightenment beliefs. To the extent that the Enlightenment represents its core set of shared beliefs, the Kemalist Republic should not have an underlying problem of 'fit' with the EU (Mango, 2004).

More problematic is uncertainty about the relative importance of market competition and social solidarity in the EU's basic values. This issue ranges France against the UK and many east European states. Potentially, the Nordic model of flexible labour markets with generous social programmes has the greatest potential to act as a magnet around which consensus might develop. However, it is by no means obvious whether, and how, existing EU Mediterranean states, regardless of Turkey, are able to emulate this model, or even whether the Nordic states will continue to be success stories. Interestingly, the debate about different social models does not take into account east central Europe and the implications of its accession on how the EU might be reinvented (Sapir, 2005). The behaviour of these new accession states and its effect on traditional members will prove to be an important variable that conditions Turkish accession negotiations. The more irritated and threatened is France by threats to its own model, the greater the potential for the country to act as a veto player.

Recent enlargements have produced major effects on the EU that will grow over the period of Turkish accession. These include the following.

Size, diversity and 'soft' power

The basic institutional structures, policy beliefs and rules of the EU were established by its six founder members, the 'north-west' core, and, within this core, France and Germany acted as the 'motor' or 'engine' of European integration (Dyson and Goetz, 2003). This historic role continued into the 1990s, most recently with the Schengen process on freedom of movement, EMU, and the single currency. When one considers their gross domestic product (GDP), financial weight and trade, they remain at the core of the EU and the Euro Area (Dyson, 2006). However, successive enlargements have made the EU more diverse in membership and raised the question of whether this traditional core's power is shrinking. Alongside the north-west core, there are Mediterranean, Nordic and now Baltic and east central European member states (with the three Baltic States being different from the four 'Visegrad' states – the Czech Republic, Hungary, Poland and Slovakia – and Slovenia different again from the others). Each has different experiences of both European integration and Europeanization, not least in the geo-strategic and historical contexts, and timing of accession. There are also awkward outliers such as the UK. Turkey will add appreciably to the EU's problems of size and diversity, because of its historically unparalleled combination of population with low per capita GDP. The key question for traditional member states is whether Turkey will prove to be another awkward outlier (and not welcome); a catalyst for a new regional grouping (say Balkan, Black Sea or eastern Mediterranean); or be assimilated into the existing Mediterranean pattern of relationship to the EU. Whichever scenario prevails, the north-west core is likely to experience a much more painful and conflict-laden relationship with the EU (Dyson and Goetz, 2003). The days in which this relationship of north-west core and EU could be characterized as simply a combination of coexistence and mutual adaptation are disappearing. This phenomenon of a 'shrinking' core is accentuated by its declining 'soft' power. France and Germany are – with Italy – the problem economies of the Euro Area. Their economic performance contrasts negatively with Finland, Ireland and Spain within the Euro Area, and with the UK, Denmark and Sweden outside it. Germany is no longer the 'paymaster' of Europe, and thus has lost a key traditional instrument to allow it to play a pivotal role in resolving EU disputes. The EU's problems of reinventing itself are accentuated by the defensiveness and fear that enlargement – and, more important standing domestic structural problems – has spawned.

Foreign and security policy

The new accession states in east central Europe, led by Poland, Lithuania and Slovakia, have defined for themselves a new proactive role in pushing an EU agenda of spreading freedom and democracy through the prospect of EU membership. This agenda is not so much inspired by pro-American sentiments as by their own historical memories as post-communist societies of isolation and suppression, and by geo-strategic interests in stabilizing their borders. The acute irritation in Paris was revealed in response to the support of most of these states (declared before EU entry) for the US/British armed intervention in Iraq in 2003. This proactive role was further developed over the Ukraine crisis in 2004, and in relation to accelerating transformation in the western Balkans. It has important implications for the way in which Turkey defines its position in relation to the EU foreign and security policy. It also means that, for the new EU member states, the Ukraine and the west Balkans are a more pressing priority than Turkey.

Cultural power

French was the traditional lingua franca language of the EU across its institutions. French models also shaped the way that EU administrative organization and culture evolved. However, over a long period, beginning with the 1973 accessions (Denmark, Ireland, the UK) the use of English gathered momentum. The tipping point was the 1995 accession of Austria, Finland and Sweden. English had become the primary working language (and was indeed to be the only working language in the European Central Bank). With it came the Anglo-Saxon terminology of management and economic organization. This development further accentuated the sense that the traditional north-west core was eroding. The Dutch, for example, had little trouble with the rise of English, compared to France. Germany and Italy were relatively indifferent. In the original Six, three states were French-speaking. In the current EU of 27 states, France's linguistic and cultural influence is diminished.

Competitiveness

The traditional core EU states possess high labour costs and generous social benefits founded on a strong belief in 'the' European 'social model'. The combination of a single European market with eastern enlargement to low-wage, low-tax states creates a fundamental challenge. Companies have major economic incentives to 'delocalize' to east central Europe and potentially beyond it, especially where low wages go hand in hand with high skill levels and good 'hard' infrastructure (such as transport) and 'soft' infrastructure (such as cultural facilities and quality). East European states have been proactive on this front too, especially through 'flat' tax systems (modelled on Estonia, these have been adopted in Slovakia and Romania and are planned for Poland). Hence political elites in the core states perceive the threat of a haemorrhaging of jobs, incomes and tax revenues, and consequent erosion of the 'social model'. Moreover, their own higher wages and social benefits are an incentive to inward migration and further pressures on labour markets and social security systems. There is, in short, a mounting problem load on the core states that is producing new questions about whether, on balance, they benefit from the enlarged and changing EU. Wages, working conditions, labour-market policies and social policies are increasingly challenged, and the discourse of wage and social 'dumping' is gathering pace. The domestic difficulties of absorbing these current pressures make the EU a less unitary actor in accession negotiations with Turkey and others and, in consequence, more complex to deal with.

EU budget

Previous enlargements, notably in the Mediterranean, have been associated with substantial increases in the EU budget. The 2004 enlargement broke this precedent. This important contextual change follows from the fiscal stresses that the richer EU states face. Germany, in particular, is no longer the EU paymaster, especially after the budgetary shock of unification. The German government has redefined its huge financing of German unification as an extra contribution to European unification. Hence, faced by tighter capping of EU revenues, future enlargements will involve a more intense and painful politics of redistribution from existing to new beneficiaries of EU spending. In consequence, the visible material gains to states such as Ireland and Spain, regardless of France and Italy, will decline. France, in particular, faces a potential challenge from Common Agricultural Policy (CAP) reforms to accommodate enlargement that are fraught with potentially negative domestic political effects. Turkish accession negotiations will be paralleled by a difficult internal EU debate on EU budget reforms, focusing on agriculture and research and development. This debate goes again to the heart of how the enlarged EU reinvents itself, represented in a shift from 'old' to 'new' spending programmes that support greater innovative capacity.

Conclusion

Negotiating Turkish accession is bound up in a complex two-way process: an extended period of asymmetry of power and 'top-down' pressures for comprehensive domestic transformation in order to comply with the *acquis* and to secure the long-term benefits of EU membership; and an EU that is changing with successive waves of enlargement, potentially in unpredictable ways. The interaction of these processes is fraught with political sensitivities in both Turkey and the EU and its member states. These sensitivities represent an acute two-level political management problem for Turkish elites, always mindful of the risks from a domestic dynamic of nationalist populism that can derail the pursuit of long-term vital national interests in the accession process. The demands on domestic political leadership are likely to be acute.

First, the length of the accession negotiations, right through to eventual Euro Area membership (say, notionally, in 2020) opens up repeated opportunities for the process to be contested domestically. Expert elites and many in the political elite will present EU accession as an 'enabling constraint' that delivers stable economic development and a pluralistic liberal democratic culture, using it to legitimize domestic reforms. On the other hand, populist political leaders will be provided with incentives to blame the EU for problematic or failed reforms, or for budgetary or foreign-exchange crises. The case will be made that, given the asymmetry of power, Turkey is getting a bad deal or its government is displaying weakness abroad. While these domestic political patterns were seen before the 2004 enlargement, notably in Poland, they did not derail the final outcome. They will not do so in Turkey so long as political as well as expert elites display deep-seated conviction that EU entry is central to national interests and the historic role of Turkey, and develop and sustain an appropriate 'communicative' discourse aimed at generating domestic public consensus (Schmidt, 2002). They will also need to recognize that economic and political costs become higher, the longer governments defer reforms. Turkey will, however, have its own versions of the Polish farmers groups and Catholic Church, institutional vehicles for an exclusive cultural nationalism and identity.

Second, Turkish accession will pose difficult questions about domestic executive, administrative, judicial and police capacity to handle the EU *acquis*, and about developing a vibrant civil society to complement the state. The key challenge is to build institutional capacity in anticipation of accession, including regional and social capacity. This issue is receiving increasing attention with successive waves of enlargement (Agh, 2004). A domestic reform agenda has to include executive capacity for co-ordination (notably in fiscal policy but also generally in EU policy), civil service reforms to strengthen professionalism, an independent and professional statistical service, reforms in the penal, legal and police systems, an increasing role for NGOs in developing and delivering policies, and the difficult question of how to empower and involve regional actors. The political risk inherent to an accession process is that a tiny expert elite leads, and this provokes a domestic 'democratic deficit' and legitimacy crisis as accession privileges and strengthens the executive *vis-à-vis* other representative institutions (Moravcsik, 1998).

Third, studies of previous EU enlargements – as well as of traditional member states – show that the effects of membership on domestic transformation are not uniform (Hix and Goetz, 2000). There is no overall 'loss' of policy autonomy, political independence or cultural identity. Some policies are transformed substantially 'from above'; and many involve considerable room for manoeuvre in design and delivery. EMU alone covers the full spectrum, from loss of interest-rate and exchange-rate policies, through a paradox of tight/loose constraints on fiscal policies, to a lack of detailed prescriptions in structural reforms (Dyson, 2000). Civil service elites in east central Europe are characterized by very small Europeanized 'islands of excellence', raising serious questions about capacity to deal with post-accession membership. National parliaments, party systems and electoral competition remain weakly Europeanized. Cultural identities show a high degree of resilience. Hence, while pressures for and processes of convergence exist, there is relatively limited and patchy convergence of administrative, judicial and even economic systems. Domestic institutional variety, contrasting degrees of exposure to international and European market competition, and weak political incentives to prioritize Europe militate against a deep domestic political impact from European integration.

Fourth, it is extremely difficult to disentangle Europeanization from globalization in domestic transformation. The single European market programme and EMU anchor global norms of open trade, market liberalization, and sound money and finance. They represent globalization in its most highly developed form (Dyson, 2006). Hence, much criticism of Europeanization is a disguised or displaced critique of globalization. Transformation of cultural identities seems to be linked more closely to globalization than Europeanization. Europeanization may accentuate and speed processes of domestic transformation, or possibly add an extra social and cultural dimension to them. It has, however, a less secure claim than globalization to be the prime mover of domestic social and cultural transformation.

Finally, Turkey is facing an increasingly diverse Europe and a difficult question of the country's role in reinventing Europe. Turkey's point of reference in defining its identity provides the answer.

There are four possible scenarios. First, Turkey occupies a *sui generis* role in European integration and Europeanization, more akin to that of the UK. She is equivocal on political and economic union, prefers opt-outs, and its political elites are on the whole Euro-sceptic and stress an identity that rests outside Europe. In this scenario, Turkey is part of, and contributes to, a 'rolling back' of collective EU action. Second, Turkey leads a new Balkan/Black Sea 'world' of Europeanization that differs from the Mediterranean and east central European 'worlds' (how it does so is yet to be defined). In this scenario, Turkey contributes its own modes of 'differentiated' integration within the EU, perhaps in particular in foreign and security policy. Third, Turkey assimilates into the Mediterranean or the east central European 'world' of Europeanization, exhibiting tiny 'islands' of technical excellence rather than broad-based assimilation, sees the EU as a welcome source of 'modernization', and adopts a passive role regarding most EU issues. In this scenario, Turkey contributes to a continuing collective 'deepening' of the EU. Fourth, Turkey experiences an extended period of confusion about its relationship to the EU, it becomes a difficult actor for others to calculate and gains a reputation for being unreliable. In this scenario, Turkey like the EU, becomes locked in a stalemate consequent on a protracted inability to reinvent itself.

The EU accession process is a historic opportunity to imagine and construct a new Turkey, although in the face of very difficult political and economic realities. Like all opportunities it may be seized or squandered by its political elites or subverted by circumstances. These elites may ultimately choose to define the EU as a threat, and this risk would be increased by insensitive behaviour on the part of EU political leaders and member states. In short, the whole process depends on wise, patient and far-sighted political leadership within the 'old' EU (including the 'new' member states) as well as within Turkey. It is by no means clear that such leadership is in abundant supply in the EU institutions, in the existing EU member states, or in Turkey. Indeed, on a more pessimistic note, one might wonder whether it can be supplied in modern media-centred democracies.

68 *Reinventing Europe?*

References

Agh, A. (ed.) (2004) *Post-Accession in East Central Europe: The Emergence of the EU-25*, Budapest: The Hungarian Centre for Democracy Studies.

Dyson, K. (2000) *The Politics of the Euro-Zone: Stability or Breakdown?*, Oxford University Press.

Dyson, K. (ed.) (2002) *European States and the Euro: Europeanization, Variation and Convergence*, Oxford University Press.

Dyson, K. (ed.) (2006) *Enlarging the Euro Area: External Empowerment and Domestic Transformation in East Central Europe*, Oxford University Press.

Dyson, K. and Goetz, K. (eds) (2003) *Germany, Europe and the Politics of Constraint*, Proceedings of the British Academy 119, Oxford University Press.

Grabbe, H. (2003) 'Europeanization Goes East: Power and Uncertainty in the EU Accession Process', in K. Featherstone and C. Radaelli (eds), *The Politics of Europeanization*, Oxford University Press.

Green Cowles, M., Caporaso, J. and Risse, T. (eds) (2001) *Transforming Europe: Europeanization and Domestic Change*, Ithaca, NY: Cornell University Press.

Heritier, A., Kerwer, D., Knill, C., Lehmkuhl, D., Teutsch, M. and Douillet, A.-C. (2001) *Differential Europe: The European Union Impact on National Policymaking*, Lanham, Maryland: Rowman & Littlefield.

Hix, S. and Goetz, K. (eds) (2000) *Europeanised Politics? European Integration and National Political Systems*, London: Frank Cass.

Hughes, J., Sasse, G. and Gordon, C. (2005) *Europeanization and Regionalization in the EU's Enlargement*, Basingstoke: Palgrave Macmillan.

Knill, C. and Lehmkuhl, D. (2002) 'The National Impact of European Union Regulatory Policy: Three Europeanization Mechanisms', *European Journal of Political Research* vol. 41 pp. 255–80.

Leonard, M. (2005) *Why Europe Will Run the 21st Century*, London: Fourth Estate.

Majone, G. (2005) *Dilemmas of European Integration: The Ambiguities and Pitfalls of Integration by Stealth*, Oxford University Press.

Mango, A. (2004) *Ataturk*, London: John Murray.

Maull, H. (1992) 'Zivilmacht Bundesrepublik Deutschland. Vierzehn Thesen für eine neue deutsche Aussenpolitik', *Europa Archiv*, vol. 47; pp. 269–78.

Moravcsik, A. (1998) *The Choice for Europe*, London: UCL Press.

Pamuk, O. (2005) *Istanbul: Memories of a City*, London: Faber & Faber.

Sapir, A. (2005) *Globalization and Reform of European Social Models*, Background Paper, 9 September; www.bruegel.org.

Schimmelfennig, F. and Sedelmeier, U. (eds) (2005) *The Europeanization of Central and Eastern Europe*, Ithaca, NY: Cornell University Press.

Schmidt, V. (2002) *The Futures of European Capitalism*, Oxford University Press.

Vachudova, M. (2005) *Europe Undivided: Democracy, Leverage and Integration after Communism*, Oxford University Press.

Wendt, A. (1999) *Social Theory of International Politics*, Cambridge University Press.

4
Europeanization, Democratization and Human Rights in Turkey

E. Fuat Keyman and Senem Aydın Düzgit

A quick glance at Turkish politics and their changing nature since the mid-1990s produces two contrasting images of Turkey. The period between 1995 and 2000 shows a highly state-centric, security-orientated and crisis-ridden image of Turkey, tackling a number of serious problems, such as democratic deficit, human rights violations, the rule of law, economic instability, a legitimacy crisis, and a lack of foreign policy vision and orientation. In this period, the concomitant developments of different identity-based conflicts, namely those of the resurgence of Islam and the Kurdish problem, on the one hand, and the increasingly corruptionist and clientalist appearance of Turkish politics on the other, contributed to this image of Turkey. Contrary to this picture, however, since the year 2000 Turkey has appeared to be a country undergoing radical changes and transformations in its political, economic and cultural life. These changes have been manifested mainly in the areas of democratization and its consolidation, and the restructuring of state–economy relations in a way that creates sustainable economic growth and development. Moreover, there have emerged a number of serious attempts to make Turkish foreign policy more active, constructive and democratic, to create a more rights-based citizenship regime, and to overcome the existing regional, economic, political and cultural discrepancies and uneven developments.

What has made this sudden and rapid change possible since 2000? What are the factors giving rise to the two contrasting images of Turkey? A number of historical developments and events have played an important role in the emergence of recent changes and transformations in state–society/individual relations in Turkey. Among those of particular importance have been the February 2001 financial crisis which has been regarded as the most severe and devastating economic crisis Turkey has faced in its contemporary history; the November 2002 national election, which has brought about the possibility of political stability, as the winner of the election – the Justice and Development Party (the AKP hereafter) – formed a single-party majority government; the 2003 war with Iraq that has had a negative impact on Turkey–US relations, as the Turkish Parliament declared its disapproval of the war by rejecting what has come to be known as the March 1st bill, concerning the deployment of American troops in the south-eastern region of the country with the aim of opening the northern front for their entry into Iraq (Keyman and İçduygu, 2005).

Each of these developments in its own way has revealed the fact that the possibility of political and economic stability (as well as of internal and external security) in Turkey lies in democracy and its consolidation in state–society/individual relations. The February 2001 financial crisis made it clear, first, that there is a close link between the problems of corruption, populism, clientalism and the dominance of authoritarianism in politics; and, second, that macroeconomic stability and sustainable economic development require the restructuring of government so as to render it democratic, effective and efficient. The November 2002 national election resulted in the complete reordering of the political landscape, both by sweeping all the existing parties out of parliament and by paving the way to the single-party majority government of the AKP. In this sense, while the election symbolized the deep anger that the voters felt about the existing authoritarian, corrupt and clientalist (coalitions) government, it has also indicated very clearly that a sorely needed political stability entails a democratic governing structure that is accountable, transparent and effective in its approach to societal problems (Öniş and Keyman, 2003, pp. 95–107). Finally, the 2003 US war with Iraq and its impact on Turkey, especially on Turkish state-centric foreign policy and its security discourse, demonstrated in a clear fashion that security without consolidated democracy and sustainable economic development is no longer possible. As the justification for the war involved such so-called neo-conservative references to the export of democracy, the regime change in the name of liberty and free market, the need for a military occupation of the failed states in the name of global war against terror, it has become necessary, if not imperative, to approach security concerns by linking them to democratic consolidation and sustainable economic development. It is in this sense that the war with Iraq has led Turkish foreign policy to begin to view security, democracy and development as relational and intertwined elements of making Turkey a strong, secure and stable country.

But despite the importance and influence of all these events and developments, it is the recent deepening of Turkey–EU relations that has produced system-transforming changes and impacts on state–society/individual relations. In December 1999 Turkey was recognized officially as a candidate for full membership of the EU. In December 2002, the European Council announced that the full accession negotiations with Turkey would begin without delay if Turkey met the 'Copenhagen political criteria'. In December 2004, Turkey's constant efforts to initiate political and legal reforms, especially in the areas of human rights, and to demonstrate a strong political will to upgrade and deepen the level of its parliamentary democracy, were found by the European Council to be successful enough to announce that Turkey had met its political criteria, and consequently full accession negotiations started on 3 October, 2005. Even though there is still ambiguity and uncertainty in terms of the end result of the full accession negotiations, it is obvious that Turkey's European integration process since 2000 has been a very effective, influential and system-transforming framework underpinning democratic and legal reforms, as well as bringing about a very strong societal will and support for the reform process. In fact, as opposed to, and compared with, the 1990s, Turkey has recently accomplished a democratic reform process of a historic nature in a wide range of areas, from human rights to civilian-military relations. The reforms and legal changes include the abolition of the death penalty, the fight against torture, the enlargement of individual and cultural rights and freedoms, the fight against corruption, achieving full transparency and accountability of public expenses, and institutional restructuring in the areas of government, judiciary and government–military relations.

Democracy and human rights

At the time of writing, democratic reforms are neither complete nor fully implemented. As will be analysed later in this chapter, the implementation of the reform process is still suffering from serious problems and faces a strong institutional resistance, particularly in the areas of human rights and the judiciary. The European Commission has demonstrated both verbally and through its progress reports, its expectations of further progress in the reform process, as well as of the continuous political will of the government to enhance democratic standards and to 'harmonize Turkish legislation with that of the European Union' (Gül, 2003, p. 10). In this chapter, we shall focus on Turkey–EU relations

LIVERPOOL JOHN MOORES UNIVERSITY
Aldham Roberts L.R.C.
TEL 0151 231 3701/3634

within the context of the question of the degree to which the democratic reform process has been successful. To the extent that the Copenhagen political criteria involve 'stability of institutions guaranteeing democracy, the rule of law, human rights and respect for and protection of minorities', what is in fact at stake is not simply to ensure the existence of an institutionally working 'formal' democracy, for example, recursive and free elections, and the rights of the opposition parties – but also, and more importantly, to initiate a reform process aiming at the 'consolidation' of democracy in state–society/individual relations in a way that 'democracy becomes the only game in town' constitutionally, attitudinally and behaviourally (Özbudun, 2000, pp. 4–5). In this sense, as implicated in the Copenhagen political criteria, democracy involves an institutional guarantee of the protection (as well as the enlargement) of individual/cultural rights and freedoms.

Although, historically, democracy and human rights have been regarded as separate, even distinct phenomena, human rights today are treated as being integral to democracy (Goodhart, 2005). In today's late-modern and globalizing world, as well as in the process of European integration, it is not possible to think of democracy without human rights; nor is it possible to think of human rights without democracy. Indeed, it is through the existence and protection of the political, economic, civil and social rights by which citizens utilize their capacities and capabilities to constitute an active and participating demos, that democratic regimes both define and differentiate themselves from authoritarian and totalitarian ones. If the full realization of democracy requires the protection, promotion and enlargement of human rights, human rights and freedoms also require democracy for their protection. Moreover, the deepening and consolidation of democracy in a country depends to a large extent on the protection and enlargement of fundamental human rights (Hongju and Slye, 1999). It is for this reason that to view democracy not only as 'a political regime' based on free and recursive elections (a formal democracy) but also 'as a type of state–society/individual relations' based on the primacy of the language of rights and freedoms (a consolidated democracy) it is necessary for a country to be democratic.

It is this understanding of democracy that constitutes the basis of the Copenhagen political criteria. In this sense, to ask a candidate country to meet the Copenhagen political criteria in order to begin full accession negotiations, means the realization and implementation of democratic consolidation (or of democracy as a human right) in that country. If this is so, then in dealing with the question of the recent democratic reform process in Turkey, we should employ a substantial notion of democracy as a mode of regulation of state–society/individual relations through the language of rights and freedoms. In what follows, we provide, first, a detailed analysis of Turkey's democratic reform process from the perspective of democratic consolidation, and second, suggest that the success of Turkey's efforts to enhance and upgrade the level of its democracy depends on the employment of the principle of fairness and objectivity in Turkey–EU relations.

Turkey–EU relations and democratization in Turkey

As noted above, since 2001 in particular, Turkey has undertaken significant reforms, especially in the areas of human rights and fundamental freedoms. Although the reform process is far from complete, with legal shortcomings and problems with effective implementation still remaining, it is an irrefutable fact that the most extensive process of democratic change in Turkey's republican history is in the making. After the Helsinki Summit of 1999, the European Commission published the first Accession Partnership document in March 2000, which was followed by the preparation of the Turkish 'National Programme for the Adoption of the *Acquis*' by the Turkish authorities in March 2001. These first signs of EU conditionality provided the initial trigger for change. Immediately following the approval of the National Programme, political reform was initiated, with thirty-four constitutional amendments in October 2001, a new Civil Code in January 2002, and three 'harmonization packages'[1] being adopted in the follow-up to the Copenhagen Summit of 2002. The legislative changes introduced significant reforms, most particularly in the fields of human rights and the protection of minorities, freedom of expression and freedom of association.

These reforms were the first crucial responses to EU conditionality, passed under a fragile three-party coalition government that included the highly Euro-sceptic right-wing Nationalist Action Party (MHP) in Turkey and culminated in the Copenhagen Summit of 2002, at which the EU decided to open negotiations with Turkey as and when it had fulfilled the Copenhagen political criteria (Aydın and Keyman, 2005). The summit decision reinforced the EU's commitments by providing Turkey with the prospect that full EU membership was indeed a real possibility (Keyman and Öniş, 2004). Meanwhile, the EU has also decided to increase significantly the amount of financial assistance to Turkey. Hence, the EU's impact was not confined merely to pure conditionality but extended to cover financial and technical assistance.

Pre-accession financial assistance reached €250 million in 2004, €300 million in 2005 and €500 million in 2006 to 'help Turkey prepare to join the EU as quickly as possible'.[2] Similarly, administrative and judicial capacity-building mechanisms, primarily through the Twinning instrument, were now employed to make EU member states' expertise available to Turkey through the long-term secondment of civil servants as well as through short-term expert measures and training. The strengthening of the credibility of conditionality was reflected in the adoption of four subsequent harmonization packages and two sets of constitutional amendments, leading to the decision to open accession negotiations at the Brussels Summit of 2004. The reforms were once again geared towards improving the most-criticized aspects of Turkish democracy, such as limits to freedom of expression and freedom of association, and at curbing the strong influence of the Turkish military on domestic politics.

The political reform process did not, however, come to an abrupt end or face a serious reversal in the period following the decision to open accession negotiations. In fact, as the 2005 Progress Report on Turkey highlights, the country was found to be continuing to fulfil sufficiently the Copenhagen political criteria despite the slower pace of reform and the remaining problems with implementation. Important legislative reforms came into force in 2005, such as the new Penal Code and the Code of Criminal Procedure among others, that are expected to lead to structural changes, particularly in the judiciary (European Commission, 2005).

As can be seen from the brief description of events given above, the role of the EU in triggering the steps towards a more consolidated democratic system in Turkey is undeniable. In fact, it is evident that as the prospect of accession negotiations and ultimate accession are strengthened by the EU Summit decisions, the reform packages, new laws and constitutional amendments gain further momentum. The impact of the EU, however, cannot be assessed without a careful consideration of the internal actors and events in the country, as well as other external developments that have had an impact on the democratization process. Hence democratic change in Turkey cannot be conceptualized outside the interaction between the internal and the external.

Regarding the internal actors of change, it has to be noted that the single-party rule of the AKP following their electoral victory in November 2002 elections, has been very effective in translating the strengthening of EU conditionality into real change in the domestic sphere by deepening the reform process initiated by the previous coalition government. In fact, the advocates of a previously religious-based anti-establishment party played a significant part in political reforms because of a combination of interests and ideological concerns. First and foremost, the AKP viewed EU accession and the necessary reform process as a tool to increase its legitimacy and to guarantee its political survival *vis-à-vis* the secular establishment in Turkey. In a similar sense, the EU also provided increasing legitimacy for the AKP's heavy emphasis on democracy and the protection of individual rights and freedoms in its political ideology.

The AKP was not the only domestic actor that sought to bring change in Turkey, however. Turkish civil society also played a prominent part in promoting political reform in the country. By helping to create a strong language of rights, the EU began to take an important role in furthering changes in state–societal relations and provided legitimacy for a vast number of civil society organizations calling for a more democratic Turkey and demanding the recognition of cultural/civil rights and freedoms (Keyman and İçduygu, 2003, pp. 219–33). For example, while civil organizations have for a long time been demanding a reform of the Law on Association, change on this front has been brought about by the momentum of EU accession after the groundwork had been done by the domestic actors (Tocci, 2005, p. 81). The Turkish business community has also given support to the democratization process, both through its discourse on democratization and its associational and lobbying activities. The February 2001 financial crisis and Turkish–International Monetary Fund (IMF) relations in its aftermath played a crucial role in pushing economic actors towards realizing that a strong and stable economy requires the democratization of the state and its governing relations with society.

Reforms were also made possible by the decrease in adoption costs for traditional veto players such as the Turkish military and security establishment after the defeat of the terrorist organization, PKK, by the Turkish military. This helped significantly to create a more tolerant environment for political reform in the country, especially regarding the protection of minorities in Turkey.

An external development that helped to trigger the pace of reform in Turkey was undoubtedly the war in Iraq and the ensuing developments in northern Iraq with respect to the status of the Kurdish population. The deterioration of relations with the USA after the decision of the Turkish parliament to not to allow US troops access via Turkey during the Iraq war effectively reinforced Turkey's orientation towards the EU, particularly by the way in which it helped to decrease the traditional reliance of the Turkish security establishment on US support. The ensuing developments in northern Iraq, on the other hand, were particularly influential in triggering the debates over the rights of the Kurdish minority in Turkey in the face of the growing attraction of northern Iraq for Turkey's Kurds.

While the interaction of these factors played a crucial role in triggering democratic reform in the country, this process was not without its detractors. One can argue that there was, and still is, domestic opposition to the reform process in the country from various segments of Turkish society. These groups not only comprise the nationalist right and the nationalist left of the political spectrum, but also extend to some parts of the bureaucracy, judiciary and the security establishment. Hence there is an intense ongoing struggle inside the country between the reformists and the resistant forces that has led to the emergence of a mixed picture in the evaluation of the current state of the reform process. Certain pockets of reform have experienced slower progress than others, for a variety of reasons.

Civil–military relations constitute an area of reform where Turkey has made significant progress over the years. Various legislative reforms have been undertaken recently to align civilian control of the military with practices in EU member states. A number of fundamental changes have been made to the duties, functioning and composition of the National Security Council (NSC),[3] as well as to the conditions relating to the control of military spending, in order to increase transparency and legislative oversight.

The changes have not been solely legislative and institutional, however. Issues regarding the military and national security are now widely discussed and criticized in the public sphere. During most of 2004 there were major public debates around the National Security Political Document, prepared primarily about the developments in northern Iraq, questioning the military's role in the drafting of the document and calling for stronger legislative oversight and input. Similarly, regarding the preparation of the 2005 budget, the Minister of Defence has stated that a third of the proposed defence budget was reduced by parliamentary reviews, leading for the first time in a decade to the fall of military spending to rank second, behind education.[4]

One can also detect a tendency among the military towards a non-interventionist stance regarding various issues considered to fall under the scope of 'national security', such as the referendum over the Annan Plan in Cyprus, and Turkey's involvement in the Iraq war. The fact that the military did not try to reverse these decisions underlines the process of change in the modalities of governance in Turkey. The most recent example was provided by rising PKK activity in the summer of 2005, which once again brought debates on the role of the military to the forefront, and upon which the Chief of Staff stated in August 2005 that the 'fight against terror would take place within the framework of democratic rules'.[5]

Despite ongoing progress, it is still difficult to argue that civil–military relations in Turkey are fully aligned with EU standards. There are important issues still waiting to be addressed, such as the limited role of the Ministry of Defence, hence civilian input in decision making as well as required measures to raise awareness among parliamentarians to make full use of their increased capabilities of legislative oversight. Statements from military officials on political matters, albeit to a lesser extent, are still communicated via public speeches and press briefings.[6] This mixed picture hinges to an important extent on the fact that the role of the military in the Turkish context still lies primarily in people's beliefs and expectations. The military remains the most trusted institution in Turkey and its declarations on political issues are still respected by politicians and the population at large, showing how expectations take time to change, and requiring a deeper socialization process in the country.[7] However, the self-assessment of the military's role in Turkish politics, which was crucial to the military's acceptance of the new reforms, will help to ease the path for further change (Heper, 2005, pp. 33–44). While 'giving politics a chance' has long been regarded by the military as a high-risk strategy in the face of past experience, the EU accession process now seems to be acting as a provider of security, increasing the will of the military to move out of politics and creating a environment conducive to further reform (Tocci, 2005, pp. 73–83).

Regarding the protection of human rights, minorities and the rule of law, a more mixed picture can be discerned depending on the sub-area of reform. Turkey has been highly successful in the fight against torture and ill-treatment, largely thanks to improved safeguards for detainees. Police compliance with the new laws and regulations are now reported to be 'generally good', and there now remain only isolated incidents that can be tackled with the full implementation of the new laws (Human Rights Watch Report on Turkey, 2006). Significant problems still remain, however, primarily with respect to freedom of expression, the judicial system, freedom of association and the protection of minorities.

Freedom of expression is one of the major areas of reform, where probably the most intense struggle between the reformist and conservative elements is taking place currently in Turkey. Legislative reform in this field, most particularly through the new Penal Code, has begun to be applied in practice. A significant number of people jailed under the old Penal Code have been set free. There has been a continued reduction in the number of prosecutions, and particularly convictions, in cases that fall within the scope of freedom of expression (European Commission, 2005, p. 25). According to Human Rights Watch, as of November 2005 there were no individuals serving prison sentences for the non-violent expression of their opinions (Human Rights Watch, 2006). Despite these positive developments, however, there is still a constant emergence of new cases where individuals expressing non-violent opinions have been prosecuted, and in some cases convicted, under the new Penal Code. Article 301 of the new Penal Code is currently the major tool used by the anti-reform elements in the country to file complaints regarding expression of opinions. The Article regulates offences that involve 'insulting Turkishness, the Republic, the Parliament and state institutions'' and in fact constitutes a revised version of the infamous Article 159 of the old Penal Code by considering those statements that are not intended to 'insult' but 'criticize' as being outside its jurisdiction.

We can illustrate the utilization of Article 301 and the struggles over the reform process in this relation in greater detail by considering two cases. The first case involves the charge brought against the famous Turkish novelist Orhan Pamuk. In an interview with a Swiss newspaper in February 2005, he was quoted as stating that '1 million Armenians and 30,000 Kurds have been killed in this country'. A complaint was filed against him through a civil initiative by a group of lawyers called the 'Lawyers' Union' (Hukukçular Birliği), on the basis of the claim that the statement contravened Article 301 of the new Penal Code by 'insulting Turkishness'. After being rejected by two public prosecutors from Istanbul on the grounds that this would not constitute a legal case, their complaint was finally accepted by a third public prosecutor that agreed to take it to court. Hence a case was filed against Pamuk, requesting a three-year sentence. The decision was met with wide criticism from within Turkey as well as from the international community. The court decided in the end that the permission of the Ministry of Justice was required, on the grounds that the old Penal Code was in favour of the defendant. It needs to be mentioned that the High Court of Appeals (Yargıtay) played a crucial role in this decision, since it ruled, in the period following the opening of the case against Pamuk, that cases opened prior to 1 June 2005 – before the new Penal Code – require permission from the Ministry of Justice, and hence set a precedent for the Pamuk case. Upon the decision of the Ministry stating that it did not have the right to give permission for a trial, the court dropped the case in January 2006.[8]

The second case was filed against a famous NGO activist and journalist, Hrant Dink, on the basis of an article he wrote on the need for Armenians in Armenia and the diaspora to make peace with their identity by refusing to view Turks as their eternal Other. This complaint was also made by the Lawyers' Union, and was brought to court by a public prosecutor on the basis of the same Article 301. Dink was given a suspended six-month prison sentence and appealed to the High Court. What is most notable in this case is that the court seemed to disregard totally in making its decision expert testimony that the article was being 'misinterpreted'. Furthermore, the experts giving the testimony themselves faced prosecution, instituted once again by the Lawyers' Union.[9]

Both of these cases demonstrate that reform-resistant forces in Turkey are now working in a concerted and persistent fashion to block the reform process from within by utilizing the Turkish judicial system.[10] In doing so, they have found their main allies among some members of the Turkish judiciary and the remaining defects of the new Penal Code. The vaguely-worded Article 301 and (to a lesser extent) Article 305 (foreign aided acts against national interest) are significant, but not the only, mechanisms through which freedom of expression is curtailed. While the judges, especially of higher courts, are referring increasingly to the European Court of Human Rights (ECHR) in their decisions,[11] a fraction of the members of the judiciary also play a crucial role in the restricted interpretation of these laws, which strengthens organized resistance to reform.

Part of the explanation behind resistance can be sought in institutional/procedural matters. Many public prosecutors feel compelled to bring such cases to court rather than declare them as unmeritorious, since they perceive that their careers may be at risk from judicial inspectors – functioning under the Ministry of Justice – who may believe they are not bringing sufficient prosecutions.[12] Another important issue in this respect concerns the methodological difference between Turkish courts and the ECHR in determining whether an expression threatens public order. The ECHR takes into account four different conditions in determining whether thoughts or opinions create a real danger to public order: the content of the relevant statement; the identity of the speaker; the context in which the statement is made; and the form of the expression of the statement. Some of the decisions taken in the Turkish courts, however, still take into account only the content of the expression, thus resulting in contradictory decisions (Uygun, 2004, pp. 17–19). This problem of contradictory decisions in the Turkish judiciary is compounded even further by the two unresolved traditional ills of the Turkish justice system, most particularly the lack of proper working conditions, leading to inefficiency and the insufficient institutional independence of the judiciary from the executive.

The bulk of the explanation behind resistance, however, lies in entrenched ideological legacies. The common ideological strand among those who resist the reform process in Turkey has at its core the monolithic, exclusive, traditional interpretation of the Turkish nation and the nationalism that it inspires, loaded with the fear of separatism and partition of the country among different ethnic groups, also known as the Sevres Syndrome, named after the infamous Sevres Treaty that partitioned the Ottoman Empire among the European powers. The content of the prosecutions, be it the Armenian question or the status of the Kurdish minority, attest to this. Hence it is possible to argue that this ideological legacy is also prevalent among certain members of the judiciary, who internalize traditional state sensitivities and reflect these in their decisions.

Similar ideological baggage can also be discerned in resistance to reform attempts in relation to freedom of association and the protection of minorities in Turkey. With respect to freedom of association, the New Law on Associations that came into force in November 2004, constituted a major step in expanding the freedoms accorded to civil society organizations, by reducing the possibility for state interference, and thus helped to resolve many of the state restrictions that hampered civil society activity until recently. The most problematic aspects of the right of association, however, are very much linked to the debate on the protection of minorities in Turkey.

Regarding the protection of minorities, progress has mainly been achieved on the discursive front where the issue has for the first time penetrated into the public sphere, and on the legislative/institutional front, where certain advances have been made with respect to the status of both non-Muslim and Muslim minorities in Turkey. The 1923 Treaty of Lausanne recognizes only non-Muslim communities as minorities in Turkey.[13] The main problems suffered by these minorities have been the lack of legal personality and the impossibility of acquiring or selling property. Despite the fact that the reform packages have addressed the problem by allowing non-Muslim minorities to register the property they use as long as they can prove ownership, the regulation that was issued following the amendment required applicants to follow incredibly lengthy and cumbersome bureaucratic procedures as well as creating the mechanisms for further bureaucratic intervention in the process.[14] Moreover, it failed to bring a just solution regarding the return of their properties that had already been confiscated by the state. The new draft Law on Foundations prepared by the Directorate General (DG) for Foundations with the aim of easing these problems received much criticism, primarily from the EU. While it expanded the grounds for claims to property, the new law failed to resolve the problems of confiscation, especially of property sold to third parties.[15] The government took action to revise the draft law in January 2006, not only because of EU criticism but also because of the fear of increasing cases in this sphere at the ECHR.[16]

Therefore, progress on the right of association with respect to non-Muslim minorities has been slow and insufficient, mainly as a result of the mindsets of the bureaucracy – particularly in the DG for Foundations. The bureaucracy, who prepare the implementing regulations and deal with the activities of the associations with the authority to dissolve them, seize their properties, dismiss their trustees without a judicial decision and intervene in the management of their assets. This is driven once again by a perception of non-Muslim minorities being a threat to 'national security' that needs to be controlled strongly. Such a conceptualization also lies at the heart of the ban on the training of non-Muslim clergy, which also remains untouched by the reform initiatives. This issue figured regularly in the National Security Political Documents, apart from in the most recent one that was adopted in October 2005.[17] Similar problems have also been encountered with non-Sunni Muslim communities, most particularly the Alevis.[18] They are not recognized officially as a religious community and experience difficulties in founding places of worship despite their vocal demands.

The progress in reform was also mixed for the most numerous Muslim minorities in Turkey, namely the Kurdish minority. The eventual defeat of the PKK by the Turkish military, the emergence of EU conditionality and the growing attraction of northern Iraq for Turkey's Kurds contributed in Turkey to the increasing perception of the Kurdish problem as a minority issue with socio-economic and identity-related dimensions to it, rather than just a military matter. This led to gradual shifts in the official views on this front, leading to certain reforms that were intended to improve the lives of the Kurdish minority. In addition, there were steps such as the granting of the right to broadcast in Kurdish, the right to learn the Kurdish language in private institutions and the right to name children in Kurdish, also implemented subsequently. Human rights reforms in general have had a significant impact on the lives of the Kurds in Turkey. Despite the re-emergence of PKK terror in the spring and summer of 2005 – albeit much weaker than in the 1990s – forcing the country to walk the thin line between human rights, minority rights and security, there has been no signs of a reversal of the reform process. The Minister of Justice and Prime Minister Erdoğan have stressed on various occasions that there would be no going back on the Copenhagen political criteria (AKP, 2005).[19]

Problems remain, however, both with respect to the extension of cultural rights, and the political rights of the Kurdish minority. Language schools have been closed because of insufficient demand based on financial difficulties and broadcasting still remains limited to the Turkish state broadcasting corporation and does not cover local broadcasters despite ongoing work on this front. The situation of internally displaced persons (IDPs) still looks bleak because of economic factors and the security situation, and the Law on Compensation of Losses Resulting from Terrorist Acts adopted in 2004 has had serious delays and problems in implementation. Furthermore, the path to political representation of the Kurdish minority in the parliament is severely blocked as a result of the 10 per cent electoral threshold. This excessively high, and in effect undemocratic, threshold, a remnant of the 1980 military coup, weakens legitimate rule in Turkey and prevents the fair representation of the Kurds in parliament and their effective participation in political dialogue.

This picture shows that the shift from the traditional interpretation of the Turkish nation to a redefined notion of political community, which requires a more inclusive concept of citizenship and the recognition of cultural and ethnic pluralism in the country, is proving to be a painful process in Turkey. The reactions to an official report on 'Minority Rights and Cultural Rights in Turkey', prepared by the Human Rights Advisory Board of the Prime Ministry in October 2004, illustrates clearly the difficulties encountered in this shift. The report, which underlined the insufficiency of minority rights and cultural rights in the country, and emphasized the virtues of multiculturalism, provoked a rich debate in the Turkish public sphere. It was, however, subsequently attacked by the Ministry of the Interior as well as by some prominent members of AKP and certain segments of civil society. Ongoing cases were filed against the President of the Board and the Rapporteur, and the Board has not been in operation since. This demonstrated once again the prevalence of the Sevres Syndrome, and the problems of past ideological legacy, which are the major impediments to the internalization of the political reform process, not only with regard to the protection of minorities but also democratic reforms in all spheres in the country.

Democratization, fairness and the future of Turkey–EU relations

It is true that Turkey has demonstrated a strong political will to initialize a set of legal and constitutional changes to upgrade its democracy. Yet it is equally true that these changes have still to be implemented in state–society/individual relations. The problem of implementation – that is, the problem of democratic consolidation – still remains one of the crucial problems in Turkey–EU relations. Turkey has still a long way to go to become a democratic society, to have its democracy as a human right, and to consolidate its democracy in a way that 'it becomes the only game in town'. In order for its democracy to be consolidated, it is necessary, if not imperative, for Turkey to maintain a strong political will to implement the legal and constitutional changes it has initialized to meet the requirements of the Copenhagen political criteria. Democratic consolidation is an ongoing process of creating a type of society in which 'no one can imagine acting outside democratic institutions', and the language of rights and freedoms constitutes the basis of the regulation of state–society/individual relations. Turkey has begun its journey in this process, and the more certain and deeper Turkey–EU relations are, the more likely becomes Turkey's ability to consolidate its democracy.

It should be pointed out that the possibility of Turkey's success in the process of implementation also requires a fair and objective treatment that EU employs and displays in its relationship with Turkey as a potential full and equal member. As the former EU's enlargement Commissioner, Günter Verheugen, has suggested, Europe should 'use the same methodology and benchmarks, the same criteria and same rules' that have been applied to other new members of the EU. The EU should not have 'higher or lower standards for Turkey', and this should not involve 'double standards': 'we cannot have double standards. We cannot have 100 percent of implementations. We do not do that even with our own countries' (Dempsey, 2004). In other words, Europe should be 'fair and objective' in its view of Turkey and its full member-ship – that is, the principle of fairness and objectivity should be applied as the normative ground of Turkey–EU relations. As a norma-tive ground, the principle of fairness and objectivity entails, first, that the progress reports written on Turkey and decisions taken about Turkey's success in full accession negotiations should be *universal* and *impartial*. The EU should treat Turkey not as a special case, but as one of the candidate countries for full membership status (that is, the norm of universality). At the same time, the EU's distance to Turkey's full membership should be equal to its distance to the full membership of the other candidate countries (that is, the norm of impartiality). In concrete terms, the norms of universality and impartiality indicate that the decision about Turkey would be fair as long as it was not framed by a reference to Turkey's Muslim population or Turkey's geo-graphy. It should be based on the ability, the capacity and the will of Turkey to become a more democratic and modernized country.

However, the recent talks about Turkey in the EU have involved ref-erences to both religion and geography, as well as to the inability of Turkey to become democratic because of its Kemalist political history, which gives primacy to the state and military over society and demo-cracy. There is nothing Turkey can do about the references to religion and geography, since it cannot change its cultural identity or its geo-graphical location. Such references are culturalist, and any decision about Turkey and its place in Europe, that is taken on the basis of reli-gion and geography, would say something not about Turkey, but rather about Europe and its culturally essentialist orientation. In this case, there is not much need to discuss Turkey, more analytically, or its problems in terms of democracy and modernization, and its ability and capacity to adapt itself to Europe. But in Turkish talks, references that have been made to direct attention to the problems of democracy as human rights and its consolidation, suggesting that Turkey needs still more political reforms to be successful and to proceed in the process of full accession negotiations, should be taken seriously. Such universal and impartial references, which are political rather than cultural or geographical, require more conversation, more discussion and more dialogue about Turkey's ability to become a consolidated democracy and modern liberal/plural modernity.

Second, fairness and objectivity entail that it is *the Copenhagen criteria* – the level and nature of democratization and its consolidation in

Turkey – that constitute fairness in Turkey–EU relations. Democracy as human rights is the content of the Copenhagen criteria. The Copenhagen criteria outline the political conditions attached to membership, and involve a transition from formal to substantial democracy. As noted, this transition is in fact 'a process' that includes both the formal procedures (free and recursive elections, a multi-party system, and the ability of the opposition parities to criticize the governing party or the governing coalition in a given country) and the substantial democratization of state–society relations through the respect and protection of individual/group rights and freedoms (Pridham, 2000). Defined in this way, the logic of the Copenhagen criteria and the consolidation of Turkish democracy appear not to contradict one another, but on the contrary to be complementary processes where the former is a logical consequence of the latter. Indeed, the Copenhagen criteria can be considered as a logical consequence of the process of the making of modern Turkey which began in 1923 with the political reform process, initiated by Mustafa Kemal Atatürk and his followers.[20]

Third, a fair and objective benchmark against which to judge Turkey's success in *implementing* the Copenhagen political criteria in state–society relations should derive from an understanding of democratic consolidation as a 'never-ending process'. This means that in contrast to authoritarian and totalitarian regimes, in democratic regimes the process of implementing of rights and freedoms never ends. This is the main differentiating point between democratic regimes and authoritarian and totalitarian ones.[21] Whereas democracy involves an ongoing process of negotiation between state and society about the content and scope of rights and freedoms, this form of negotiation is limited in authoritarian regimes, and almost non-existent in totalitarian regimes. For this reason, if Europe constitutes a democratic political space, then the process of implementing the Copenhagen criteria involves not only the candidate countries, but also the existing member states, since by definition no democratic regime can include the process of implementation in its fullest form. This also means that the implementation process continues in a given candidate country during the full accession negotiations, even after receiving full membership status. In this sense, it can be suggested that the decision of the EU about Turkey would be fair if it is founded on the understanding that Turkey is demonstrating a strong political will and effort to take the necessary measures to implement the Copenhagen criteria.

The norms of universality and impartiality, the understanding of the Copenhagen criteria as embedded in the idea of democratic consolidation, and the way of thinking about the process of the implementation of the Copenhagen criteria as a never-ending process, together constitute what can be called 'the principle of fairness and objectivity' in Turkey–EU relations. It should not be forgotten that, while Turkey's political will is essential, if not imperative, to make the possibility of democracy as human rights an achieved reality, there is no doubt that the fair and objective approach that Europe employs in its view of Turkey is also of utmost importance to Turkey's success in its full accession negotiations. The more Turkey–EU relations are framed by the principle of fairness and objectivity, the more likely does Turkey's success in achieving democracy as human rights become. While recognizing that the negotiation process is a highly technical endeavour dependent on successful harmonization with the EU acquis, one should also be aware of the fact that the 'political' is still apparent in the pre-accession period through the linking of successful compliance with the Copenhagen political criteria with progress in the accession negotiations.[22] A fair and objective evaluation hence becomes crucial not only for the consolidation of Turkish democracy but also for successful accession negotiations. The choice here is not only Turkey's, but also Europe's...

Notes

1. A term of reference for a draft law consisting of a collection of amendments to different laws designed to amend more than one code or law at a time, which was approved or rejected in a single voting session in the parliament.
2. European Commission Representation to Turkey, *EU-Funded Programmes in Turkey: 2003–2004*, December 2003 (http://www.deltur.cec.eu.int/english/eufunded2004/01eufp04.pdf).
3. NSC is a formal institution dominated traditionally by the military, charged with the duty of preserving values such as the territorial and national integrity of the state, and the modernizing reforms of Kemal Atatürk.
4. 'Eğitim Bütçesi Savunmayı İlk Kez Aştı (The budget for education has for the first time exceeded the defence budget)', *Hürriyet*, 1 July 2004. Despite the fact that military spending increased by 0.5 per cent in the 2006 budget, education spending was higher than defence expenditure for the second successive year.
5. 'Özkök'ten OHAL Yalanlaması: Böyle Bir Talebimiz Hiç Olmadı (Özkök denies OHAL allegations – the declaration of the state of emergency – 'We Never Made Such a Demand'), *Zaman*, 31 August 2005.
6. See 'Turkish Civil–Military Relations and the EU: Preparation for Continuing Convergence', Final Expert Report of a Task Force convened under the aegis of a project on 'Governance and the Military' organized by the Centre for European Security Studies (CESS), in association with the Istanbul Policy Centre (IPC), November 2005.

7. The intense focus of the media, academia and political elites on NSC meetings in the wake of decisions such as the one to send troops to Iraq in the autumn of 2003, the decision to re-launch negotiations on Cyprus and to favour referenda over the Annan Plan as well as on NSC reactions to Northern Iraq and rising PKK terrorism constitute key examples in this respect.
8. 'Orhan Pamuk Davası Düştü (Orhan Pamuk case has been dropped)', *Radikal*, 23 January 2006.
9. 'Hrant Dink'i yine Anlamadılar (Once again they did not understand Hrant Dink)', *Radikal*, 13 December 2005; 'Sözde' İfade Özgürlüğü: Hrant Dink'e Altı Ay Hapis (Freedom of expression in theory: 6 years' prison sentence for Hrant Dink)', *Radikal*, 8 October 2005.
10. These are not the only cases filed by the Lawyers' Union. Among others is a case against Joost Lagendijk, Member of the European Parliament and chairman of the EU-Turkey Joint Parliamentary Committee, for his statements on the Pamuk case on his visit to Turkey during the first trial, a case to block Dink's claim to appeal and various other cases against Turkish journalists writing on the Pamuk and Dink cases (on the grounds of attempting to influence the judiciary on the basis of Article 19/2 of the new Press Law).
11. Between January 2004 and November 2005, the courts have referred to the ECHR in 224 judgements. See *Turkey: 2005 Progress Report*, European Commission, Brussels, 9 November 2005, p. 17.
12. Based on an interview with Oktay Uygun, Istanbul, April 2005.
13. The Treaty grants non-Muslim minorities (represented by approximately 25,000 Jews, 3,000 Greeks and 5,000 Armenians) substantial negative rights as well as positive ones. Most significantly, the Treaty gives non-Muslim minorities the right to equal protection and non-discrimination, the right to establish private schools and provide education in their own language, the conditional entitlement to receive government funding for instruction in their own languages at the primary level in public schools, the right to settle family law or private issues in accordance with their own customs, and the right to exercise their religion freely.
14. Since January 2003, only 341 of 2,285 applications for registration of property have been accepted.
15. 'Vakıflardan Bu Kadar Artık Gözler Hükümette (The foundations have done their part, now it is the government's turn)', *Radikal*, 15 April 2005.
16. 'Vakıfta AB'ye Uyum (Harmonization with the EU in foundations)', *Radikal*, 1 January 2006.
17. 'Gerekirse Asker Yine Göreve (The military on duty if needed)', *Radikal*, 26 October 2005.
18. There are an estimated 12–20 million Alevis in Turkey.
19. See the official website of the Justice and Development Party (AKP) (www.akparti.org.tr), 29 July 2005.
20. For a detailed account of the connection between the Copenhagen criteria and the political vision of Mustafa Kemal Atatürk, see Senem Aydın and E. Fuat Keyman 'European Integration and the Transformation of Turkish Democracy', CEPS EU-Turkey Working Paper Series, No. 2, Centre for European Policy Studies, Brussels (http://shop.ceps.be/BookDetail.php?item_id=1144).

21. For more detail about democratic consolidation, see Michael Goodhart, *Democracy as Human Rights*, London: Routledge, 2005.
22. See EU Commission (2004) *Communication of 6 October 2004 from the Commission to the Council and the European Parliament: Recommendation of the European Commission on Turkey's Progress Towards Accession.* The Communication states that 'The Commission may also recommend suspending the negotiations if there is a serious and persistent breach of the principles of liberty, democracy, respect for human rights and fundamental freedoms or the rule of law on which the Union is founded. If such a recommendation is made, the Council may, by a qualified majority, decide to suspend negotiations.'

References

Adalet ve Kalinma Partisi (AKP) (2005) various documents, www.akparti.org. accessed 29.dol2000.

Aydın, S. and Keyman, E. F. (2005) 'European Integration and the Transformation of Turkish Democracy', CEPS EU–Turkey Working Paper Series, No.2, Centre for European Policy Studies, Brussels (http://shop.ceps.be/BookDetail.php?item_id=1144).

Centre for European Security Studies (CESS) (2005) 'Turkish Civil–Military Relations and the EU: Preparation for Continuing Convergence', Final Expert Report of a Task Force convened under the aegis of a project on 'Governance and the Military' organised by the Centre for European Security Studies (CESS), in association with the Istanbul Policy Centre (IPC), November 2005.

Dempsey, J. (2004) 'EU appeals for fairness over Turkish talks', *Financial Times*, 28 May. http://search.ft.com/ftArticle query Text=Jody+dempseyage= true.id=040528000920page=1.

EU Commission (2004) *Communication from the Commission to the Council and the European Parliament: Recommendation of the European Commission on Turkey's Progress Towards Accession*, COM (2004) 656 Final, 6 October 2004.

European Commission (2005) *Turkey: 2005 Progress Report*, Brussels, 9 November; http://www.europa.eu.int/comm/enlargement/report_2005/pdf/package/sec_1 426_final_en_progress_report_tr.pdf).

Evans, T. (2001) *The Politics of Human Rights*, London: Pluto.

Goodhart, M. (2005) *Democracy as Human Rights*, London: Routledge.

Gül, A. (2003) 'My Government Has Delivered', *International Herald Tribune*, 12 December, p. 10.

Heper, M. (2005) 'The European Union, The Turkish Military and Democracy', *South European Society and Politics*, vol. 10, no. 1, pp. 33–44.

Hongju, H. and Slye, R. (eds) (1999) *Deliberative Democracy and Human Rights*, New Haven, Conn: Yale University Press.

Human Rights Watch (2006)*Human Rights Watch Report on Turkey*, (online) 18 January 2006 (http://hrw.org/english/docs/2006/01/18/turkey12220.htm).

Keyman, E. F. (2006) *Remaking Turkey*. Oxford: Lexington.

Keyman, E. F. and İçduygu, A. (2003) 'Globalization, Civil Society and Citizenship in Turkey: Actors, Boundaries and Discourses', *Citizenship Studies*, vol. 7, no. 2, pp. 219–33.

Keyman, E. F. and İçduygu, A. (eds) (2005) *Citizenship in a Global World: European Question and Turkish Experience*, London: Routledge.

Keyman, E. F. and Öniş, Z. (2004) 'Helsinki, Copenhagen and Beyond: Challenges to the New Europe and the Turkish State', in Mehmet Uğur and Nergis Canefe (eds), *Turkey and European Integration: Accession Prospects and Issues*, London: Routledge.

Öniş, Z. and Keyman, E. F. (2003) 'Turkey at the Polls: A New Path Emerges', *Journal of Democracy*, vol. 14, no. 2, pp. 95–107.

Özbudun, E. (2000) *Contemporary Turkish Politics: Challenges to Democratic Consolidation*, Boulder, Colorado: Lynne Rienner.

Pridham, G. (2000) *Dynamics of Democratization*, London: Continuum.

Tocci, N. (2005) 'Europeanization in Turkey: Trigger or Anchor for Reform?', *South European Society and Politics*, vol. 10, no. 1, pp. 73–83.

Uygun, O. (2004) 'Freedom of Expression under the ECHR and Turkish Law', Paper presented at the Human Rights General Assembly: European Convention of Human Rights and Turkey, Istanbul, 17–19 May.

5
The Economics of the Accession Process: A Multidimensional and Policy-orientated Approach for Turkey

Esra LaGro

> The solution does not at all lie in a rejection of globalization or a retreat into new forms of autarchy, but in the deliberate invention and building of a new institutional setting that will govern the process of increasing interdependence and integration among countries, regions, and peoples of the world. (Derviş, 2005, p. 6)

Turkey has started accession negotiations with the EU. This major step towards Turkish membership of the EU implies many changes and challenges for both sides, and undoubtedly creates complexities. It also means that Turkey has to follow the EU agenda more closely than ever in order to comply with the requirements of the accession process. Simultaneously, the EU is evolving very fast within the global order, in which not only the gap between developed and developing states but also the gap between 'haves' and 'have-nots' in individual societies and nations increases. The efforts to overcome these gaps and the need for more convergence in the enlarged union are reflected within the EU and its individual member states *vis-à-vis* specific policy choices, and provides a strong incentive to accelerate reforms at all levels, as manifested in the recent efforts of the Barosso Commission.

This chapter argues that the necessity of an integrated and multidimensional approach to the challenges relevant to the present and future reform agenda of the EU is relevant for Turkey in general, and for the accession process in particular. The first section will present a brief overview of the Turkish economy in the context of the accession process. Second, the concepts of stability, competitiveness and legitimacy, as well as their interrelatedness, will be explored with reference to the three main EU agendas to which they correspond, with particular emphasis on the Lisbon agenda. Third, the challenges for Turkey during the accession negotiations and the possibility of the future Lisbon conditionality and policy requirements stemming from it will be discussed. Fourth, the implications of structural reforms in terms of modernization and legitimization of Turkey with reference to economic governance and industrial policy will be put forward. Finally, further policy concerns *vis-à-vis* accession negotiations will be presented with a view to providing food for thought for the future, especially for policy-makers.

The chapter builds on a framework for analysis that has been developed by Jones (2005) and Rodrigues (2005) concerning the EU, and attempts to apply this to the Turkish accession process. Jones emphasizes the relationship between three different agendas of the EU reform processes, that is, the Maastricht, Lisbon and Laeken agendas. These agendas stand for three main aims, specifically stability, competitiveness and legitimacy (Jones, 2005, p. 1). This is in line with Rodrigues who, while commenting on the Lisbon mid-term review, asks the question 'Europe for what?' She highlights the fact that the discourses referring to the past rationale of European integration are no longer viable among the younger generation of EU citizens, who take peace and stability for granted. Therefore, the EU and its member states face the challenge of finding a new target. Rodrigues points out that, in order to direct the expectations of citizens, the EU needs to focus on 'sustaining their living conditions in a global economy, making Europe a stronger player in improving global governance, and creating a more democratic and effective political system' (Rodrigues, 2005, p. 1).

Although the interrelatedness of these three concepts concerns mainly the EU reform process, they are also highly relevant to Turkey. There are two main reasons for this. First, Turkey, being a long-time associate member and having engaged in the accession process, has to adopt the entire *acquis* and must implement the required reforms. Therefore, Turkey is already a part of the future EU processes and agendas. Second, as both Jones and Rodrigues have pointed out, in all member states the success of the envisaged reforms depends largely on attaching them to clearly identifiable projects; in this case, the project being the EU and its future (Jones, 2005, p. 4; Rodrigues, 2005, p. 1). Europe is, undoubtedly, the anchor for the reform process in Turkey, since Turkey identifies itself with the future of the EU.

Thus this chapter argues in favour of the relevance and significance of these concepts and processes for Turkey throughout the negotiations and beyond, while drawing parallels to some of the similarities arising from both internal and external challenges, with specific reference to the EU. This, in turn, brings us to the possibility of a Lisbon condition-ality that exists apart from the Copenhagen criteria. Turkey needs to address issues pertaining to the Lisbon agenda on the way towards full membership. Hence Turkey needs to develop a sound long-term strat-egy and the necessary governance structures in order to catch up with the EU, while simultaneously solving its own problems as a middle-income developing country with inherent infrastructural problems. One viable strategy in this context would be an industrial policy based on the consensus of the actors involved, which will also improve social cohesion. Thus the objectives of stability, competitiveness and legiti-macy could be achieved, and the long-term economic and social burden of the accession process divided evenly between the 'haves' and the 'have-nots' in Turkish society.

Turkey, economic policies and the European economy

In the context of economics, there are several intriguing questions con-cerning Turkey's membership of the EU. Will Turkey be an asset to the EU economy with its dynamism and growth potential? Will Turkey – given its huge size and population – be a liability for future EU budgets? Will the young population of Turkey immigrate to Europe and constitute a threat to the EU job market? Could the entry of Turkey create a backlash to the EU's competitiveness and weaken the EU economy in the global context? These and other questions have been asked in Western Europe, and there are examples where negative projections have been used to oppose the opening of accession negoti-ations. The aim of this section is neither to attempt to reinvent the wheel nor to answer all the above-mentioned types of question. Furthermore, it is hardly possible to do this type of projection for the future, given the possibility of unforeseen external or internal events. The purpose of this section is to give an overview of the Turkish economy and to highlight the findings of some of the previous studies that were conducted to answer the above-mentioned questions.

The economic policies in Turkey can be viewed in rough terms within just two time frames. The first covers the period between 1923 and 1980, and the second is the period after 1980. During these two time frames the Turkish economy followed global cyclical develop-ments, and continued its efforts to develop and sustain growth, basic-ally from scratch in the aftermath of the establishment of the Republic in 1923. The period prior to the 1980s was generally marked by the well-known import substitution model, together with efforts to create an industrial basis and private capital accumulation in line with strategic development plans covering five-year periods. However, by the end of the 1970s the Turkish economy was in recession – as was the global economy – and needed macroeconomic stability. The neo-liberal economic trend of the 1980s led to structural reforms in order to overcome inherent difficulties. In 1980, the government announced relatively radical reforms, not least aiming at replacing the import substitution model with an export-led growth model, thus strengthening the liberalization of the economy and integration with world markets. However, as has been the case with developing countries around the world, this process has not been smooth in Turkey either. The main reason has been that the implementation of neo-liberal policies in Turkey lacked the immediate necessary economic governance infrastructure that would back up these types of policy. Therefore, the ups and downs experienced in the years that followed were not a surprise, and they continued until very recently. The unquestioned merit of the neo-liberal policies, partially because of the international conditionality imposed by the IMF and the World Bank (in line with the ideological trend of the time), led Turkish policy-makers towards radical policies, but unfortunately the much needed structural reforms did not follow with the same weight and speed. The outcome was successive crises leading to an increase in public debt, high inflation rates and balance of payments problems, which were remedied mainly by government choices pointing to their short future discount rates. Despite the negative issues invoked by this evolution and the crisis-prone nature of the economy, Turkey continues to be on the right track. The Customs Union established with the European Union as of January 1996, the macroeconomic stability programme began and sustained in the aftermath of the 2001 crisis, and the recently opened accession negotiations with the EU are clearly important incentives for improved governance and functioning of the Turkish economy.[1]

Following the crisis of 2001, the GDP of Turkey fell by 7 per cent and inflation rose up by 70 per cent. Since then, however, the Turkish economy has been stable as a result of the firm implementation of the Stability Programme by two successive governments, including the one at the time of writing. The main outlook of the Stability Program announced by the former Minister of the Economy, Dr Kemal Derviş, which put Turkey back on track, was based mainly on four pillars.[2] The first was *transparency*. The main problem behind the crises was identified as relations between state and society, and between politics and the economy. The rent seeking behaviour of the actors involved was

identified as sustaining only the negative consequences of these relations (Derviş, *et al.*, 2006, pp. 102–3).[3] The second pillar was the *long-
term planning and quality of governance structures*. The programme not
only targeted stability but also a restructuring of economic governance
in Turkey in order to avoid future problems in balancing the economy.
The third pillar was sustaining *the trust of the private sector and international investors in government*. Finally, a revolutionary *change in the structure of state owned banks* was to be implemented.

The principles introduced by Derviş and his team are also in line
with today's reality, and the process that began back in 2001 could be
considered as the stepping stone of the future of the Turkish economy,
and of the accession process. When the almost institutionalized *rent
seeking structure* could also be further destroyed, there is no obstacle
before Turkey facing the challenges to come during its encounter with
the EU.

Aiming at providing an overview of the economic state of affairs,
Tables 5.1 and 5.2 below show data concerning the Turkish economy
prior to the crisis in 2001 and in the aftermath of the crisis.[4] The data
are indicative of present facts regarding the Turkish economy, and
provide some clues for the future. Table 5.1 shows that Turkey, despite
the 2001 crisis, has a significant annual growth in GDP. Table 5.2 indicates the trade and current account balance of Turkey between 1999
and 2005 – that is, from EU candidacy to the negotiation process.
Despite its flaws, the potential of the Turkish economy should not be
underestimated, and the remarkable performance in the aftermath of
the 2001 crisis is indicative in this respect. The World Bank report
states, for example, that 'the public sector primary balance moved to a
surplus of 6.8 percent of GNP by 2004, from a deficit of 2.5 percent in
1999, enabling a reduction of gross public debt from 108 percent of
GDP in 2001 to 77 percent in 2004' (World Bank, 2006a, p. 2). However, as is further emphasized in the report, the pace of reform should
be continued.

Box 5.1 shows the main issues concerning the overall performance of
the Turkish economy in general and with regard to the EU accession
process in particular. These issues have been the focus of an extensive
debate. Therefore, a selected number of studies and debates will be
highlighted below, since they are important for the future economics
of accession negotiations. When these studies are examined, it is clear
that, in most cases, there is a balanced view of the Turkish economy
and a largely optimistic outlook concerning the future.[5]

Table 5.1   Overview of the Turkish economy

Year	2000	2003	2004
People			
Population, total (millions)	67.4	70.7	71.7
Population growth (annual %)	1.7	1.5	1.4
Life expectancy at birth, total (years)	68	68.6	69.9
Fertility rate, total (births per woman)	2.6	2.4	2.2
Literacy rate, adult total (% of people ages 15 and above)	–	–	97.7
Economy			
GNI, Atlas method (current US$ billions)	201.2	197.8	269.0
GNI per capita, Atlas method (current US$)	2980	2800	3750
GDP (current US$ billions)	199.3	240.4	302.8
GDP growth (annual %)	7.4	5.8	8.9
Inflation, GDP deflator (annual %)	49.9	22.5	9.9
Agriculture, value added (% of GDP)	15.4	13.4	12.9
Industry, value added (% of GDP)	25.3	21.9	22.4
Services, etc., value added (% of GDP)	59.4	64.7	64.7
Exports of goods and services (% of GDP)	24	27.4	28.9
Imports of goods and services (% of GDP)	31.5	30.7	34.7
Gross capital formation (% of GDP)	24.5	22.8	25.7
States and markets			
Time required to start a business (days)	–	38	9
Market capitalization of listed companies (% of GDP)	35	28.4	32.5
Fixed line and mobile phone subscribers (per 1,000 people)	512.1	661.9	750.5
Internet users (per 1,000 people)	37.1	84.9	142.5
High-technology exports (% of manufactured exports)	4.8	2	2
Global links			
Merchandise trade (% of GDP)	41.3	48.5	53.1
Net barter terms of trade (year 2000 = 100)	100	99.1	102
Foreign direct investment, net inflows (BoP, current US$)	982.0 million	1.8 billion	2.7 billion
Long-term debt (DOD, current US$ billions)	84.2	98.3	108.2
Total debt service (% of exports of goods, services and income)	35.4	38.6	35.9
Official development assistance and official aid (current US$ millions)	327.2	164.8	257.0
Workers' remittances and compensation of employees, received (US$)	4.6 billion	729.0 million	804.0 million

Source: World Development Indicators database, World Bank (2006b).

Table 5.2 Trade and current account balance 1999–2005, from EU candidacy to the negotiation process (in US$ millions)

	1999	2000	2001	2002	2003	2004	2005
Exports (by ISIC)	26,587	27,775	31,334	36,059	47,253	63,167	73,122
Textiles and clothing	9,828	10,031	10,341	12,148	14,995	17,338	18,637
Machinery, electric-electronic and vehicles	5,120	5,853	7,262	8,881	12,802	18,585	21,870
Machinery & equipment	1,272	1,439	1,617	2,117	3,159	3,965	4,915
Electric-electronic	1,463	1,787	2,041	2,632	3,168	4,459	5,076
Vehicles	2,386	2,627	3,605	4,132	6,474	10,161	11,879
Imports (by BEC)	40,671	54,503	41,399	51,554	69,340	97,540	116,048
Capital goods	8,727	11,365	6,940	8,400	11,326	17,397	20,236
Intermediate goods	26,854	36,010	30,301	37,656	49,735	67,549	81,320
Consumption goods	4,820	6,928	3,813	4,898	7,813	12,100	13,926
Memo: energy imports*	5,375	9,529	8,339	9,204	11,575	14,407	21,164
Export/Import ratio (%)	65.4	51.0	75.7	69.9	68.1	64.8	63.0
Trade balance	−14,084	−26,728	−10,065	−15,495	−22,087	−34,373	−42,926
Trade balance as a percentage of GDP	−7.6	−13.4	−6.9	−8.4	−9.2	−11.4	
Exports of services	16,800	20,364	16,030	14,783	19,025	22,928	25,854
Transportation	2,900	2,955	2,854	2,795	2,184	3,267	4,016
Tourism	5,203	7,636	8,090	8,479	13,203	15,888	18,152
Other	8,697	9,773	5,086	3,509	3,638	3,773	3,686
Imports of services	9,313	8,996	6,900	6,904	8,520	10,144	11,850
Transportation	2,101	2,463	2,021	1,934	2,707	4,331	5,313
Tourism	1,471	1,713	1,738	1,880	2,113	2,524	2,872
Other	5,741	4,820	3,141	3,090	3,700	3,289	3,665
Current account balance	−1,344	−9,819	3,390	−1,524	−8,036	−15,604	−22,852
Current account balance as a percentage of GDP	−0.7	−4.9	2.3	−0.8	−3.4	−5.2	

Note: * SITC Rev. 3 code, which includes 32 coal, coke and briquettes; 33 petroleum, petroleum products and related materials; 34 gas, natural and manufactured; 35 electric current.
Source: World Bank Report (2006a).

Box 5.1   Main issues concerning the Turkish economy in the EU accession process

- Improving economic governance: alignment with the *acquis* and its implementation during the accession negotiations
- Sustaining macroeconomic stability
- Balancing existing regional disparities
- Increasing trade with the EU: extension of customs union towards agriculture and services
- Sustaining foreign direct investment (FDI) flows and increasing them to comparable levels with the size of the Turkish economy
- Sustaining high growth level
- Investing in the education of the young population
- Improving global competitiveness

The report of the Independent Commission on Turkey provides a view of the economic opportunities and challenges *vis-à-vis* Turkey. The report confirms that the macroeconomic instability of Turkey might be a problem. However, developments after 2001 indicate that despite 'this crisis ... [being] a serious setback; it also showed its [Turkish economy's] resilience, dynamism and stability' (Independent Commission Report, 2004, p. 36). The implementation of the Stability Programme, supported by the IMF, showed immediate positive results: 'within a year growth resumed at over 7 per cent, inflation dropped significantly, the debt to GDP ratio declined, the Turkish lira regained its value, and foundations for a sustainable economic upturn were in place' (ibid.). On the other hand, the report mentions the challenges and provides a 'to-do' list for Turkey. First, Maastricht criteria on macroeconomic stability must be followed closely. Second, the relatively low levels of foreign direct investment (FDI) should be increased. Third, bureaucratic inefficiency and corruption must be diminished. Fourth, GDP and GDP per capita should be increased. Fifth, existing regional disparities should be improved. Sixth, agricultural policy needs to be reformed. The report also highlighted the fact that the impact of Turkish accession to the EU on the economic front will be negligible, since it amounted to less than 2 per cent of the EU's GDP by 2004 (Independent Commission Report, 2004, p. 37).

A thorough economic assessment of the Turkish accession was also made by a leading think tank – the Centre for European Reform (CER), which relied partially on the findings of the Independent Commission

Report. The author of the report, Katinka Barysch, emphasizes that the likely impact of the Turkish economy will be negligible if accession occurs, and this impact will be positive rather than negative. Turkey already has a customs union with the EU and is thus already better prepared than the CEECs but Turkey is also 'prone to swings in investor confidence'. This would make anchoring the Turkish reforms to the EU in the way that the new member states did difficult (Barysch, 2005, p. 7). Barysch further comments that Turkish workers will not have access to the EU labour market before 2020. The EU countries might by then in fact be looking for a dynamic workforce. As a final assessment, she highlights the fact that if the EU cannot realize the much-needed reforms until 2015 or 2020, Turkey might not want to join a problematic union that is unwelcoming (Barysch, 2005, p. 8).

Another leading think tank, the Centre for European Policy Studies (CEPS), has also run a research programme on the Turkish accession, and several reports were prepared pertaining to the different aspects of the Turkish accession process. According to the CEPS study, the evaluation of the Turkish economy is rather difficult because of its heterogeneity. Consequently, some sectors are productive and can without any problem compete already with the EU, but others cannot. However, if the productive sectors can expand further to accommodate surplus labour from the agricultural sector and other relatively unproductive sectors, 'the Turkish economy should be able to reach the level of new member states in not too distant future' (Derviş *et al.*, 2004b, p. 106).

The EU Commission report entitled *Issues Arising from Membership Prospect of Turkey* generally highlights the fact that the accession of Turkey has both challenges and opportunities. Accordingly, the impact of the Turkish economy will be negligible, and the process of 'negotiations should help the continued efforts of Turkey to ensure macroeconomic stability and promote investment, growth and social development. Under these conditions Turkey's GDP is expected to grow more rapidly than the EU average' (EU Commission, 2004a, p. 4). The regional disparities would be a problem for cohesion policy. However, Turkey's full accession to the internal market would be beneficial, depending 'not only on the fulfilment of present obligations under the customs union but also on the principles of good governance to be adopted for the economy as a whole' (EU Commission, 2004a, p. 4). It is further emphasized that accelerated growth in Turkey will improve the investment opportunities of EU companies as well as increase the exports of the EU-25. Next, the report highlights that 'a possible increase in labour supply, stemming from migration from Turkey, could contribute to some additional growth' (EU Commission, 2004a, p. 16). Finally, there is one significant recommendation that should be emphasized – that is, in order to benefit from the population dynamics of Turkey, the EU should invest in education and training in Turkey in the decades to come (EU Commission, 2004a, p. 4). This investment might indeed make a difference, leading to a win–win situation.

There are several studies along similar lines regarding the economics of Turkish accession to the EU, most pointing to the main conclusions as presented above. Clearly, sustained macroeconomic stability and the improvement of economic governance are not enough to achieve sustainable growth for Turkey. As has been pointed out by Acemoğlu (2005), the incorporation of China, India, Pakistan and Indonesia into the world economy means more competition for middle-income countries such as Turkey. Therefore, Turkey needs to achieve more in order to increase its competitiveness, both in a global context and *vis-à-vis* the EU. One recipe in this framework would be to implement a well-designed industrial policy to enhance stability, competitiveness and social cohesion (which would also increase the level of legitimacy). This strategy will be discussed in further detail in the following two sections.

Stability, competitiveness and legitimacy in the EU, with reference to the Lisbon strategy

As mentioned at the start of this chapter, Jones (2005) and Rodrigues (2005) highlight the concepts of stability, competitiveness and legitimacy – all three being related to successful EU economic governance. Having started accession negotiations with the EU, Turkey is also part of these processes. It is therefore important to reflect on these concepts, with a view to the accession negotiations.

The stability concept was introduced in the Maastricht Treaty (TEU), characterized by the well-known Maastricht criteria and the preparations towards the launch of the euro. The macroeconomic stability targeted in this way was partially a reaction towards the periods of instability in the 1970s and the first half of the 1980s. The Stability Pact has its own problems concerning the implementation targets of the individual member states; however, the launch of the euro has clearly been successful. As it is emphasized in the above mentioned studies, the Maastricht criteria, including the stability concept, are important for the Turkish accession process.

The concept of competitiveness was added to the agenda of the EU leaders with the famous Lisbon summit, where the European leaders pledged to stimulate economic growth and employment, and make Europe the most competitive knowledge economy in the world by 2010. However, five years on from the decision, Europe was nowhere near these ambitious targets. Therefore, a mid-term review of the Lisbon strategy was prepared and a renewed Lisbon strategy adopted during the Spring Council of 2005. Undoubtedly, the renewed Lisbon strategy will be on the agenda of the Turkish accession negotiations, as part of Copenhagen conditionality if not anything else.

The concept of legitimacy was a conclusion of the Laeken summit, where the European leaders underlined the importance of 'bringing European people closer to the Union'. For the purposes of this chapter and perhaps beyond, we should distinguish between macro- and micro-level legitimacy. Employment of the term macro-level legitimacy makes it possible to talk about the legitimacy of the EU in the eyes of individual member states; for example, to what extent the open method of co-ordination is useful or not. Micro-level legitimacy has more to do with debates on the future of Europe, and the extent to which individual citizens are incorporated into the EU project as firm supporters of the grand European project of a federal Europe if not now, then in the foreseeable future. If we view citizens as being like customers of the state, this is more of a 'customer satisfaction' concept than an ideological outlook, and has to do with how the Europe project is sold to the EU citizens, and how well they accept this. This is also true for Turkey. The success of the negotiations and their final outcome depend on how well the EU process is perceived, understood and owned by Turkish citizens.

The Barosso Commission made the Lisbon agenda and its integration to the existing EU policy structure a top priority of its working programme. Since then, and even before the mid-term review of Lisbon strategy, a number of important reports were prepared by High Level Groups in order to point out strengths and weaknesses of the European economy, especially in comparison with the USA and other global players, in addition to several official policy documents and studies prepared in order to streamline an industrial policy for the EU.[6] Moreover, an extensive debate began concerning economic governance measures to be adopted to achieve the targets of the Lisbon strategy. One of the important landmarks in this context has been what is popularly known as the Sapir Report (2003). In their detailed assessment of the Sapir Report, Pelkmans and Casey assert that 'the Sapir report provides a detailed overview of the challenges and identifies problems and possible solutions for the EU. It is a call for higher economic growth in the EU. It is also an agenda-setter' (Pelkmans and Casey, 2004, p. 1). The agenda that is outlined for the EU is sixfold and provides a detailed assessment of these issues. First, the single market should be made more dynamic. Second, investment in knowledge should increase. Third, the macroeconomic framework for the EMU should be improved. Fourth, the policies for convergence should be optimized. Fifth, the governance structures should be more effective. Finally, EU-budget allocations should be restructured (Sapir *et al.*, 2003, p. 4). This report is not only about an economic assessment of the EU *per se*, but it also questions existing and possible new modalities of good governance at several levels in the EU and its member states. Despite the fact that both its timing and content have been an issue for debate, the report is still one of the important assessments of economic governance in the EU. Although the content of this report remains largely unknown in the Turkey, it is important for the country, since it provides a thorough analysis of the European economy, thus providing clues for future alignment with the EU.

The well-known Kok Report (2004), which also served as a background and framework of analysis during the European Commission's mid-term review of the Lisbon strategy in 2005, puts forward several issues as recommendations. Accordingly, the EU Council should take the lead in optimizing the Lisbon strategy, and the member states should become more committed to the success of the process. Next, the EU Commission should act as a facilitator and review the policies implemented in the member states, while the EU Parliament is called on to actively monitor the process. Finally, the relevant social actors should participate actively in the implementation (Kok Report, 2004, p. 8). This last item in the report is probably the most significant one from the perspective of the accession process, since it points to a culture of corporatism. Turkey does not have a corporatist culture in the way it has developed in Western Europe since the 1950s. This therefore creates a deficit in economic governance. Thus Turkey needs to develop its own model of corporatism and involve all relevant societal actors in reform processes in order to sustain not only the economic reforms but also social cohesion.

The Kok report also calls for 'sustained political determination' in terms of reaching the Lisbon targets and achieving high levels of growth while strengthening social cohesion. Indeed, the key phrase for the Lisbon strategy is *political determination* on the part of the individual

EU member states. The EU Commission, throughout Turkey's screening process has evaluated the level of political determination concerning several chapters, and it will be further emphasized with reference to industrial policy in the next section.

The EU Commission prepared a study concerning the economic costs of non-Lisbon[7] also followed by several other studies concerning achieving high growth and sustaining social cohesion in the EU – the way to reach the Lisbon targets. In this perspective, another important highlight is the Community Lisbon Programme launched by the Commission following the mid-term review of the Lisbon strategy, which emphasizes the importance of knowledge and innovation for growth, and the ways to improve employment levels in Europe (EU Commission, 2005b, p. 3). The programme pledges to review both the actions to be taken during the individual member states' national Lisbon programme implementations and the EU level. This programme should actually serve as a framework for Turkey, and Turkey should prepare a national Lisbon programme, not only because it will become part of the conditionality but in order to invest in the country's own future.

It is evident that the EU needed to reform itself, especially prior to and following the 2004 enlargement. However, these reforms could only be legitimised through their links to EU citizens. First, the success of these reforms can only be sustained if the citizens own them, and second, if the reforms cannot be communicated to EU citizens, domestic political populism would take over and would lead to an increase in Euro-scepticism. The same is true for economic and political governance in Turkey. Clearly, the three above-mentioned concepts – stability, competitiveness and legitimacy – constitute the pillars of economic governance in Turkey and of the EU–Turkey accession process. The next section will further discuss these highly relevant issues.

From Copenhagen criteria to Lisbon: too many targets and policy agendas and too short time for achievement

Copenhagen conditionality has for more than a decade been an important policy tool for the European Union *vis-à-vis* candidate countries, enabling the alignment of prospective member states. The vagueness of these conditions has been, and still is, giving the EU the necessary room for manoeuvre, while at the same time keeping the candidates anchored. Turkey will not be an exception.

Two of the Copenhagen criteria are especially important for the Turkish accession process. The first is the existence of a free market economy with capacity and competence to compete in the single market, and the second is the ability of the EU to absorb new members. These two criteria, especially the second, present Turkey with several challenges, not least if we read the criteria in reverse order. On the one hand, it has political and policy related meaning, and on the other, it has an economic meaning. The political context leaves the issue of full membership of Turkey completely in the hands of EU member states regardless of the conditionality fulfilled with the projected public referenda, rising nationalism, and Euro-scepticism in Europe. The economic meaning of the absorption capacity of the EU relates to the fact that, with the recent entry of ten new members, the Union's capacity has become saturated and the future will be very difficult for Turkey since Turkey itself matches these countries in size and population. In this case there is only a single option remaining for Turkey – to read this criterion in a different way (that is, to make the country an indispensable economic partner of the EU), since the EU seems to unable to absorb Turkey.[8] While achieving this target, stability, competitiveness and legitimacy concepts – the structural components of EU economic governance – should be treated along EU lines throughout the EU accession negotiations. This seems to be the only recipe for full membership and sustainable development on the part of Turkey, given the fact that there are too many targets and policy agendas, and relatively little time to catch up with the EU as well as enhance the absorption capacity of the EU for Turkish accession. This discussion of the Copenhagen criteria continues below, with the three policy agendas of the EU – namely Maastricht, Lisbon and Laeken, and in this context their relevance for the targets to be achieved on the part of Turkey during accession negotiations.

As is well known, the Maastricht agenda is about macroeconomic stability, and Turkey has achieved remarkable macroeconomic stability since the crisis of 2001, has implemented a variety of structural reforms, and the programme is continuing. The stability concept is also important when several reports and studies about Turkey's possible accession to the EU are reviewed, as mentioned above. In this context, given that the current macroeconomic stability programme anchored to IMF conditionality is continued consistently, it is possible to foresee that the Maastricht agenda will not be a main concern for Turkey's accession in the absence of large and unexpected external events affecting the global economy. Also because, eventually, IMF conditionality will be replaced by that of the EU. Thus, stability, the first structural component of EU economic governance, is not likely to be a major problem for Turkey in the immediate future.

The Lisbon agenda, however, is different, and will be more difficult than Maastricht agenda for Turkey, concerning its present and future implications; therefore it is the main focus of this chapter. The Lisbon agenda is almost always considered to be primarily an overall economic reform process, but in fact it has highly political and socio-cultural components covering a wide arrange of issues to be resolved on the way to becoming the most competitive knowledge economy in the world. The political component is in itself very complex and delicate, and interrelated with the socio-cultural structure of individual member states. In the EU, the much needed reform to increase competitiveness in the global context and modernization of policy structures are left to the context of open method of co-ordination: which means that the achievements of the member states as a whole will be definitive for the success of the EU as a global player. And behind all these arguments the traditional trade-off between federalists and inter-governmentalists is also manifest.

The concept of competitiveness in general, and with reference to Lisbon in particular, needs to be worked upon further. This, from our point of view, has to be put in the framework of a sound industrial policy defined both according to individual needs and the structure of Turkey (as in the case of the EU member states), and according to the Lisbon criteria. The question arises, perhaps, as to why Turkey would embrace the Lisbon criteria even before becoming a full member. The answer is simple and twofold. First, Lisbon targets seem to be the next line of criteria that Turkey will face during its difficult encounter with the EU throughout the negotiation process. The governance structures of the EU are evolving and also its *acquis*, and the EU's target is to be the most competitive economy in the world, which would bring us back again to the Copenhagen criteria, the ability to compete in the internal market. Implicitly, the existence of a competitiveness gap would create problems *vis-à-vis* the absorption capacity of the EU. Second, Turkey should embrace these targets on its way to sustainable development, with or without full membership of the EU, since the Lisbon criteria in fact amount to an overall reform package.

As mentioned above the Laeken agenda refers to legitimacy, and I have divided the concept as micro- and macro-level legitimacy. In this context, the Turkish government needs to develop its reform process in a way that legitimacy is ensured at both levels for the success of the reform process throughout the accession negotiations.

Before we proceed to the next section, it is also useful to consider the comments of the EU Commission on strengthening industrial competitiveness in Turkey. The Commission emphasizes that Turkish industrial policy is being transformed since the coming into force of the customs union, and the Turkish economy is currently more open to competition. The regular reports of the Commission in 1999–2001 related to the negative consequences of global developments on Turkish industry; small improvements in the privatization process; and the efforts to establish and sustain macroeconomic stability. In the 2002 regular report, the Commission highlighted the fact that there has been little improvement concerning industrial policy in Turkey, in particular with reference to SMEs. In the 2003 regular report some progress was noted concerning industrial policy, which coincided with the preparation of the Industrial Policy document prepared by the Turkish government that year. In 2004, again some improvement *vis-à-vis* the Community's industrial policy was noted, but this was considered to be insufficient in the regular report. In its *Recommendation* for the opening of accession negotiations with Turkey in October 2004, the Commission underlined that Turkish industrial policy is largely in line with EU principles, but efforts should be made in terms of restructuring the economy. Next, the problem of low levels of foreign direct investment should be tackled, and, the SMEs' access to finance should be improved (EU Commission, 2004b, p. 16). With reference to these and other evaluations mentioned in this context, the next section offers a modest assessment, with further policy recommendations for Turkey. Clearly, the EU process alone is not the solution to existing infrastructural and other problems of Turkey (see Chapter 6 for further discussion of this).

A sound industrial policy and economic governance: their implications for Turkey's internal process of modernization and external legitimization

In the light of previous discussions, it is evident that Turkey has to define an overall industrial policy. Proponents of a neo-liberal discourse claim that having no industrial policy is the same as having an industrial policy, the idea being to let the free market govern. This is a well-known argument. Whether it is a feasible policy for Turkey is another question (see Chapter 6). But one thing is certain: if there is no sound industrial policy, the gap between the 'haves' and the 'have-nots' will increase on such a scale that Turkey, despite its great potential, will not be able to achieve a structured development of its economy and there-fore be doomed to failure.

In this framework, an industrial policy document/outline entitled 'Industrial Policy for Turkey: Towards EU Membership' was prepared in 2003 in co-operation with many institutions in order to provide an overview of the state of affairs in Turkey.[9] This policy document was based on Turkey's 8th Five Year Development Plan, and was submitted to the EU Commission within the framework of harmonization with the *acquis*. However, the relevant societal actors in Turkey have barely considered this document in their attempt to create a wider consensus concerning its implementation.[10] The focus of the industrial policy document is on manufacturing, and the objective of the industrial policy in Turkey is to increase competitiveness and productivity while at the same time sustaining growth. This, in principle, seems a good idea, but the outlook presented in the document shows that there are policies for industry but no overall co-ordinated industrial policy that takes into account the needs of relevant groups or institutions. This aspect is important in the sense that each EU member state has its own model of corporatism, and the absence of such a model constitutes a weakness for Turkey. Although the proponents of orthodox liberal economy would oppose the creation of an industrial policy, there is a need for co-ordinated action in the shape of such a policy in order to sustain long-term growth while enhancing social cohesion and decreasing regional disparities.

When the screening documents are examined, it can be seen that the questions asked by the EU Commission of the Turkish government are in line with one of the main arguments of this chapter. The Commission wished to know to what extent industrial policy was important to Turkey, asking the question, 'How much is industrial policy a political priority?'[11] This is an important question, and it cannot and should not be answered simply; it should be thoroughly thought through and debated. This also points to the issue of political determination, men-tioned previously with reference to the Kok Report. The Commission has been assessing the political determination of Turkey with this question.

The need for a sound industrial policy also manifested itself in a recent speech by the Vice-President of the European Commission, Günther Verheugen.[12] He points out important issues, and emphasizes that 'We [the EU] need more than ever before an active industrial policy that keeps industry in Europe ... One further point – an active industrial policy does not stop at the borders of the old EU; it also applies to the new Member States' (Verhaugen, 2006, p. 3). It is possible to extend this argument to future member states as well. Hence, the negotiation process should be perceived as being broader than the *acquis* and Copenhagen criteria alone. It concerns a serious transformation process and is not a magic wand that will solve all problems. It is for Turkey to decide, and immediately if possible, what kind of targets should be aimed for in different time periods, and at what speed the process can progress.

Conclusion: further policy concerns *vis-à-vis* the accession process

Clearly, the European Union is one of the most important anchors for Turkey in the reform process. But knowing this fact is not enough on its own; strategic planning and implementation are needed, especially with regard to the Lisbon strategy. An active industrial policy is the *sine qua non* of the accession process, not only in order to catch up with the EU but also to enhance development in Turkey.[14] In this framework, one of the prerequisites of a sound economic policy is further democratization as well as developing a corporatist culture. Concerning the economics of Turkish accession, there is a need for institutional and structural capacity-building – in other words, better public and corporate governance. Improved governance and increased transparency should be coupled with the restructuring of industry and defining strategic targets to this end. These would all help to stimulate the internal modernization process and help public legitimacy immensely. Finally, an important issue is who will pay the cost of harmonization and alignment to the EU throughout the negotiation process and beyond? Taking the current budgetary deals within the EU into account, it is obvious that the main part of the costs will be paid by Turkey itself. However, the cost of this encounter should be divided evenly across all segments of society, with a view to decreasing the gap between the 'haves' and the 'have nots'. Only then will the targets be achieved with optimum results, and the EU's important aims of economic governance – that is, stability, competitiveness and legitimacy – can also be achieved by Turkey.

Notes

1. For recent empirical work, see Kaminski and Ng (2006).
2. For a detailed discussion, see Derviş *et al.*, 2006.
3. For detailed discussion of rent seeking behaviour and its consequences, see Chapter 6 in this volume.

4. The data are from the World Development Indicators Database, and the *World Bank Country Memorandum Report 2006*, which was prepared to give an assessment of the Turkish economy on the eve of launching the accession negotiations.
5. For further details concerning the economics of Turkish accession, readers are recommended to consult the following studies: Derviş *et al.*, 2004a; Ülgen and Zaharadis, 2004; Lejour *et al.*, 2004; Gros, 2005; World Bank Country Memorandum, 2006.
6. Several policy documents and studies are made available through Screening Documents in this context.
7. See the EU Commission (2005a).
8. This idea might seem simple, and it can perhaps be responded to in a negative way, but it is worthwhile considering. Because Turkey will not be able to continue for too long with IMF conditionality, which in any case does not help its development problems, the EU process thus provides a better anchor in the medium and long term. The view that the IMF recipes are not always sustainable is discussed in further detail in the next chapter.
9. The industrial policy document is important and will probably be reviewed during the negotiation process, not least because the current version of the policy is far from being satisfactory. For a better overview, see SPO (2003).
10. The institutions that were involved in the preparation of the document are as follows: State Planning Organization; Ministry of Industry and Trade; Undersecretariat for the Treasury; Undersecretariat for Foreign Trade; the Secretariat General for EU Affairs; the Small and Medium Sized Industry Development Organization; the Turkish Patent Institute; the Union of Chambers of Commerce, Industry, Maritime Trade and Commodity Exchanges of Turkey; and the Confederation of Turkish Craftsman and Artisans.
11. Indeed the view we advocate here concerning a broad-based industrial policy for Turkey has been confirmed in a 2006 report of a Special Ad Hoc Committee on Industrial Policies created by the State Planning Department (SPO) within the framework of the 9th Five-Year Development Plan. Compared with the 2003 policy document created within the framework of the 8th Five-Year Plan, the report this time partially takes into account the criticism that industrial policy should be based on broad consensus of all the parties involved in the process. The report highlights the necessity of 'industrial policies' as a tool for integration of Turkish manufacturing industry to global economy. However, the report does not go beyond a set of recommendations (SPO, 2006).
12. For further on this issue, see *Screening Documents for Chapter 20: Enterprise and Industrial Policy, Country Session Turkey, Questions and Answers*, 4–5 May 2006.
13. 'Competitiveness – the answer to restructuring and competition', speech delivered by Günter Verhaugen, Vice-President of the EU Commission responsible for Enterprise and Industry, EP debate on restructuring in the EU industry, Brussels, 4 July 2006.
14. The need for a sound industrial strategy has become even more clear with the opening of negotiations on Chapter 20 'Enterprise 2nd Industrial Policy' in March 2007.

References

Acemoğlu, D. (2005) 'Political Regimes, Institutions and Growth', Keynote speech delivered during TUSIAD-Koç University Economic Research Forum International Conference on Sustainable Growth Strategies for Turkey, Istanbul, 17 June 2005.

Barysch, K. (2005) *The Economics of Turkish Accession*, London: Centre for European Reform Publications.

Bartlomiej, K. and Ng, F. (2006) 'Turkey's Evolving Trade Integration into Pan-European Markets', World Bank Policy Research Working Paper 3908, Washington DC: World Bank, May.

Derviş, K., Asker, S. and Işık, Y. (2006) *Krizden Çıkış ve Sosyal Demokrasi*, 2nd edn, Istanbul: Doğan Kitap.

Derviş, K. (2005) *A Better Globalisation: Legitimacy, Reform, and Governance*, Center for Global Development, Washington DC: Brookings Institution Press.

Derviş, K., Gros, D., Öztırak, F., Bayar, F. and Işık, Y. (2004a) 'Relative Income Growth and Convergence', CEPS EU–Turkey Working Papers 8, Brussels: CEPS, September.

Derviş, K., Emerson, M., Gros, D., Ülgen, S. (2004b) *The European Transformation of Modern Turkey*, Brussels: CEPS.

European Commission (2004a) *Issues Arising from Turkey's Membership Perspective*, EU Commission Staff Document COM (2004) 656 Final, Brussels, 06.10.2004.

European Commission (2004b) *Recommendation of the European Commission on Turkey's Progress towards Accession*, Communication from the Commission to the Council and the European Parliament, COM (2004) 656 Final, Brussels, 06.10.2004.

European Commission (2005a) *The Economic Costs of Non-Lisbon. A Survey of the Literature on the Economic Impact of Lisbon-type Reforms*, Directorate General for Economic and Financial Affairs, European Economy Occasional Papers, No. 16, Brussels.

European Commission (2005b) *Communication from the Commission to the Council and the European Parliament Common Actions for Growth and Employment: The Community Lisbon Programme*, COM (2005) 330 Final, Brussels.

European Commission (2006) *Economic Forecasts*, Directorate General for Economic and Financial Affairs, European Economy No. 2, Brussels, Spring.

Gros, D. (2005) *Economic Aspects of Turkey's Quest for EU Membership*, CEPS Policy Brief 69, Brussels: CEPS.

Independent Commission on Turkey (2004) *Turkey in Europe. More than a Promise?*, Report, Brussels.

Jones, E. (2005) *European Economic Governance: Forging an Integrated Agenda*, Chatham House Briefing Paper, IEP BP 05/02, London.

Kok Report (2004) *Facing the Challenge: Lisbon Strategy for Growth and Employment*, Report of the High Level Group Chaired by Wim Kok, Brussels, November.

Lejour, A. M., de Mooij, R. A. and Capel, C. H. (2004) *Assessing the Economic Implications of Turkish Accession to the EU*, The Hague: Netherlands Bureau for Economic Policy Analysis (CBP), Document No. 56.

Pelkmans, J. and Casey, J.-P. (2004) *Can Europe Deliver Growth? The Sapir Report and Beyond*, CEPS Policy Brief No.45, Brussels: CEPS (http://shop.ceps.be/downfree.php?item_id=1092).

Rodrigues, J. M. (2005) *The Debate Over Europe and the Lisbon Strategy for Growth and Jobs*, Background Paper, 23.08.2005 (http://www.pes.org/downloads/The_debate_ over_Europe_050826.pdf).

Sapir, A. *et al.* (2003) *An Agenda for a Growing Europe: Making the EU System Deliver, Report of an Independent High Level Group established at the initiative of the President of the European Commission* (other members of the group: Philippe Aghion, Giuseppe Bertola, Martin Hellwig, Jean Pisani-Ferry, Dariusz Rosati, José Viñals and Helen Wallace), Brussels, July (http://europa.eu.int/comm/dgs/policy/advisers/experts_groups/ps2/docs/agenda_en.pdf).

SPO (Republic of Turkey, Prime Ministry State Planning Organization) (2003) *Industrial Policy for Turkey: Towards EU Membership*, Ankara: SPOC.

SPO (Republic of Turkey, Prime Ministry State Planning Organization) (2006) *Industrial Policies*, Special Ad Hoc Committee Report (Sanayi Politikalan, Özel İhtisas Komisyon Raporu), Ankara: SPO.

Ülgen, S. and Zaharadis, Y. (2004) *The Future of Turkish–EU Relations*, CEPS EU–Turkey Working Papers 5, Brussels: CEPS, August.

Verheugen, G. (2006) 'Competitiveness – the Answer to Restructuring and Competition', Speech delivered during EP debate on restructuring in EU industry, Brussels, 4 July.

World Bank (2006a) *Turkey – Country Economic Memorandum – Promoting Sustained Growth and Convergence in the EU (Vols 1 & 2)*, Washington, DC: World Bank.

World Bank (2006b) *World Development Indicators Database*, Washington, DC: World Bank, April.

6
The Economic Challenges of the Accession Process: The Matter in Question

Erol Katırcıoğlu

This chapter brings into focus a crucial debate that has existed for a long time in Turkey, while also being a complementary to Chapter 5 in this volume. The matter in question in this debate is where Turkey stands with regard to economic development. It is a question that will remain throughout the accession process and beyond. How can Turkey sustain a free market economy and adjust to globalization and the EU accession process while at the same time continuing to be a developing economy? The first section will identify the debate, and thus also the challenges of the EU accession process, while the second section will highlight, in parallel with the EU process, the challenges of globalization for Turkey and present an overview of the choice of industrial policies on the part of the government. Next, the insufficiency of these approaches, and possible positive and negative outcomes for Turkey will be presented. Finally, the proposition of sustaining an optimal reform process will be discussed. In this context, democracy, good governance and legitimacy will be emphasized as prerequisites of economic reform.

The challenges facing Turkey during accession negotiations with the EU and beyond

In September 1999, a well-known American economist, Edward C. Prescott, gave a speech entitled 'Will Turkey catch up with the industrial leaders?' at the 3rd International Economy Congress organized by the Middle East Technical University in Ankara. His immediate answer to this self-posed question was in the affirmative. However, he had predetermined one condition, that the forces, which he had named the *insiders*, needed to be destroyed. He put an emphasis on the word *destroyed*, because according to Prescott, *insiders* constituted the sectors that were mainly responsible for the *inefficiency* that undermined the business practices as well as those who determined the prices for their own services. The most important point of his criticism is that these constitute a segment in society that is protected from external competition by the government.[1]

Prescott further suggested that, if Turkey is to reach the living standards of the Western industrialized countries, the main requirement is to change the structure of these groups nourishing *inefficiency* in the economy. Therefore, the question as to how a more transparent and persistent economic infrastructure can be maintained, and the question as to how a more transparent and accountable government structure can be created are in fact being recognized as different facets of the same question. As noted above, Turkey has been debating this issue for a long time, and as debate continues on this subject, and illegal relations between some government, political and business segments have become more apparent over time, there has been inevitable pressure for more transparency. In this way, the idea of breaking the interwoven cleavages between politics (state) and the economy (market) completely, and leaving economic activities to the *market* alone is being considered seriously. The catchphrase, 'Less government and more market involvement' is becoming widely used. Various markets, mainly the stock market, in evaluating whether a political proposition is right or wrong, respond to this.

But the significant question is, how will Turkey develop? It is true that the Turkish economy is, more or less, a *market economy*; however, by the same token, it is also true that it is a *developing* economy. In this case, what will become of the problems in areas that are considered to be the infrastructure of a society, such as poor urbanization, inefficient health and education, and unequal income distribution? Will it be sufficient to leave these problems to the market to be solved? Or, will it be necessary to get the government involved?

Turkey and the globalization process: the significance of the local

The year 1980 was a turning point in the Turkish economy, and thus also of Turkish society. The Turkish economy, which up to that date had been more of a closed economy, opened its doors to the world economy. The more Turkey opened itself to the world, the more the effects of the world economy, and therefore of globalisation, have been felt.

The most important characteristic of globalization is the flexibility introduced in many areas. Being able to move capital in considerable amounts from one point to another in the world; the moving of companies very quickly from regions with high production costs to those with lower costs; the use of the internet, fast communication tools, and new trading opportunities such as e-commerce can be listed as examples of this flexibility. It is true that the flexibility introduced by the globalization process goes beyond the borders of the nation-states and reduces differences between countries to a certain extent, but it also increases the gap between different segments of society (see Chapter 5). Indeed, it is possible to observe similar developments also in the case of Turkey. In particular, as the economy integrated more to the world with the adoption of the decision to liberalize its markets in the 1980s, and the decision on the customs union in 1996, the pressure of external competition caused the Turkish economy to develop a much more flexible structure. Later, the reforms implemented as part of the 'structural adjustment programme' being carried out in co-operation with the IMF and the World Bank after the economic crisis of 2001, and those implemented as requirements of the accession process for the EU have led Turkey to become closer to the global world. However, problems of development have still not been solved despite these steps being taken and reforms implemented.

It is a well-known fact that general public opinion in Turkey is not very critical of globalization as in the matter of market. Even though people are not against globalization in general, they do not differentiate particularly between globalization and development. To put it more clearly, they have an unquestionable belief that globalization would inevitably provide development. However, there are no real examples that would justify the belief that being more integrated into the global world would solve the problems of development. If, for example, the South American experience is taken into consideration, it is apparent that Argentina could not succeed in this.[2] Argentina, as is well known, was in total collapse at the end of the 1980s. The government had become bankrupt, the national currency had lost its value, the wages were so low that they were not even enough to meet basic needs, and violence was everywhere in society. To solve these problems, a 'structural compliance programme' was implemented under the leadership of the IMF. The programme was initially very successful and provided speedy improvement. Indeed, Stiglitz had even defined Argentina as the 'top student' of the IMF (Sugden and Wilson, 2003, p. 16). However, by the year 2000, Argentina was suffering another crisis. In 2001,

40 per cent of the population was living below the poverty line. Argentina's globalization process is a live example of how globalization in a country, where development problems have not been solved, can cause social collapse. Therefore, considering globalization as a tool in the development process the driving force would be a much more realistic approach from the point of a genuine development process.

On the other hand, the international institutions related to Turkey's globalization process, such as the IMF, the World Bank, and the EU, do not accept this approach. According to them, what needs to be done is to implement the required reforms in order to enable the market mechanism to work better. These reforms will give way to development through maintaining macroeconomic stability; in other words, these institutions suggest that these reforms will also provide development. The IMF and the EU have a similar approach in this context. The Structural Adjustment Programme, which has been in existence since 2001 with the IMF, contains reforms leading to the optimization of the free market economy.[3] Naturally, the barriers to the market mechanism need to be removed, and the market needs to function better. Nevertheless, as was noted above, the realization of these reforms might not be sufficient to solve the developmental problems. In other words, Turkey may sustain a place in the global world with the implemented reforms and those yet to be implemented; but, this place may not be the one that Turkey desires, because the global world has a hierarchy in itself, and the position that Turkey will find itself in this hierarchy will not be in the upper levels as long as the long-standing structural problems are not solved.

A very simple rule-of-thumb calculation can be made to indicate how serious Turkey's existing problems really are. Turkey's per capita income was €7,000 in 2004, against an average of €23,500 for the European Union. Again, let us assume that Turkey has a 5 per cent growth rate annually, and the EU a 2 per cent growth rate. How many years will it take Turkey to catch up to the same degree of welfare as in the EU countries? The answer is, almost forty years. Considering the fact that Turkey cannot grow at 5 per cent every year, and that the EU will grow at more than 2 per cent annually reflects a more likely situation, which would mean that this period would even be longer. This is only a simple calculation; however, the result is true and clear: the economic performance Turkey has achieved to date has not been sufficient to reach the welfare level of Western European countries, because it is not possible for Turkey to develop through a globalization process that does not have any other objective than enabling a better-functioning market mechanism.

In fact, perceiving globalization as a provider of development *per se* is in essence reducing this process to very simple terms. For a company to be able to be competitive worldwide, it is vital for that company to have a very strong economic environment and infrastructure in every sense – in other words, it needs to be *developed*. It follows from this that globalization needs a well-developed *local* economic environment. In other words, being successful in the globalization process is directly related to how developed is the *local* basis.[4] Therefore, the sound development of globalization in Turkey depends to a great extent on how well the Turkish local basis is developed. So, the local basis in Turkey developed enough to carry a sound globalization? It is very hard to give an affirmative answer to this question. Instead of providing various statistics on the matter, it would be more beneficial to look at the regular reports of the European Commission. The quoted passages below summarize the results from the evaluations done within the framework of the Copenhagen economic criteria:

> Turkey has made considerable progress in addressing the most urgent imbalances in the economy, yet the process of achieving a functioning *market economy is not completed*.[5] ... The quality of education, health, and infrastructure needs to be improved in order to enhance the competitiveness of Turkish human and physical capital and to allow for a decline in the present social and regional differences. (EU Commission, 2000, p. 31)

Or as stated in another report:

> Turkey *has made progress* [my emphasis] in improving the functioning of markets and in strengthening the institutional framework for a fully functioning market economy. However, macroeconomic stability and predictability has not yet been achieved to a sufficient degree ... As a result of decades of insufficient spending on education and human capital development, the overall level of education of the Turkish labour force is relatively low. (EU Commission, 2003, p. 52)

These remarks state that on the one hand, a functioning market economy has not been developed in Turkey, yet on the other hand (despite the fact that in the most recent yearly reports the Commission has accepted that Turkey has a free market economy), investments must be made for the development of education, health, and other infrastructure. How can these problems relating to the local basis of

Turkey, which hardly has a fully functioning free market economy, be solved within the market economy alone?

The importance of industrial policies

As can clearly be seen from the discussion above, it is not enough for Turkey to leave the globalization process to the market economy alone. Because the problems that Turkey encounters are not related solely to not having a functioning market economy or not, they are also linked to having structural problems that require the involvement of the public sector or even more directly, the government and state apparatus, because of their very nature. Hence it is possible to say that Turkey's development, and catching up with Western countries requires the involvement of volitional decisions along with the market. This brings us to the issue of industrial policies.

Industrial policies in essence constitute a concept defining policies for the purpose of conscious, intentional and volitional development of the industrial structure. The intention is not to discuss this concept, which has been a never-ending argument, especially between liberals and social democrats, in detail here.[6] Still, it will be appropriate to take this matter into consideration in order to summarize existing approaches that also reflect the debates in Turkey.

There is no need for industrial policies – the *laissez-faire* liberal approach

For those who have ultimate faith in the market mechanism, an industrial policy is not a matter worth discussing. According to these individuals, any kind of (governmental) intervention in the market mechanism creates a diminishing effect on social welfare, since a market economy produces the highest welfare as long as it functions freely. Indeed, intervening in such a mechanism producing the highest welfare naturally can only decrease that welfare. According to advocates of this opinion, industrial policy is just another name given to protective policies one way or another. Protective policies, on the other hand, neither increase the welfare nor discipline the industrial structure. Therefore, industrial policies should not be permitted. Industrial policies may diminish the social pain by supporting some industries at their collapsing stage, as well as their workers, but a fast operation can be a less painful solution.

According to the advocates of this view, there are some consequences of the intervention of the government in the economy. The most argued point is that those who govern the country – namely, politicians and bureaucrats – are disconnected from the market processes, which prevent them from reaching the right decisions. For example, when a new technology is to be selected, it will be hard for them to make the right decision, since they will not have sufficient information on what type of technologies are present in the market, and which would be the most suitable for existing conditions. Furthermore, it is impossible for the government to establish clear-cut criteria for concessions to be granted to firms within an industrial framework. Therefore, since it is not clear as to whom and why these concessions will be granted, these policies turn into mechanisms that cultivate corruption.

Industrial policies are necessary under the leadership of the government – leaving a role for the governmental approach

Those who defend the necessity for industrial policies maintain the opinion that the liberal market economy does not function as laid down in theory and competition is prevented within the market itself. In order to stop the loss of wealth that arises from the distortion of competition, they claim that it is necessary for the government to interfere with the markets. Indeed, for various reasons, the market economy may not function properly to maintain the best distribution of resources. In particular, the firms having invested in sectors where the costs are relatively high may quite naturally obstruct the entry of new companies and/or of new technologies; or the ones that have pre-viously entered the sector may try to prevent new entries by abusing their dominant position; or a small number of large firms can collude easily and earn supra-normal profits. In all these cases, the liberal market economy will not function as defined in textbook theory, and the intervention of the government in such markets will increase social welfare.

Apart from such market failures, in cases where the markets do not produce certain goods or services (such as education) sufficiently, or where some goods impose extra cost – not to their producers, but to society – for example the cost of dealing with environmental problems caused by the firms – the intervention of the government always results in improving welfare. On the other hand, in the event that certain goods and services are under a natural monopoly, the produc-tion of such goods or services by the government, or regulation of that market by the government again enhances social welfare. Additionally, the market conditions in certain sectors, which need to be restructured, may not be appropriate for such changes to be applied only by the market (for example, shipyards with old technologies, coal mines and so on). In such markets, with the existence of a limited number of players, the decision to exit from the industry should not be taken independently. In this case, it might be necessary for the government to intervene and to facilitate the transformation process.

Insufficiency of the approaches: the possible positive and negative outcomes

The most important argument of those opposing the industrial policies is that such policies create or facilitate a *rent-seeking* relationship among politicians, bureaucrats and businesspeople. Indeed, between a politician who acts with the intention of being re-elected, a bureaucrat whose goal is to secure his/her place in the government mechanism, and a businessperson, who wishes to grow by laying his/her hands on the resources of the government, corrupt relations can easily be developed. Therefore, industrial policies, no matter what their purposes, inevitably encourage rent-seeking behaviour. Such comments have been made in Turkey for a long time, as they have with regard to a lot of developing countries, and, as has been mentioned above, they receive much support from the general public. The incentive of rent-seeking created by the intervention of the government not only impairs the possible contribution of the government to the development process, but also other developments such as the introduction of technologies. In particular, in the event of a firm holding a natural monopoly, technology makes only one firm viable in a certain sector, and the involvement of government policies other than regulation can, because of a lack of competition, hamper incentives to do research on new technologies – for example, the satellite and wireless technology changed the natural monopoly condition of the cable communication market, and the requirement for government intervention in this field ceased as a result.

On the other hand, it is an important fact that a market economy does not function on its own as foreseen by economic theory. In addition to the abuse of a dominant position or a distortion of competition by firms who enter collusive agreements between themselves, the problems created by a few holding the power to make strategic decisions require public intervention in the development process. The economic power gathered in the hands of a few players prevents, in one way or another, the right decisions being made related to the utilization of resources, and impedes development (Cowling and Sugden, 1998). In these instances, even the policies to open the economy to the outer world or to create competitive pressure through imports will not be effective on their own. They can enable the continuation of the poor structure that exist by various means (such as the conduct of importing by the actors in the market themselves holding a dominant position). The existence of such groups that can protect themselves on their own, and which Edward Prescott defines as *insiders* also requires the existence of public policies.

The approaches mentioned briefly above have their own strong points theoretically. It should be underlined here that all politicians, whether liberal or not, are under pressure from the economic actors, and the preferences of the politicians who desire to be re-elected are transformed into policies in the end. Very often, the politics conducted are mixture of both approaches. Therefore, in reality, it is not possible to find a purely liberal or a classical industrial policy in today's world.

What kind of industrial policy?

In a globalizing world, as foreign trade volume has increased, the meaning of trade has also started to change. According to conventional trade theory, international trade was realized through the logic of comparative advantage based on factor endowments. The country that produced a certain commodity at a lower cost, by exporting this commodity to another country, and by importing the one it produced at a higher cost, could earn more profit. However, in the 1980s, it became apparent that almost 60 per cent of the commodities in world trade constituted those that did not have any comparative advantage (Helpman and Krugman, 1987). In other words, the comparative advantage became recognized not only as a result of the production factors the countries had, but also a result of the implemented industrial and trade policies. In short, increasingly the opinion found acceptance that the comparative advantage was not a given in society; and on the contrary, it could be created artificially by conscious preferences (Cowling and Sugden, 1998).

This new theory, namely *strategic trade theory*, while focusing on the new opportunities and some new difficulties in the globalizing world, also signalled a new industrial policy approach. If the comparative advantage could be created by the conscious preferences of a society, then a new industrial policy taking this view into consideration would accelerate the development of a country. With this new approach, it may be possible to implement some new incentive policies geared towards enabling certain powerful firms in the domestic market to be successful in the international market. For example, promoting the production or the research and development (R&D) activities of the big firms that are the champions of the domestic market, or protecting the domestic market with certain non-tariff barriers may make it possible for these firms to gain an advantage over their competitors in the international market. In this way, even though supporting the firms with high market power would decrease the consumer surplus, such a loss can be compensated by the monopoly rents to be obtained by the same firms in the international market. Therefore, in a more general sense, we can say that supporting the national champions of a country through industrial policies orientated towards increasing their input efficiency and protection from the foreign trade has an importance that can affect a country's place in the international division of labour.

When the disadvantages of previously mentioned classical industrial policies are taken into account, it is apparent that this new approach is a new opening before the countries. Above all, this new field of policy, when formulated more appropriately according to the rules of the market economy rather than targeting the very rules of the free market, has a stronger legitimacy than the classical approach. This policy can be viewed as a new approach to be utilized to strengthen the *local basis* in order to help the national firms gain an advantage in international competition.[7]

One can assert that this new trade policy has two basic flaws, regardless of the fact that it has emerged as a new field of policy, and has been implemented in various forms. First of all, this policy is not exempt from the rent-seeking tendencies that can arise between the politician, the bureaucrat and the businessperson, which is also one of the flaws of classical industrial policy. And, second, a country supporting its own national champion will inevitably cause the governments of other countries, where competitive firms are situated to retaliate and this may prevent the gains expected from this policy.[8] Therefore, in order to propose a strategic trade policy and an industrial policy to be legitimate policies to strengthen the local basis of a country, these flaws should be eliminated or diminished as much as possible. This aspect will be commented on further in the next section.

Sustaining optimal reform process: democracy and legitimacy as prerequisites of economic reform

We have tried to make it clear above that in today's world, *market economy* alone would not be sufficient to catch up with the degree of welfare of the developed countries with respect to infrastructure, labour, technology and environment for developing countries. In order to achieve this target, the society needs to utilize its own means through conscious preferences; in other words, it must implement industrial policies (see Chapter 5 in this volume). Indeed, no matter which perspective is adopted, it is evident that we do not have an adequate basis for Turkish firms to be successful in an international competitive environment. The social problems, infrastructure and urbanization problems in Turkey prevent firms from participating fully in globalization.

On the other hand, corruption and abuses that Turkish society has had to face for some time now displays another truth about the country. It has become clear that rent-seeking behaviour is very common and the management concept of the government has been utilized to support this kind of behaviour. In such an environment, how can we propose the industrial policies, the necessity of which have been stated previously? Indeed, to what extent is it possible to utilize these industrial policies without the creation of any rent in an environment where government power is being abused? These questions indicate clearly that a new path needs to be taken. In other words, a new approach is required, which, on the one hand, will enable industrial policies to trigger the development of the country, and on the other, these policies will not lead to corruption.

In real sense, there is no simple prescription for such an approach. Today, the necessity of eradicating corruption and having a transparent economy and government administration should not cause us to abandon the idea of industrial policies. What we need to do is to start a new societal discussion and a new search by considering the disadvantages of these approaches. The main goal of this chapter is to contribute to the discussion by putting forward certain ideas geared towards the establishment of such a model, rather than by introducing the model itself.

As has been mentioned above, the solutions to developmental problems require conscious and purposeful volitional decisions. In other words, the solution to the problems defined here as development problems (such as poor urbanization, insufficient infrastructure and education services, and unbalanced income distribution in areas constituting the infrastructure or the local basis of a society), require volitional decisions to be taken by society as a whole as well as the market. Who will take these decisions? In the light of the discussions above, since such decisions have traditionally been accepted as decisions that involve the government, they will have to be taken by politicians and bureaucrats.

As generally accepted by the economists, since 'decision-making always works in favour of the decision-makers' (Zeitlin, 1974), politicians and bureaucrats will always benefit from this situation. However, since the decisions involving the society also need to maximize the interests of the whole society, decisions made by limited number of politicians and bureaucrats result in strategic failure, as Branston *et al.* put it. Such failure is a situation, like market failure, where public intervention is required (Branston *et al.*, 2002).[9]

Therefore, it is necessary that the model to be established to solve the development problems takes the democratic contribution of the whole of society as its starting point. The following recommendations constitute some of the qualities and benefits of such a model, which is to be established according to the perspective outlined:

- Such a model has to be democratic enough. In other words, in today's world, where it is impossible to know everything and the cost of obtaining specialist information has increased, making the right decisions has acquired a dimension involving more than individuals. Therefore, a new industrial policy in line with development targets needs to be established based on a new organisation including all (local and national) parties. This approach will be one that is participatory concerning the representation of different views and that has the least possibility of wrong decisions because of its richness of opinions.
- In such an organization, all parties should have a place as parties to the problem (sector). Among these parties, depending on the nature of the problem (sector), bureaucrats, employers, representatives of labour unions, scientists, consumer representatives and other related social groups should also participate.
- In these organizations, since the representatives of the parties take on responsibility through election, responsibility is distributed more consistently, and this in turn increases the credibility of the organization.
- Such an organization will not only eliminate the consequences of decision-making at the government level, but will also eliminate the consequences of decision-making in a poorly-functioning market. With this characteristic, accurate decision-making will be achieved.
- Of course, in addition to all these, in such organizations, which will be established with the participation of different people from different sections, it is evident that the rent-seeking behaviour will be minimized.

This kind of organization, the basic principles of which have been described above, can be similar to formations, that have become widespread in the EU in recent years, although not including carrying all the principles entirely. The core concept here is *network governance*. In Europe, there are already organisations of this kind, such as the Third Italy, Cluster and Filiers, which have been formed in order to eliminate the disadvantages of the state–economy axis, in the context explained here, and which have attained a certain level of prevalence at the local, national and association levels.

Conclusion

This chapter has been the expression of a search, although an open-ended one, for the purpose of better adjustment to the process of globalization, while at the same time trying to cope with the accession process of Turkey to the EU. The question of how Turkey can adjust to this relatively faster world and, as mentioned above, to the EU, involves companies, unions and all kinds of organizations and countries as well as individual Turks. The urge to survive is perhaps the strongest of all. Therefore, knowing and understanding the conditions of the new world is more than anything else closely related to the urge to survive. Because of this, we are now trying to find solutions a number of questions, some of which the Turkish government and society have already solved, and some they have not. Turkish society needs to solve its existing problems as soon as possible. In the search for solutions for the Turkish economy and society, it is vital to develop a model for the organization of industrial policies that is more democratic, more participatory and more creative than the models seen until now.

Notes

1. Edward Prescott, METU 3rd International Economy Congress, Ankara, 1999.
2. For comments regarding the globalization of Argentina, see Sugden and Wilson (2005).
3. As is well known, the Copenhagen criteria are: the existence of a functioning market economy, and the capacity to cope with competitive pressure and market forces within the Union.
4. This shows that globalization and localization are not conflicting, but rather are complementary processes.
5. Italics are mine.
6. Wolf (1988) can be seen for a through evaluation of both views.

LIVERPOOL JOHN MOORES UNIVERSITY
LEARNING SERVICES

7. For example, it is possible to influence technology by providing firms with R&D support, quality of labour by contributing to education expenses, trade by establishing new standards, and competition by utilizing the competitions laws. One of the examples, that summarized this new industrial policy the best, is the example of the Airbus–Boeing aircraft firms. Germany, the UK, and France decided to manufacture the Airbus aircraft by creating a consortium against Boeing, the world leader in the manufacture of medium-range commercial aircraft. This initiative made it possible for the European aircraft industry to gain a competitive position *vis-à-vis* America. The support that Europe gave to Airbus, determined the success of Airbus in this competition. This determination also increased the cost of Boeing's efforts to prevent the entry of Airbus.

8. One of the most important advocates of *Strategic Trade Theory*, Krugman (1987), later stated 'No one has set forth empirical evidence providing that protection or export incentives provided considerable gains' and changed his position (Krugman and Smith, 1994, p. 7).

9. In this study, while the authors emphasize the importance of taking strategic decisions, they also argue that the taking of such decisions by a limited number of people would result in 'strategic failure', and that this would require public intervention.

References

Branston, J. R., Cowling, K. and Sugden, R. (2001) 'Corporate Governance and the Public Interest', Warwick Economic Research Papers series, No. 626. http://www2.warwick.ac.uk/fac/soc/economics/researchpapers.

Cowling, K. and Sugden, R. (1998) 'The Essence of Modern Corporation: Markets, Strategic Decision-Making and the Theory of the Firm', *Manchester School Papers*, vol. 66, no. 1, pp. 59–86.

EU Commission (2000) *Regular Report on Turkey*, Brussels: European Commission.

EU Commission (2003) *Regular Report on Turkey*, Brussels: European Commission.

Helpman, E. and Krugman, P. (1987) *Market Structure and Foreign Trade*, New York: MIT Press.

Krugman, P. (1987) 'Is Free Trade Passé', *Journal of Economic Perspectives*, vol. 1, pp. 33–144.

Krugman, P. and Smith, A. (eds) (1994) *Empirical Studies of Strategic Trade Policies*, Chicago, Ill.: Chicago University Press.

Prescott, E. (1999) 'Will the Middle East Catch up to the Leaders?', Keynote paper delivered at the 3rd Economic Congress of METU, Ankara.

Sugden, R. and Wilson, J. R. (2005) 'Economic Globalization: Dialectics, Conceptualization and Choice', *Contributions to Political Economy*, vol. 24, pp. 13–3.

Yeldan, E. (2001) *Küreselleşme Sürecinde Türkiye Ekonomisi*, Istanbul: İletişim Yayınları.

Wolf, C. Jr. (1988) *Markets or Governments*, London: MIT Press.

Zeitlin, M. (1974) 'Corporate Ownership and Control', *American Journal of Sociology*, vol. 79, no. 5, pp. 1073–119.

7

Socio-cultural Dimensions of Accession Negotiations

Pulat Tacar

The Turkish accession negotiations, which began in October 2005, will last for ten to twenty years and can be considered as important for Turkey as the era of modernization reforms that followed from the establishment of the modern Turkish Republic in 1923. The coming years will beyond doubt be crucial for Turkey's place in the world of the twenty-first century. The twenty-year forecast was made by the French president, Jacques Chirac, in order to calm anxieties triggered by the decision to start accession negotiations. Furthermore, he wanted to emphasize that nothing is decided with regard to Turkey's full membership. Even after a technically successful conclusion of the negotiation of thirty-five chapters of the *acquis,* all member states governments will have a decisive say concerning the start and end of each chapter. Eventually, the final decision might be taken by EU citizens through *referenda* in several member states, including France and Austria. Turkey is constantly reminded that, even if it complies with all the EU rules and standards, the EU member states reserve the right to take a final political decision concerning Turkish membership. Hence, both Turkey and the EU will have an option to reconsider whether membership is a desirable or feasible option and, obviously, the positive and negative aspects of membership can be evaluated more realistically in 2017 or 2027.

In order to fully capture the complexity of this difficult encounter, this chapter is divided into four main sections. While the first section presents general reflections on the accession process, the second compares the modernization and accession processes. The third section provides a detailed analysis of Europe's changing political landscape, and discusses challenges of an ethnic or cultural nature. The final section explores the models of governance of multi-culturalism with a view to providing a different perspective for both the EU and Turkey.

Reflections of the accession process

It is not clear what the majority of the Turkish public truly knows about the EU criteria and positions, and what membership will really mean for them; for example, which sovereign rights will be transferred to Brussels, and what the pros and cons of EU membership will be. Basically, there are contradictory views on the positive and negative effects, even about the impact of the customs union. Some analysts claim that the customs union has damaged the Turkish economy; while others claim that it has strengthened it. Currently, a considerable number of the Turkish people want to join the Union, believe that it is a big step in the modernization process of the country or that the EU will bring more welfare, better health and life conditions, and more freedom. Some expect that membership will open the doors of the labour market in Europe. In contrast, the dark side of the moon has not yet been considered seriously.[1]

Some European leaders prefer the idea of a partnership agreement, something between full membership and a kind of association. Some of them, like the CDU leader the current Chancellor in Germany, Angela Merkel, call this a 'privileged partnership' but without defining it clearly. What these leaders probably have in mind is a sort of buffer zone or a *limes* similar to neighbouring areas of the Roman Empire.[2] But Turkey already has a special relationship with the EU, because it is the only country that entered into a customs union without being a full member of the union. Hence it is by no means clear what kind of option is left to make sense of the concept of privileged partnership. In fact, the Turkish public finds it difficult to understand European politicians who claim that, because its capital is Ankara, Turkey is not European, or, because the great majority of its population is Muslim, the country belongs to another civilization. After all, Ankara also was the capital of Turkey when the Association Agreement was signed and ratified. In addition, EU member states knew about the size of the Turkish population and the country's economic potential before accession negotiations began.

Some conservative and nationalistic circles in Turkey cultivate the idea that the EU plans to divide Turkey and redefine its territorial integrity. This is one of the Euro-sceptic discourses. Naturally, the EU will not gain anything by dividing Turkey. But the EU and the member states may have a slightly different concept with regard to minorities, the role of the army, the place of women in society, and so on. Furthermore, one should not forget that the EU, in its dealings with

Turkey, will defend the Union's interests as well as the interests of the individual member states. In other words, the EU should not be expected to be neutral in its dealings with non-members. Even if the national interests of some EU members do not totally match the long-term interests of the Union, the EU will support its members. This can be seen in the case of the Greek Cypriot government vetoing regulations drafted by the Commission in order to govern free trade relations with Northern Cyprus.

It is important to emphasize that the integration process implies that a considerable amount of power will be transferred from the nation-state to the EU. This means that several decisions with regard to daily life, the economy, trade, the quality of food, health systems, the environment, labour regulations and so on will be taken not in Ankara, but in Brussels, and these rules will come into force on the day of their publication in the *Official Journal of the European Union*. The decisions of the Union's Court of Justice are also definitive. Furthermore, not only the *corpus* of the decision, but also the *considerata,* has the force of law.

When negotiations came closer, the EU expressed its expectations about Turkey in stronger terms. These mainly underlined the importance of the union's *acquis* as well as compliance with the Copenhagen criteria: in other words, EU conditionality. Most expectations stemming from the European Commission and the European Parliament are of a political nature, and some might regard them as interferences in the internal affairs of Turkey. Furthermore, some member states have tried to obtain concessions from Turkey on bilateral issues – for example, concerning Cyprus, the Aegean issues and so on. These states will consider such concessions – that is, solving these problems in their favour – as a prerequisite for the continuation of accession negotiations as it was clear in the talks prior to the December 2006 EU summit.

Until full membership is granted, Turkey will face many of these situations. But, as mentioned above, even if all the pressure is dealt with and all the demanded concessions are met, European citizens will make the final decision regarding Turkish membership. The institutions to decide on the faith of Turkey will not be national parliaments on the recommendation of their respective governments, but the peoples of Europe and, of course, one must not forget, the European Parliament, which is gaining power exponentially within the EU institutions. For example, a citizen in Austria might say: 'the Turks came up to the doors of Vienna and ruined everything here in 1683 so I don't want them in the Union now'; another European citizen might say:

'Turks are not Christian, they are Muslim, and I don't want them to join us.'[3] Furthermore, the former president of France, Valéry Giscard d'Estaing openly said that 'the capital of Turkey is not in Europe, so Turkey is not in Europe. If the Turks join, that will be the end of the European Union.'[4] The former French president did not ask the same geographical question with regard to Nicosia, the capital of Cyprus. These few examples are meant to show that the perspective of Turkish membership is blurred and carries a good deal of uncertainty.

It is clear that the insistence on the open-ended character of negotiations with Turkey and repeated reference to alternatives other than full membership will remain hanging over Turkey like a 'sword of Damocles', right until the end. This will have extremely serious psycho-sociological consequences, creating an atmosphere of insecurity in Turkey and beyond during a period when Turkey has a great need of stability, especially because of the development of the Turkish economy and the related need to attract foreign investments. Such political and psychological pressures amount, from time to time, to discrimination and they shake the trust of the Turkish public. Recent polls show that enthusiasm regarding membership is decreasing in Turkey (and in the EU). When the pressures caused by the problems of accession and their effects on the public become more visible, it is likely that this negative trend will become more pronounced.

The 'negotiations' might easily be called 'setting the rules of compliance to the *acquis*'. Thus the process of accession differs from other diplomatic negotiations or commercial bargaining. Turkey does not face a give-and-take situation, characterized by negotiations between equal partners. Furthermore, room for manoeuvre is limited, especially for Turkey. Most previous enlargements were made in packages. Turkey has deliberately been left out of these and will be pushed alone 'into the lion's cage' – that is, the referendum process. But the one who wants to join a club must go along with the rules set by the existing members or give up the request for membership. In this type of a negotiation process, one cannot expect friendly relations, justice or equity between parties. We are in a situation where the stronger party dictates its will, and the Turkish public must be prepared for this. Unfortunately, the Turkish public is not used to this kind of dictation and if it feels its national pride has been hurt, it may react unpredictably.

During the accession negotiations, Turkey and the EU will decide on how Turkey should comply with the 80,000–100,000 pages of the *acquis*. Ambassador Murat Sungar, the former Secretary General for European Union Affairs of the Prime Ministry, stated in one of his speeches that in fact not even 15 per cent of the translation of the *acquis* has been completed. During the negotiations, exceptions concerning the timing of the compliance with the *acquis* will be considered. Within European law this is called 'derogations', the postponement of a rule of the EU law for a defined period of time. For example, if Turkey becomes a member, the postponement of the free movement of labour will be subject to such a derogation. The fundamental rule of the EU single market is the free flow of goods, services, capital and labour. Thus there should not in the future be any permanent derogations concerning the fundamental principles of the EU, otherwise Turkey will not be given the status of (full) member of the EU.

So far, the demands for possible political and economical concessions have been presented. There are also undoubtedly important lessons to be drawn from the past enlargements especially for the most recent rounds of the process *vis-à-vis* the individual member state demands.[5]

The accession process as a modernization process

According to some analysts, the main objective of the accession process is to become a modern society. The EU is merely instrumental in Turkey's reaching that ultimate goal. According to other analysts, EU membership means more integration with the European value system. In spite of the fact that the acceptance, preservation and encouragement of both national and regional identities constitute a fundamental EU principle, membership must be seen as a process leading to a new, superior identity. In fact, this also points to the difference between those wanting a federal Europe and others who prefer a confederate Union, and the issue has yet to be resolved within the Union. Unless Turkey amends its laws and regulations, which at the time of writing are incompatible with the EU *acquis*, it will not be able to become an EU member or an advanced economy. Turkey then risks being left to play in the second league of nations.

Under the current circumstances, Turkey needs to start an active and effective information campaign with regard to the implementation of EU norms and standards. The best way to do this is to let public authorities, local administrations and non-governmental organizations work together. The reforms should not be presented as patronizing or unfair arrangements. The Turkish population should understand that the reforms will benefit both individuals and society as a whole. This can be achieved through wisely planned information policies. Despite the inherent difficulties, the Turkish nation can and should come out of this bumpy, painful process of accession.

Most probably for reasons attached to the predominant religion in Turkey, the general public believes that treaties, once concluded, are binding for ever. But in international law, the principles called *Pacta sunt servanda* have a counterpart called *Rebus sic stantibus*.[6] Today, Turkey faces this reality. For example, according to the Additional Protocol concluded between the EEC and Turkey, a provision on the free flow of labour should have been implemented as of 1 November 1986. At that date, the EU refused to comply with its engagement and declared that, because unemployment had increased in Europe, and the labour market conditions had changed, their commitment to the free movement of Turkish labour could not be honoured.

Changing political landscapes and ethnic and cultural challenges

Throughout Turkey's long accession process, Turkey and the EU countries will experience three or four elections, and different governments will come to power in every country and the new governments will probably have different approaches to Turkey's accession to the Union. The membership pattern will also change. The Union might encounter more difficulties than expected with the accession of Romania and Bulgaria. Finally, the evaluation concerning Turkey's compliance with the EU *acquis* may lead the accession process to a dead end. In fact, it can easily be seen that some EU members pursue a policy directing Turkey to a *privileged associate member* position, or a neighbouring country status, which was not foreseen in the *acquis*. This will be unacceptable to Turkish governments as well as to the representatives of the NGOs and the academics in the country. But, when the time comes, one may understand that to jump off a moving train is extremely difficult. To counter such a situation one needs other leverages.

Some of those opposing Turkey's accession claim that Turkish society has different values. This 'different values' thesis has become even more popular in recent years. However, when speaking of the Union's values, those that are written in documents, constituting the political and legal basis of the Union, should have priority compared to the unwritten values. A very broad framework can be drawn when speaking of values, but these are bound to be subjective and cultural. Some, such as the French philosopher, Edgar Morin, say that the foundations of European values lie within the Jewish–Christian religions and Greek philosophy, together with Roman laws.[7] Yet we also know that some Roman Catholics strongly oppose references to the Jewish religion in this context.

One of the opposition factors concerning the Turkish values is the fact that the great majority of Turks are Muslim, even though the state is secular. There are other factors as well, yet, if we need to classify cultures, I would suggest classifying the Turkish culture under the heading 'Eastern Mediterranean'. The EU has proved that it does not deny the Eastern Mediterranean culture when it accepted the Greek Cypriots as full members of the Union.

Currently, millions of Turks are already EU citizens and contribute to the diversity of the EU, and the EU recognizes cultural diversity among its citizens. The European nations have a very rich ethnic, religious, linguistic, regional and traditional diversity. The EU promotes the recognition, respect and preservation of this diversity and tries to eliminate all kinds of discrimination within and outside its borders, especially in candidate countries. During the accession process, Turkey will need to accept and implement these values.

Problems can arise when some citizens or members of a minority see the principle of diversity as a tool for dividing a country. There are signs of possible tensions in this respect in current member states – for example, in the expectations of the Basques and Catalans in Spain, and the Corsicans in France. In Turkey, the declarations of some ethnic Kurdish citizens also cause tension. However, it is possible to consider and implement minority rights, included in the Copenhagen criteria and underlined in several annual reports of the Commission, as well as in the decisions of the European Parliament, under the framework of, 'recognizing, preserving and promoting diversity' and 'the prevention of all kinds of discrimination'. In other words, Turkey, or France, should not be forced to accept any minority within the nation except the ones defined by international treaties. On the other hand, Turkey should continue to prevent all kinds of discrimination of its citizens by implementing legal and administrative actions. Positive discrimination for different cultural groups may also be considered. In order to meet the demands of different cultural groups, the creation of an environment of trust is a *sine qua non*. One cannot share without having a feeling of trust. Finally, measures taken to promote diversity should not be used by those who benefit from them to endanger the unity and integrity of the state. In this respect, the primary task of the state should be to eliminate legislation that prevents its citizens from using their rights and freedoms and make sure that everyone has access to the rights and freedoms enumerated in the European Human Rights Convention and its additional protocols. Respect for and compliance with the decisions of the European Court of Human Rights (ECHR) is another must. The summit decisions of the Organization for Security and Cooperation in Europe (OSCE) should also be respected.

The 10 per cent national barrier for national elections can be seen as damaging justice and equity. However, Turkish legislation makes securing stability a priority. There are also demands coming from EU partners with regard to the freedom of religion. It must be possible to implement some of these demands as long as they have a legal ground – for example, the right to worship, the right to minorities to own property and so on. Turkey does not deny that minorities, recognized and mentioned in the Lausanne Treaty, have the same rights concerning educational institutions and foundations as all other citizens. Turkish laws and decisions of its Justice Department can be challenged by the ECHR when necessary and applicable. However, the EU will lose its credibility if it treats minorities in the member states in the Union and other countries differently. One example can be given with regard to the violation of the rights of the minority living in western Thrace in Greece. These rights stem from both the Lausanne Treaty and the European Human Rights Convention. The members of the minority there speak Turkish and consider themselves to be Turks, but they are not free to call themselves Turks. In this fashion, their identity is oppressed. In some cases they may even be condemned because of that. The fact that the Union does not do anything about these human rights violations creates a loss of credibility in the eyes of Turkish public opinion.

Another issue that Turkey will face during the accession negotiations is the Cyprus problem. After the creation of the State of Cyprus – through the London and Zürich Agreements – the then President of Cyprus, Archbishop Makarios, attempted to render them inoperative even before their ink had dried. His objective was to change the status of Turkish Cypriots from equal co-founders to the status of a minority. The Greek Cypriot government also pursues this attitude with patience; they are in no hurry. They have become an EU member and have the European Union's legal and political support behind them. Now they plan, during the accession negotiations, to get all the political concessions they want from Turkey. The recent EU decision not to open negotiation chapters relevant to Greek Cypriot political position speaks for itself.[8]

Another issue is the correct reading and translation of the *acquis*. Since Turkey has not been doing its homework properly, unawareness of the scope and the true meaning of the rules have been much more controversial. A concrete example in this context would be the last sentence of the Copenhagen criteria:

> Accession depends on ... the existence of a functioning market economy as well as the capacity to cope with competitive pressure and market forces within the Union ... the ability to take on the obligations of membership including adherence to the aims of political, economic and the monetary union ... *the ability of the Union to digest the new member* while preserving the European integration process must also be to the best interest of the Union as well as the candidate country.[9]

In November 2004, there was confusion in Turkey when an impact analysis concerning Turkey's membership to the EU was requested from the Commission. To some analysts, this decision qualified as a new condition for accession. In reality, it was not, because the ability of the Union to accept new members has always been part of the *acquis*. In any case, an impact analysis is also urgently needed for Turkey: the Turkish public has the right to know what the costs of complying with EU standards and norms will be for Turkey, and how this will be financed.

According to World Bank experts, compliance merely with the environmental *acquis* above implies that Turkey will need to spend about a €40 billion, and compliance with environmental norms will increase production costs for the Turkish business community. Owners of some small and medium-sized enterprises have explained that they do not have the ability to comply with EU environmental standards at present or in the foreseeable future, primarily because of infrastructure problems. This will put further pressure on the need for Turkish public infrastructure investments, contributing to a higher level of employment. However, the implementation of EU norms will make lay-offs inevitable, because an increase in production costs will have a negative effect on exports, which will result in an increase in the unemployment rate.

Complying with and implementing the agriculture standards of the EU will have a negative effect on the Turkish agricultural sector. It will be necessary to amend the heritage clauses of civil law concerning the size of farms. There is a vital need for the Turkish primary sector to comply with EU policies regarding agriculture, stock-breeding and fishery standards as soon as possible. In Turkey, hidden employment in the agricultural sector – is around seven million. The average size of farms is small, and EU countries generally do not have farms as small as those in Turkey. Productivity in the agricultural sector is only about an eighth of the average in the EU. The brutal truth is that Turkey will have to educate and reallocate some ten million people from agriculture to the industrial and services sectors. Some of these people, who will have to leave the rural districts, will not have the skills it takes to find jobs in other sectors. This will inevitably trigger social unrest and increase income gaps among the Turkish population. The government will have no choice, but to implement unpleasant policies in this field, and at the same time experience the loss of public political support. The result will be a lower level of economic and social stability, perhaps even instability, which in turn will deter foreign investors from investing in the Turkish economy.

Unfortunately, Turkey will not receive much support from EU funds to balance this negative development. The times have gone when former candidate and present member countries, such as Ireland, Greece, Portugal and Spain, received large funds from the EU. The new member states have consumed most of the EU's resources. In fact, it is understandable that they do not want to share the already diminished amount of funds with Turkey. Finally, it does not seem that any member country wishes to raise its contribution to EU funds, largely for political reasons, allied to the current economic recession in the Euro Zone.

The negotiation process is complicated, needing both expertise and patience. The opening and closing of every chapter will need to be agreed by all the 27 EU member states. As in all negotiations, the representatives from these countries will be subjective in their demands and evaluations, and will be looking out for their own benefit. Most of the EU's member states, especially the majority of the new ones, do not yet fully comply with the EU *acquis*. When they were accepted as members, some of their deficiencies were not taken into consideration. But for political reasons, even the smallest from Turkey's side may well be used to delay the accession negotiations. This will create a level of frustration in Turkish society, and worst of all may drive the majority of the Turkish public away from wishing that Turkey becomes a member the EU. We already know that there are groups both inside and outside Turkey, who aim at achieving this outcome. Turkey must be prepared for the tough attitude of some governments, who will demand bilateral political concessions from Turkey, and for others who, for historical, religious or cultural reasons, are not willing to accept Turkey as a full member of the EU.

The effect of these developments on Turkey's economy and public order must be planned in advance, and remedies found in sufficient time to deal with these matters. It is evident that an economy that bears a burden of about US$300 billion in foreign debt and has a constantly rising current foreign trade deficit, will easily be affected by negative shocks. This is a consideration that is especially important for foreign investors, who seek stability in the countries in which they consider to invest.

During the accession negotiations, Turkey's implementation will be under the supervision constant of the EU Commission and the EU member states. Turkey needs to be prepared for regular information and disinformation campaigns, and should patiently follow the objectives set of by the various Turkish governments that are to follow in the next twenty years. The long and painful process will have serious political, social and psychological effects on the Turkish public. The EU's rules and standards will significantly change the way everyday life is led in Turkey. During these future developments, Turkey may face many political provocations, which will increase the difficulties it will encounter. This requires a fundamental change of thinking in society. It has to be kept in mind, that the Turkish *sine qua non* objective is not only accession to the EU, but also to reach the standards of a modern society. Finally, the governments of Turkey must understand that keeping the accession process only within a political-bureaucratic framework will not be sufficient to overcome the negative image of Turkey in European public opinion. In order to change the 'bad image' and to underline the positive aspects of Turkish diversity, intensive scientific, artistic and cultural relations should be established and continued with its European counterparts. In this context, the next section focuses on the Turkish experience of the governance of multiculturalism. I believe that through its rich cultural heritage and cumulative experience, Turkey can make an invaluable contribution to the EU, while winning the hearts of the *Turco-sceptics*.

Governance of multiculturalism in Turkey and the EU

Hardly any country is homogenous in terms of ethnicity, race, religion, sect or language. In the present world, discord between different ethnic or religious groups is the main factor behind misunderstandings and conflict. Social scientists tend to agree that conflicts surfacing as a result of plurality in multicultural democratic societies can either be eliminated or de-escalated by means of prudent policies.

Assimilation practices

In the pre-modern period, the first priority of nations was to establish a state and preserve it. Leaders of these countries believed that, without a strong central state, they would be torn apart. Accordingly, they view ethnic or religious differences – in other words, minorities – in Turkey as a threat to the unity and integrity of the Turkish economy. Historically, this perceived threat was reinforced when groups belonging to these minorities revolted against the central authority or had a role to play in the delicate geo-strategic balance of which the country was a part. As for the minorities, they experienced doubt and reservation *vis-à-vis* the majority among which they live. They do not want decisions concerning their rights to be made once and for all by the majority. Hence, they seek international guarantees to protect these rights.

The first reaction of societies experiencing ethnic and religious division is to follow a policy of forced assimilation of those elements that are different, to guard against the fragmentation of the country. Assimilation uses both direct and indirect means to remove cultural diversity. Those who see assimilation as a solution do not accept the existence of minorities or the expansion of existing differences. Even in the case of minorities, whose existence has been recognized through agreements, every kind of legal or administrative measure is taken in an attempt to deny them recognition.

Modern states also find that centralized power is important. The policies they rely on concerning minorities, seen as a threat to the centre, include simple exclusion, assimilation and integration. At times they deny there are differences, and refuse to grant minority rights, opting for assimilation instead. However, this can have the consequence of contributing to struggles for democratization that emerge as a process of decentralization in plural societies. Undeniably, there is a direct link between decentralization and democratisation.[10]

Nevertheless, while assimilation has been a common practice historically, it would be difficult to find a country in which it has been a complete success. Even if assimilation policies seem to be successful in the short term, differences will resurface in some way or another. It is not easy to extinguish shared memory. Policies designed to eliminate differences will not only contribute to tension and conflicts, but they may also bring about uprisings, as has been witnessed in France.

Integration policies

Countries that are able to appreciate this possibility prefer to solve the problem through policies of 'integration'.[11] There are various approaches to or interpretations of the concept of integration. People have attempted to compare integration to a 'mosaic', a 'melting pot', and so on. There may be many reasons to opt for integration. Most of them relate to the maintenance of security, the enforcement of power discrepancies present among those entering into integration, mutual interests, or the replacement of conflict with a reduction in tension. During integration, the parties to the process preserve their own social values and unique cultures. A sound integration should not deprive individuals or groups the right to be different.[12]

It is through reconciliation that the post-modern EU, of which Turkey wants to become a part, is trying to design integration policies and regulations pertaining to living together. In the event that the implementation of these regulations is endangered, country responses can go as far as interfering in the internal affairs of one another – as was seen in the case of the reaction shown to Jörg Haider's party in Austria. The other fundamental elements of the EU include: the rejection of the use of force in conflict resolution between member states; the gradual lessening of the importance of borders between countries belonging to the Union; and the increase in regional co-operation in matters that extend beyond the borders of the countries.

Europe is moving towards a new legal and socio-political order. This, and its post-modern nature, have not been adequately understood, examined or discussed in Turkey. This new order is seen by those, who in their wildest imaginations could not dream of Turkey stepping outside the boundaries of the traditional definition of a state, as consisting of 'elements that would undermine the state'. Compared to the pre-modern state or the modern state, the problems of minority and diversity in this new order are solved in a very different way. States attaining the stage of post-modernity increasingly devolve certain responsibilities to sub-national units, including regional administration, civic organizations or associations. Other state functions are transferred to international institutions such as the EU and the North Atlantic Treaty Organization (NATO). Moreover, the transfer of this authority is made easier by implementing policies of governance of diversity. States are rapidly losing their centralized features. As a result of this, minorities are resolving their own cultural, religious and linguistic problems without the intervention of the state. The responsibility of finding and administering the expenditure necessitated by affirmative action are increasingly left to regions or groups of people. Consequently, the transfer of resources from the majority to the minority is being reduced, with regional administrative and civic organizations being left to find ways of raising the requisite funds. In the area of economic and social development, the state has been reduced to playing the role of a partner, catalyst and facilitator rather than the provider of growth or development. The state will just provide the legal framework within which minorities deal with their own linguistic, religious and cultural matters. It will ensure the participation of minorities in the decision-making process that determines regulations concerning them. This is in fact one of the basic principles of participatory democracy. Within the framework of state or regional administrations, the vast majority of minorities in the post-modern, liberal, democratic European states have a rather important degree of autonomy with respect to their own cultures, language and religion. However, attention must be drawn to the fact that, despite attempts at attaining self-government, most have remained more formal than substantial. France, for example, which for constitutional reasons does not legally recognize the presence of minorities, has emphasized decentralization and broadening the transfer of authority to regional administrations. Within this context, France has set up the 'National Council of French Languages and Cultures'. As a result of these developments – not to mention the cost of maintaining the self-governed diversity – the desire for self-government by the minorities living in the liberal-democratic states of the EU has declined in recent years.

For countries that are part of, or have decided to become part of, the EU, assimilation is no longer a legal or administrative option. Therefore, for countries rejecting affirmative measures to some segment of their population – because such practices are unconstitutional or because they do not recognize the status of minorities (for example, France and Turkey) – it is necessary to find solutions to the difference problem within the framework of multiculturalism or diversity governance.

European attitudes towards diversity

While European countries are moving in the direction of economic and political integration, they aim at preserving and developing cultural diversity. In many European countries, assimilation is characterized as cultural genocide. Among European countries with a federal government, reactions concerning this issue are even greater. The aim of European countries is averting the eradication of diversity and differences, and protecting those who are different or constitute a minority from assimilation. In 2001, the then president of the EU Commission proclaimed that, 'Across Europe, there is in general no majority; we are all minorities.'[13]

The countries forming the EU have carried their cultural differences with them to the Union, and see the preservation of this cultural diversity as a condition for their unity. In the eyes of Europe, there is no single culture of Europe, but rather there are *cultures* of Europe. The principle of the preservation of diversity and difference is a fundamental norm of member states. Each of the individual countries also consists of an aggregation of cultures. Cultural difference is considered not as an element of division but rather of enrichment. According to the norms, while preserving and developing these, care is taken not to compromise the integrity of the states or the culture of the people constituting the majority in the country. For example, the learning and use of that country's official language or languages will be an obligation on all citizens. Similarly, the existence of an official state language or languages will in no way serve as an obstacle to the use and development of different mother tongues. The problem that awaits a solution is who is going to meet the expenses involved in this practice. In some countries, the cost of education, teacher training, the printing of textbooks, radio and television broadcasts, translation and translators are met through the public budget. Some believe, however, that these expenses should be borne by the social groups concerned.

Turkey's attitude towards European norms on minorities and diversity

European countries have, by forming norms and standards through national laws and international communiqués and agreements, created morally, politically and legally binding obligations with respect to diversity and minorities. It is clear that Turkey has dragged its feet in this area very much, that the contents of these communiqués and agreements have not been examined closely by the Turkish public or politicians. The norms and standards of the countries of the EU with whom Turkey wants to integrate have not been translated into Turkish, published, announced to citizens, or been subject to public discussion. The documents concerning this subject remain in the files of the ministries. Another main reason for this is the ruling of the Turkish Constitution, rejecting the distinction of minority–majority among the citizens of Turkey, and the psychologically prohibitive environment formed by decisions made regarding this matter in light of the contents of the Constitution. However, Turkey attended all the conferences, and was on the committees that prepared these European norms and standards, and thus was party to their contents. It did not object to the communiqués or agreements prepared. The only action it took was to state its reservations about the compatibility between the norms and standards and the Turkish Constitution, and the articles of engagement of the Lausanne Treaty. On the other hand, Turkey has not signed or approved the Minority or Regional Languages Agreement, or the Council of Europe Minorities Protection Outline Agreement, both of which were prepared by the Council of Europe with the participation of Turkey. The reason for Turkish officials treating this matter with velvet gloves is that they fear the division and break-up of Turkey, which is what the terms difference, diversity and minority, and the practices associated with them, amount to, given the obligations (to preserve the integrity of the country) laid out in the Constitution. The break-up of Yugoslavia and the inability to stop terrorism in the Basque region, in spite of the broad autonomy granted to the Basques, are examples that cannot be overlooked. Moreover, the wounds of the armed struggle in the south-east of Turkey are still fresh.

To sum up, I believe that the European mindset with respect to difference and diversity, as well as European lifestyle, is something with which Turkish public opinion and politicians alike should become familiar. Moreover, there needs to be a profound exchange of ideas. Without either being done, Turkey runs the risk of being confronted by severe confusion and misunderstandings in the future. And there is one point that must not be forgotten: just like Turkey, the countries of Europe are themselves extremely careful and sensitive when it comes to the matter of protecting the integrity of their countries. The challenge is to find an appropriate level of tolerance. Administrators who keep the threshold high justify this by pointing to Turkey's sensitive position – that is, lagging behind regarding the cultural and social values among the Turkish public, and the country's geo-strategic position.

The Copenhagen criteria and minority and diversity issues

The EU did not create norms respecting differences, diversity and minorities solely on its own. It was the norms established within the framework of the Council of Europe and the OSCE that became the norms adopted by the Union. The conditions, labelled the Copenhagen criteria, stipulated that countries wishing to become members have to accept these norms, demonstrate respect for 'democracy, the rule of law, human rights and minorities, and in this regard, provide the institutional stability that would protect these rights'. The term *stability* needs some explication. What is wanted from candidate countries is not some 'fly-by-night', 'here today and gone tomorrow', kind of conformity but rather continuity. These criteria must become an integral part of the life of society. What is necessary is a complete change in mentality.

The aim of the Copenhagen criteria is that accession states do not eliminate minorities, differences and cultural diversity. A policy of denigrating or disregarding identities cannot breed social harmony. The majority in a country should not ostracize or attempt to assimilate the minority. Every effort should be made to avoid squeezing citizens who are different or diverse in terms of language, religion, race and culture to become part of a homogenous group. Minority views ought to be respected, and the threshold of tolerance should be adjusted upwards, but the idea is that recognition, protection and development of difference or diversity should not reach such irrational proportions that national unity or the integrity of the country is jeopardized. This criterion is one of the limits imposed by the European Protection of Human Rights and Freedoms Agreement.

The boundaries of freedom, which encompasses the expression of difference, are quite broad within the Europe with which Turkey wants to integrate. Provided that ideas expressed do not advocate the use of force or violence, or threaten the use thereof, they are not restricted. The restrictions laid out within the confines of the agreement are not based on subjective criteria but rather objective ones. For example, France (as is the case with Turkey) does not accept minorities for constitutional reasons. But as a consequence of the freedom of expression and the right to form associations, France has political parties or political movements that demand regional autonomy or freedom, and these parties can participate in parliamentary elections. This is just one example of the boundaries of freedom that can broadly be defined.

A correct reading of the Lausanne Treaty:[14] the case of diversity

In the Turkish Constitution, no minorities other than the ones specified in the Lausanne Treaty or the Bulgarian Friendship Agreement are recognized in the country. Minority rights in Turkey are considered within the framework the Lausanne Treaty, under the heading of Protection of Minorities, Articles 37–45. It is assumed that the Treaty covers only non-Moslem Turkish citizens. A reading of articles of the

Lausanne Treaty show that the following articles refer to non-Moslem Turkish citizens:

- Rights pertaining to travel and migration (Art. 38/3);
- Civil and political rights (Art. 39/1);
- Establishment and management of any kind of institution, and the use of one's own language and worship there (Art. 40);
- Teaching in native languages (Art. 41/1; 2)
- Respect for customs and traditions in family life and personal status (Art. 42/1); and
- freedom from coercion with respect to acting in accordance with convictions (Art. 43).

The other articles in the treaty ensure rights for all Turkish citizens, or anyone else living in Turkey, who speaks a language other than Turkish. There are rights subsumed under the heading Protection of Minorities of the Lausanne Treaty that apply not only to non-Moslem Turkish citizens, but to all citizens. For example, all citizens are to be considered equal, regardless of religious belief. Accordingly, each citizen is entitled to certain civic rights – particularly the right to work as a civil servants and to be promoted. Moreover, no restrictions are to be imposed on the choice of area of employment (all under Article 39). Citizens also have the right to use whatever language is desired in carrying out either personal or commercial transactions (Article 38/4).

These rights have the force of law. No institution, regulation or procedure can oppose or contravene the articles of the Lausanne Treaty. It has been agreed that no law, code or regulation of the Turkish Republic can be considered superior to these articles. Hence, we should emphasize that the articles of the Lausanne Treaty represent a kind of 'human rights guarantee' directed towards the preservation of cultural diversity in a country.

Measures that states can take concerning diversity governance[15]

There is no single model for the preservation and development of diversity. Every country has different solutions according to its institutions, history, social values and cultures of the different groups that comprise the nation. France, the UK and Spain have even gone as far as permitting the enactment of diverse legislation in various regions with the result that practices differ from one area of the country to another. For example, in the UK, there are distinctly different governance models in Northern Ireland, Scotland and Wales. This is because the roots of conflicts in these nations of the UK are distinct. Pragmatic solutions were found that take into consideration the idiosyncratic characteristics of the citizens living there, the diversity having its origins in history, and the problems arising from this. Various rights have been devolved to the separate regions: the transfer of executive authority to Wales; tax assessment authority to Scotland; and the right of Northern Ireland to maintain institutional ties with the Republic of Ireland, provided the province remains within the UK. In France, similar arrangements have been made with its Overseas Territories and the island of Corsica. In France, decentralization is at the top of the list of solutions, and significant devolution to regional governance has been achieved.

When speaking of diversity governance, the most important measures are the rules governing the prevention of discrimination. It is a national and international obligation to treat every citizen equally, without regard to ethnic origin, race, colour, language, religion or sex, and avoiding discrimination between citizens. Hence, states must remove elements in their codes and laws that have discriminatory effects.

Apart from this, the state may take specific measures to protect and develop the differences manifested in people who are distinct from the majority in such areas as mother tongue, religion and ethnic origins. It can also grant parliamentary representation quotas to minorities. Such measures are referred to as *affirmative action* or affirmative *discrimination*. Those advocating the principle of affirmative action point to insufficient recognition by the government of the existence of diversity or minorities. They demand that governments provide various kinds of assistance –financial, administrative or quotas – to individual members of minority groups or their associations. OSCE communiqués adopt a principle of discrimination that does have a negative impact on the majority.

Because of similarities in constitutional principles, another example from France can be provided:

> The existence of racially, linguistically, or religiously based groups on French territory is not recognized. This notion is inspired from the principle that all citizens are equal before the Constitution. The Constitution supports the principle of the unity and indivisibility of the country. The principle of the unity and equality of the French people precludes any entertainment of notions of differences based on ethnic criteria.[16]

However, this principle does not prevent citizens, whose mother tongue is other than French, from being taught their own languages in school. Neither does it hinder broadcasting in these languages via radio or television.

In order to safeguard cultural diversity in the country, France has considered the matter within the framework of regional cultures and dialects. In 1951, the possibility of learning regional languages and dialects in school was granted officially through the Deixonne Law. This law also made provision for carrying out research and doing doctoral work on the subject of regional cultures. In 1999, while indicating its reservations, France signed the European Charter for Region and Minority Languages.[17] However, because some of the articles of the Charter were deemed to be contrary to the French Constitution, the Constitutional Council did not approve it. Even without using the term 'minority right', the General Assembly of the United Nations Educational, Scientific and Cultural Organization (UNESCO) adopted the Cultural Diversity Communiqué in 2001, and thus paved the way to peaceful coexistence and the enjoyment of individual rights.

The Constitution of the Republic of Turkey (1982) supports the principle of the unity and indivisibility of the nation. In its various decisions, the Constitutional Court of the Turkish Republic has repeatedly declared that no minorities exist other than those laid down by the Lausanne Treaty and the Bulgarian Friendship Agreement. Nevertheless, Turkey has also taken its first steps towards allowing radio and television broadcasts in languages other than Turkish, and the teaching of different mother tongues by private institutions. Practices designed to preserve diversity will have a chance to succeed, provided that norms are properly implemented and rights, guaranteed by the Constitution, are not restricted or otherwise obstructed by unrealistic laws or regulations.

In summary, regimes respecting human rights should adopt the requisite regulations that recognize, protect and develop cultural diversity, and should make it possible for governments to put these regulations sincerely into practice. This is as much a political and legal obligation – for example, from the point of view of candidates of the EU – as it is ethical. By reinforcing the richness of sub- and supra-identities, most societies can protect the integrity of their countries more consciously, while at the same time living in unity and solidarity. Turkey has considerable experience in terms of its cultural heritage and cultural diversity, and this can be useful in the context of designing solutions to EU diversity.[18] Being under the EU conditionality does not imply that only

Turkey should learn. It is a two-way process, and governance of diversity is an integral part of this process now and will be in the years to come.

Notes

1. It should be emphasized that the author of this chapter is not against Turkish EU membership. Furthermore, I sincerely believe that the EU desires an economically and politically strong, stable and democratic Turkey as a partner. This chapter is written to indicate the difficulties ahead for both sides in the accession process.
2. According to F. Bolkenstein, former EU Commissioner, 'Turkey should be kept outside the European Union to act as a buffer protecting Europe from Syria, Iran and Iraq; the former Soviet Republics of Moldova, Belarus and Ukraine should be excluded, to insulate Europe from Russia' (Bolkenstein, 2004).
3. This is not fiction; and those who followed the TV programmes at the beginning of October 2005 on several European television channels will remember that it really happened.
4. In an article entitled 'Return to Reason' in *Le Figaro*, he put forward reasons why Turkey should be left out of the EU.
5. Here, it is considered to be useful to present a witnessed event during the accession of Spain and Portugal to the EC. It was during the last week of November 1984. I was supposed to present my credentials as Ambassador, Permanent Delegate to the President of the EC Council. I was waiting in the hall of the EU Council. It was a historic day. Not because I was presenting my credentials, but rather because the final and formal decision concerning the membership of Spain and Portugal was to be taken. The doors of the meeting room opened at 18.00 hours. The Foreign Affairs Ministers of Spain and Portugal, who had also been waiting in the same room, got up for the celebration ceremony. Unfortunately, there were still some minor problems. Apparently, during this final meeting, one of the EC members requested a payment of a compensation (a kind of 'bahshish' I was told) of US$2 billion in order to say 'yes'. Also, another EC member expressed its wish to restrict the fishing areas in the Atlantic where Spanish fisherman had been fishing for hundreds of years. The Spanish Minister of Foreign Affairs, who wanted to refuse such additional concessions, who thought he should return to Madrid, was contacted by telephone by the Spanish prime minister, and instructed to stay and to accept these new conditions on the expectation, that Spain would eventually change this situation on the occasion of future enlargements. There was a lesson to be learned from this.
6. This principle means that, when conditions change, treaties may be amended according to the new situation; in other words, a treaty shall not be binding for ever and under every condition.
7. See Morin (1988).
8. Ambassador Gündüz Aktan has touched this issue in one of his articles in the *Radikal* daily with the following words: 'Both the Greeks and the Greek Cypriots will end up losing everything, because they do not know where to stop.'

9. As is well-known, in June 1993 during Copenhagen European Council, the EU member states defined the Copenhagen criteria for admission of new members to the EU.
10. For more on this debate, see World Bank (1997).
11. I use the expression 'to become integrated' in the sense of forming a new molecule out of the nuclei of different peoples and groups, whereby the original characteristics of the distinct, individual nuclei are to some extent preserved while at the same time they are united with other nuclei – eventually, forming a brand-new molecule that has a supra-identity that transcends all the other separate identities. Accordingly, 'becoming integrated' is the coming together of different groups to create a relatively homogenous social unity and to create a super-identity.
12. Of course, this is what is ideal. But it is not the picture we get in reality. Particularly with respect to economic and social factors, economically weak minorities find their cultures reduced to the level of folklore. For further information, see Endruweit (1983, p. 261).
13. See Prodi (2000).
14. The Lausanne Treaty is also known as the Treaty of Peace with Turkey, which was signed on 24 July 1923. See Meray (1993) for details.
15. For a detailed discussion on this, see Tacar (2004).
16. For details, see ECOSOC (1991).
17. The European Charter for Regional or Minority Languages (ECRML) is a European treaty (CETS 148) adopted in 1992 by the Council of Europe to protect and promote historical regional and minority languages in Europe.
18. See Tacar (1996) for a detailed account of diversity governance in Turkey.

References

Bolkenstein, F. (2004) *The Limits of Europe*, Belgium: Lannoo Publishers.

ECOSOC (1991) Document: E/CN/4/1991/53, 5 March 1991.

Endruweit, G. (1986) *Elite und Entwicklung*. Frankfurt am Main: Peter Lang.

Giscard D'Estaing, V. (2004) 'Return to Reason', *Le Figaro*, Paris, 25 Novermber.

Meray, S. L. (1993) *Lozan Barış Konferansı: Tutanaklar, Belgeler*, İstanbul: Yapı Kredi Yayınları (Lausanne Peace Conference – translated into Turkish).

Morin, E. (1988) *Europa denken*, Frankfurt am Main and New York: Campus.

Prodi, R. (2000) 'Inauguration Speech' at the European Monitoring Centre on Racism, Vienna, 7 April.

Tacar, P. (1996) *Kültürel Haklar: Dünyadaki Uygulamalar ve Türkiye için bir Model Önerisi* (Cultural Rights: Implementations around the World and a Model Proposition for Turkey) Ankara: Gündoğan Yayınları.

Tacar, P. (2004) 'The Governance of Multiculturalism', in *The European Union for the World Leadership: Towards New Global Governance?*, E. LaGro (ed.), Istanbul: Turkish Society for Quality Publications.

World Bank (1997) 'The State in a Changing World', *World Development Report 1997*, Washington, DC: World Bank.

8
From Vision to Reality: A Socio-cultural Critique of Turkey's Accession Process

Nedret Kuran-Burçoğlu

Turkey's accession to the EU will be a long and complex political process in which economic and socio-cultural problems will have to be addressed as well as possible solutions found. This process will undoubtedly be a challenge for both Turkey and the EU, since both will have to adapt themselves to a relatively new environment – that is, of 'living together' and 'sharing certain values'. This chapter focuses on what has been, and still is, almost always overlooked about the socio-cultural aspects of a prospective Turkish full membership of the EU through the medium of a conceptual framework, and a corresponding evolutionary approach. The perspective presented here is also an attempt to go beyond well-known debates in this context using an imagological analysis throughout. Consequently, the chapter provides a discussion on the socio-cultural aspects of the accession process of Turkey to the EU and, by looking at previous experiences, the first section highlights socio-cultural constraints that people in Turkey and in the EU will have to face during the process as well as the potential cultural conflicts. Subsequent sections elaborate on present socio-cultural issues with an evolutionary approach, and present suggestions on potential areas of co-operation that will be beneficial for both sides, thus facilitating the accession process.

Difficulties of living together with the 'other/s'

While considering Turkey's accession to the EU, it is of utmost importance for both parties to be aware of what kind of socio-cultural constraints there are on both sides that have to be conceptualized and dealt with during this transitional phase. One of the main impediments both to joining a union, and accepting a new member in a union is the inherent doubt in accepting the idea of living with the 'other'. However, this is not an easy task. It requires good will, a lot of patience, willingness to understand the 'other', empathy for the 'other', perseverance to accomplish an agreement, and an effort on both sides to overcome the mutual preconceived ideas and clichés about the 'other'. History is full of conflicts and wars between countries, nations and groups of people who did not succeed in living together. As the famous philosopher of the German Enlightenment, Immanuel Kant, once stated, 'The state of peace among men ... is not the natural state (*status naturalis*); the natural state is one of war ... A state of peace, therefore, must be established' (Kant, 1795).

Four steps leading to peace

Kant was right in stressing the necessity for effort in 'creating' peace. This is a long process involving four steps. First, *getting to know the 'other/s'* – that is, one has to be willing to learn about the 'other/s' culture, religion, rituals, traditions, way of life, conventions, values, likes/dislikes which can be achieved through an intercultural dialogue with the 'other/s', including joint projects, concerts, exhibitions, seminars, travels, sports and other joint activities. Through interaction with the 'other/s', one will also strengthen one's own identity. Second, *learning to respect the 'other/s*: one has to acknowledge and respect the 'other/s' diversity – that is, his/her ethnicity, race, religion, gender and culture, as well as ideas and thoughts, and be 'inclusive' rather than exclusive in this respect. While starting joint activities, as above, the universal values and common concepts that are shared with the 'other/s' should be emphasized, rather than the differences. In this context, fair treatment of the 'other/s' is extremely important, as it leads to solidarity and creates a sense of trust as well as accountability in the 'other/s'. Third, *creating awareness about potential threats to solidarity*. Along with the second step, consciousness should be raised in human minds about the dangers that threaten solidarity among people:

- deeply rooted negative and/or distorted images and ideas about the 'other/s'; and
- manipulation through the use of stereotypes that may lead to discrimination, segregation, xenophobia, racism and ethnic cleansing. The 'intentions and strategies behind concealed or overt provocations against the 'other/s' should be spotted with a critical approach, revealed and explained to public to prevent potential conflicts with the 'other/s'.

Fourth, *the sustainability of peace.* Conflict prevention (through raising consciousness about the dangers of manipulation and splits that might lead to animosities), and conflict resolution techniques – through trying to solve existing problems with a cool mind and through empathy, solidarity and trust in the 'other/s', thus achieving coherence and accountability by respecting the 'other/s' rights, values, ideas, thoughts and diversity – should be brought into play the instant peace is under threat. Only through the implementation of these steps, can peace and stability be achieved and sustained in communities.

Socio-cultural experiences of European countries on joining the EU

If the history of the EU is examined carefully, starting with the European Coal and Steel Community (ECSC) that was set up in the 1950s, it is possible to identify the complexity of integrating several European countries into the ECSC and to the EEC from a socio-cultural point of view, and the same is also true today through successive enlargements. More than fifty years have passed since the EU's inception as the ECSC, and a lot of effort and energy have been put into the integration of 27 countries, the population of which share a common religion, history and values. However there is still some hesitation about them becoming united 'under the same umbrella' with the members of the other European countries they still consider to be 'others'. The initial purpose of the EU was to prevent another war in Europe that would lead to even worse problems than the Second World War had caused. As is well-known, although the ECSC resulted in the successful integration of the members' coal and steel resources, the reasons for its formation in 1951 were primarily political. It is useful to remember that Robert Schuman developed plans for the ECSC for two major reasons: first to meet US demands that West Germany be rebuilt to help deter aggression by the Soviet Union, and second, to allay France's fears of renewed aggression by a rearmed Germany. This is understandable because, over the centuries, Germany and France had fought repeatedly over access to coal and steel resources in border areas such as Alsace-Lorraine (Cohn, 2005, p. 4). Thus the initial aim of the ECSC's foundation was, as stated in its Preamble, 'to create, by establishing an economic community, the basis for a broader and deeper community among peoples long divided by bloody conflicts'.[1] The Community was consolidated in 1967 through the Merger Treaty and has taken its current shape as the European Union based on the Maastricht Treaty (1991). Following the Eastern Enlargement with ten new members, and with the accession of Romania and Bulgaria, the Union is now a large regional bloc.

The transition from being a European country to a member state of the EU has not been easy for member states or their citizens. Difficulties were caused by different social habits, customs and conventions – traditions as well as behaviour patterns that individuals did not want to change. These were partially determined by their religious, ethnic, regional or national identities, and the scepticism they had mutually formed against each other over the course of their history. The wars they had waged had left deep marks in the memories of Europeans, and the impact of modernism had left its traces on the national and ethnic identities that they had formed *vis-à-vis* one other, thus Euroscepticism still seems to be an issue in Europe (see Chapter 9 further on this). Many Europeans are hesitant about giving up their sovereignty and being united under supranational institutions, as the essential trust between one and the other is missing, and needs to be developed. This situation demands a thorough analysis of a range of political, socio-economic and cultural factors.

The expectations and visions of the Europeans for their future: the outcomes of an extensive research project – Plan Europe 2000

In this context, it would be worth elaborating on the results of an international research project in which visions for the future of Europe were expressed. The research project was entitled *Plan Europe 2000: Between Hopes and Anxieties*. The project was initiated in 1994 by the European Cultural Foundation and was implemented in three phases. One of the phases of the project involved four workshops at the College of Europe in Bruges. In the workshops, students discussed with scholars from different disciplines of humanities and social sciences the politics, economy, social systems and environmental issues in Europe, and expressed their hopes and anxieties for the continent's future.[2]

The anxieties described can be summarized as:

> environmental issues; the manipulation of human beings through the media; reluctance to participate in social life; loss of human values; rise of nationalistic, racist and fundamentalist tendencies; decrease of tolerance; replacement of economic competition by the hegemony of world markets; increase of power of illegal organizations; social alienation leading to loneliness of individuals, increase in unemployment rates; unequal distribution of wealth, money and employment; cleavage of the gap between wealthy and poor coun-

tries; emergence of new polarizations in the communities; dominance of technology on human beings; decrease in creative thinking; incapability of finding solutions to newly arising problems; and the idea of a 'common' Europe. (Kuran-Burçoğlu, 1994)

The hopes can be summarized as:

confidence and hope in the idealism of youth and in the common sense of the elderly people; hope that the grown-ups will one day take the initiative to improve the current situation of social inequalities; globalization of the idea of civil initiative; increase in the activities of non-governmental organizations, such as Greenpeace, Amnesty International, the Pen Club, Helsinki Citizenship Assembly; sustainability of democratization under the leadership of the youth; emergence of international trustworthy and accountable institutions and mechanisms, increase in precautions for environmental issues; development of new models and strategies in education; expansion of the concept of life-long education; encouraging human beings to take initiatives to create their own future; to develop a new concept of work; willingness to share work and responsibilities; willingness to learn from past experiences; and the idea of a 'common' Europe. (Kuran-Burçoğlu, 1994)

In the cultural panel of the workshop, there were two concepts that were believed to be fundamental to the idea of Europe – that is, *pluralism* and *multiculturalism*. It was recommended that these concepts should be appropriated, and intercultural co-operation be fostered by civil society.

Reflections on the unifying strategies of the European Union

It is interesting to compare current trends with those of the 1994 project. As indicated above, 'the idea of a common Europe' was listed then, both among the hopes among the anxieties, which shows that people were hesitant about the potential outcomes of this togetherness. However, certain concepts that were in the foreground in the 1994 workshop, such as accountability (leading to mutual trust); pluralism (legal recognition of the equality and co-existence of different political values and behaviours); multiculturalism (coexistence of different cultures and cultural practices); development of new educational models (leading to more interaction and dialogue among the youth of various countries); initiative of civil society organizations (leading to peace among societies); expansion of life-long education (to increase consciousness at all levels of society); and the sustainability of democratization under the leadership of youth (to guarantee the future of democracy by being alert to the threat of domination and any kind of oppression) have been encouraged through projects sponsored by the European Commission, the Council of Europe, UNESCO and the European Cultural Foundation. In these projects, and in exchange programmes, such as Erasmus, Socrates and Leonardo, dialogue between peoples and cultures as well as intercultural co-operation are foreseen that will eventually lead to recognition of the 'other' and building of 'trust' in the 'other'. Unity in diversity is another concept that has been adopted to bring people of different cultures together, but it has been politicized and distorted.

With the adoption of these concepts, together with an anthem, a flag, a map, a passport and a common monetary system, as well as certain common values, such as the respect for human rights, democracy, rule of law and a free market economy, the EU has made a great attempt at inventing a new identity for itself and uniting its members. However, some member states show resistance to certain issues, and to the interpretation and internalization of some concepts. Pluralism, multiculturalism, and unity in diversity are such concepts that, because of their connotations, may lead to practices that do not conform to their initial purpose.

Pluralism, in a broad sense, necessitates the recognition and equal legitimation of cultural differences that are shaped within the framework of different life practices in the public and political sphere.[3] This foresees that individuals can develop independently their identities without being forced to conform to the cultural identity they have inherited. The dynamic identity that individuals develop through interaction with the 'others' is pluralistic, as it incorporates the possibility of change (İnsel, 2001). In this respect, the adoption of the concept of pluralism would pave the way for mutual change and facilitate the integration of people coming from different cultures. However, a certain intention and readiness is needed from everybody to achieve this. Besides, the concepts of 'independence' and 'equality', by definition, create ambiguities concerning their limits and specification.

The idea of multiculturalism has different connotations. It may mean communities living side by side and on an equal basis, each keeping to its own traditions and values, and practising its own culture without much interaction with the other communities. In this case, the individual cultures are preserved, but since there is little or no interaction and exchange between these communities, they remain isolated from each other, which may lead to alienation among them. Multiculturalism may also mean a gathering of people from different cultures who are assimilated by a so-called 'higher' culture that is the dominant culture of the larger group. Here, people lose their initial cultural identity and accept the values of another, existing, culture in the society in which they continue to live. This type of practice may lead to the hegemony of one culture and subordination or extinction of the other cultures, at the end of which identity problems and feelings of alienation may arise in human beings coming from cultures different from the dominant one. Multiculturalism is also used in another sense to describe a situation in which people coming from various cultures live together without losing their own culture, but at the same time respect the culture and diversity of the 'other/s' and try mutually to learn about the culture of the 'other/s', thus enriching their own culture.

As indicated above, the term 'multiculturalism' used in the first and second senses has drawbacks, leading to the isolation and alienation of people, or resulting in assimilation and losing an individual's own culture that may lead to identity problems, whereas its third meaning seems to provide an ideal situation from a socio-cultural point of view and thus should be adopted by the EU as a preferred principle. However, its implementation seems to be difficult as it harbours the potential danger that one of the cultures in the group may dominate the others. The third interpretation became popular during the 1990s. However, because of the term's two other slightly negative connotations, as well as the difficulty of its practical implementation, people have become suspicious about the concept.

The principle of unity in diversity also poses problems of ambiguity and needs to be well-defined. Does it mean that people of various cultures, races and nations, who have various ethnic, religious and political identities, would live side by side under the auspices of the EU without mixing with the 'other/s'? This type of co-existence of divergent groups with complete indifference towards the 'others' culture may lead to the formation of ghettos which would constitute a serious potential threat to the larger society in which these groups live. Or does unity in diversity mean that people with all the different socio-cultural aspects listed here would live in peace under the auspices of the EU through keeping their diversity, but also interacting with each other on an equal basis without discriminating against any culture? This, naturally, would be the ideal situation. However, human nature is unfortunately not that humane and graceful, or ready to accomplish such harmonious coexistence with people of diverse socio-cultural backgrounds. Here, the problem lies in the difficulty of achieving 'equality' among the groups, because, in practice, there are always 'some groups' that are more-equal than others'.[4]

It is remarkable that parallel to the promotion of peace-cultivating concepts and principles (pluralism, multiculturalism and unity in diversity, as discussed above) by the proponents of the EU, tendencies of racism, discrimination and religious fanaticism have, paradoxically, increased in Europe since the mid-1990s. There are several reasons for this. One of the main reasons was initiated by the events of 11 September 2001 and the following spread of terrorism in Europe. Bombings in London and Madrid were realized by terrorists, who came mainly from Arabic or Muslim countries. This resulted in the association of terrorism with Islam and has led to the emergence of a fear of Islam in Europe. This, in turn, fed religious fanaticism and fundamentalism among both Christians and Muslims, and has increased mutual aggression.

Samuel Huntington's widely-read book, *The Clash of Civilizations*, seems to have foreshadowed all these conflicts. Furthermore, rising unemployment rates leading to criminal actions of marginalized people in Europe, the reluctance of migrants to leave their ghettos and begin interacting with the societies they live in because of a lack of trust, and the unwillingness of the more privileged Europeans to share their resources with others whose diversity they would not like to recognize or respect, increased feelings of animosity in Europe. However, the discrepancies are felt not only between the founders of the EU and Europe's 'others', but also among the members of the EU itself. Negative votes cast by the French and Dutch public for the European Constitutional Treaty and the UK's refusal to accept the newly introduced euro coinage, signify that there are also conflicting interests among the member states themselves. Any solution requires great effort, patience and time.

Turkish reflections on the cement that binds Europeans together – the outcomes of an intellectual debate on the future of Europe

So far, attempts to unify EU member states have been highlighted – that is, the European countries that we believe have shared a 'common cultural heritage'. In the following, the ideas, concepts and movements that are considered to constitute this 'common heritage' will be presented, in order to provide a contemporary overview of discussions that are the outcome of international interactive workshops questioning the future of the EU.[5] The workshop results are significant in several ways; also, they were organized ten years after the above-mentioned workshops in Bruges on the future of Europe, thus in some way they provide comparative data overtime. The items presented below were answers to the following question: 'What are the main founding pillars on which European cultures are based?'[6]

'a common history', 'Greco-Roman culture', 'Roman law', 'Christianity, Christian values and morality', 'evangelic individualism', 'humanism', 'Renaissance and Reformation', 'Enlightenment and the philosophical thoughts that are associated with it: rationalism, positivism and modernism', 'secularism', 'postmodernism', 'the idea of a nation', 'economic growth and capitalism', 'leisure', 'Social Contract (Magna Carta) and the ideas that are associated with it', 'Declaration of Human Rights' and the 'French Revolution' with the principles of liberty, equality, fraternity/solidarity that are strongly tied with it. (Kuran-Burçoğlu 2004a, p. 149)

This list shows how a group of highly educated Turks and Europeans share general impressions of Europeans' 'common' cultural roots. However, in spite of all the socio-cultural 'commonalities' that characterize Europeans, they still seem to be somewhat hesitant about uniting with their fellow Europeans within the EU, and identifying themselves as members of this supranational union. How then, can the Turks, who we assume have different socio-cultural practices, values and experiences, and who have been perceived as the 'other/s' throughout European history by the Europeans – be accepted into this Union? Furthermore, how will the Turks identify themselves with the members of this supranational entity? Finally, what kind of socio-cultural constraints will both sides have to face before this union can be accomplished? These questions require a historical analysis of the perceptions of the Turks and Europeans about each other. How can the gap between these perceptions be bridged in order to pave the way for an EU with Turkey as a future member state?

The impact of previous socio-cultural experiences in the European Union on Turkey's accession process

In this section, two major phenomena will be discussed: first, the recent history of the image of the Turk in Europe, and the current impressions Europeans have of the Turks will be elaborated on. Second, the significance of the representations of Turks that is tied to the evolution of the image of the Turk in Europe will be put forward. In this context, the media through which the representations are spread, and images created, will be presented.

A glance at the recent history of the image of the Turk in Europe

Images of the 'other/s'[7] and identities are formed as well as transformed over the course of time in various spaces that preoccupy human minds, and thus influence human thoughts and actions. The socio-cultural analysis of these images in the course of history (a *diachronic* research and its evaluation) as well as a comparative analysis of their current state in various countries (a *synchronic* research and its evaluation with a supranational approach) can highlight a great many issues that underlie and shape inter-religious, inter-ethnic, inter-cultural, inter-regional and international relationships. Such *imagological research* on the image of the Turk in Europe has revealed the results summarized below.[8] After mentioning the general features of this image in Europe, an analysis of its recent transformations from the eighteenth century to the present will be provided, with a view to providing a perspective for the current circumstances.[9]

Major determining factors of the change of images

In the course of their presence in Europe over 700 years, the image of the Turks had been formed and reformed for a variety of reasons. The determining factors of these changes can be summarized as: the geographical proximity of the Ottoman Empire/Turkey to the country in which the image was formed; wars (victories and defeats); religious differences; cultural aspects, conventions and traditions; conflicting social norms and value judgements; human psychology; existing previous images; positive or negative stereotypes and clichés of the Ottomans and Turks in the minds of the Europeans; political strategies, and 'hidden agendas' of the decision-makers inside and outside the country; and the impact of representations (Kuran-Burçoğlu, 2003, p. 23).

The impact of Islam on image formation

During the expansion period of the Ottoman Empire well into the fifteenth century, the Turks were considered as 'others' in Europe, because of their expansionist character and their religion. This was the image of an 'enemy', who was 'cruel', 'barbaric' and 'devastating', and considered to be 'a potential threat to Christianity'. Until the Koran, the holy book of Islam, was translated into European languages in the Middle Ages, these people were considered to be 'heretics' by Europeans. After realizing the 'universalistic claim' of this religion, however, the adherents of it came to be considered as the 'enemies of Christianity' in the eyes of Europeans. They were thought of as the

> devil incarnate, or the wrath of God and represented as such in visual sources with the symbols of a scourge, or a whip, representing the punishment of God inflicted upon the Christians who either seemed to have neglected to obey God's commands, or misinterpreted the religion according to their own earthly interests. This was the interpretation of Martin Luther, the initiator of the Protestant Church, in the speeches he made in 1529 and 1541, in which he invited the pious Christians to wage war against this enemy who was 'considered to undermine the integrity of Christianity.[10]

Although there have been major conflicts of interests and great schisms among the different sects of Christianity throughout its history in Europe, in the case of a threat of war against the Ottomans Christians became united as they considered Muslims to be their 'common enemy' because of their different faith.

Here it should be also noted that the terms 'Ottomans', and 'Turks', have been used interchangeably in most of the European sources, without making any distinction between them, and Islam was associated with them. Ottomans and Turks were seen as the representatives of this religion and were considered to be the 'enemy of Christianity'.

Public perceptions

In contrast to the perceptions of the European clergy and the ruling classes, European public impressions of the Turks seemed to be favourable in the Early Modern Ages which was reflected in the Carnival Plays that emerged as a new genre in the Middle Ages in Central Europe among German-speaking people. The German author Hans Rosenplüt's two plays, entitled *Des Türken Fastnachtspiel* and *Ein Lied von dem Türken*, are two examples that reflect positive images of the Turks. In these secular plays, staged in 1454, a year after the Conquest of Constantinople by the Ottomans, the 'Great Turk' (the Sultan of the Ottoman Empire) was shown as a 'just and brave Emperor' who would 'go to war with his soldiers' and whose 'subjects are treated well'. 'They wouldn't have to pay tribute' to their Emperor. The temporal and spatial context, as well as the medium in which these positive images appeared, were significant: first, it was the time when the Ottomans exercised great power in Europe; indeed, it was just a year after their great victory in 1453. Second, the play was staged in Germany at Carnival time, when people were usually allowed to say what they wanted – they could even criticize their rulers without being punished. Third, the popular play exemplified a 'concealed threat' for the rulers of Europe who would not go to war themselves but let their subjects go, and who would collect high taxes from them.[11] Fourth, the play was a popular entertainment for ordinary people, thus it had a great impact on the masses and was therefore considered to be a potential danger for the rulers of the time, in particular, and for the integrity of Christian society in general. Another image that was widely shared among the public of Central Europe – and which was reflected in the folklore, ballads, songs and baroque plays – is the image of the 'lustful Turk' who chased after European women, and undermined the Christian norms of chastity and love.

Significant historical dates that induced transformations in the image

The dates of certain incidents in the history of the Ottoman Empire as well as in the history of Europe – that is, the dates of important victories and defeats of the Ottoman Empire, as well as the Proclamation of the Turkish Republic constituted turning points for the image of the Turks in Europe. Some of these dates were:

1071   Occupation of eastern Anatolia by the Seljuk Turks. This marked the beginning of the westward expansion of the Turks, which induced great 'horror' in Europe. The horror was increased with the other victories of the Ottomans on the European continent that followed: Nicopolis (1396); Varna (1444); and Kosovo (1448). The Ottomans were described as 'devastating', 'cruel' and 'barbaric heretics', as 'the enemy of Christianity' who would kill men, women and innocent children without hesitating, in cold blood'.

1453   The Conquest of Constantinople by the Ottomans/the end of the Eastern Roman Empire. With this incident, horror in Europe *vis-à-vis* this enemy reached its climax. The Europeans lost hope of ever preventing the Ottomans from occupying the Continent. The images differed. Positive and negative images prevailed side by side. There was also an exaggerated image of an 'undefeatable powerful enemy' who was considered to be the 'evil fate of Christianity'.

1571   The Defeat of the Ottoman navy in Lepanto, Italy, by joint European forces comprising Venetian, Spanish and Papal forces. This event was celebrated greatly in Europe as it was a 'common victory' against the enemy, and it marked the decline of the Ottoman hegemony in the eastern Mediterranean Sea.

1683   The defeat of the Ottomans at their second Siege of Vienna by the European army under the leadership of the Polish Prince Sigismund. This event marked the end of the 'undefeatable Turk' in Europe, but other negative aspects of the image prevailed.

1699   The Conclusion of the Karlowitz Treaty between the Ottoman Empire and the Holy Union of Austria, Poland, Venice and Russia. This Treaty marked the start of the decline of Ottoman power in Central Europe. From this date onwards, the so-called 'Eastern Question' started to occupy the European agenda. Plans were made on dividing the Ottoman Empire. The image of the 'sick man of Europe' who was going to die soon, emerged and soon became a cliché among the enemies of the Ottoman Empire until the end of the War of Independence, at the end of which the Turkish Republic was proclaimed by Mustafa Kemal Atatürk, in 1923.

1923   The Proclamation of the Turkish Republic by Mustafa Kemal Atatürk, which marked a new stage in the history of the Turks.

Significant historical events in Europe that transformed the image

Certain social, philosophical and political developments that took place in Europe after the eighteenth century to the present day have caused changes in the perceptions of the Europeans regarding the Turks. The most important are the following: the German Enlightenment; the Turchophilie Movement; colonialism; the emergence of the nation-state; and the migration of Turkish guest workers to Europe. Certainly, there were others, such as the trade relationships with Britain, friendly relationships with the French Court, positive cultural relationships with the Dutch ambassadors and so on that cannot be elaborated on here.

Towards the end of the seventeenth century, together with the rise of bourgeoisie, a new movement started to spread from France all over Europe. This was called *Turchomania* or *Turchophilie*. The manifestation of the movement in the works of art, music and literature was called *Turquerie*. The Turkish way of life was adopted as a life-style; Turkish way of dressing became fashionable; and parties were organized which people attended in Turkish robes and kaftans made from silk and embroidered Turkish fabrics. European music was also influenced by this movement: Mozart's famous opera *The Abduction from the Seraglio*, the genre called *alla Turca*, as well as the adoption of certain musical instruments in European music are the results of this impact. This movement also influenced European literature, and a new genre of tales emerged that reflected the mystery of the Orient with its picturesque descriptions, fantasies and supernatural creatures. *Turquerie* had a positive impact on the image of the Turk in Europe.

The same is true for the *German Enlightenment*, which emerged in the eighteenth century in Europe with the ideas of Immanuel Kant. Through this new philosophy the idea of tolerance was introduced to Europe by the German philosopher and author, Gotthold Ephraim Lessing (1729–81), in his play entitled, *Nathan der Weise*. Lessing expressed in this play that the three heavenly religions of Judaism, Christianity and Islam were equal, and that all of them preached virtues to human beings. This can be considered a turning point in European opinions about Islam and Judaism, as it introduced a completely new objective perception about these two religions.

On the other hand, the start of *colonialism* had a negative impact on European perceptions concerning the Turks, because it brought the condescending, so-called Orientalist gaze, coined by the late Edward Said in his famous book *Orientalism*. The impact of this look could be observed in the image of 'the sick man of Europe' (that is, the Ottoman Empire) as well as in the paintings of the Orientalist painters and in the European discourse about the Turks during the late nineteenth and early twentieth centuries.

The emergence of the *nation-state* in Europe also affected the image of the Turk. Various communities within the Ottoman Empire: Greeks, Bulgarians, Romanians, Yugoslavs and Albanians, while striving for their independence from the Ottoman Empire and fighting to set up their nation-states, formed their new national identities by 'othering' the Turks and ascribing all negative aspects to them. As Gerard Delanty also stated in his book *The Invention of Europe*, the Turks had served throughout their existence in Europe since mid-fifteenth century the purpose of the Europeans to define their identities by 'othering' them (Delanty, 2001; see also Delanty and Rumford, 2005). At first they were 'religionwise' the 'others'; this situation slightly changed in the early Modern Age, they became 'culturewise' the 'others'; and finally, after the emergence of the nation state they became nationwise the 'others'.

Another important phenomenon that had a vast impact on European perceptions of the Turks was the migration of *Turkish guestworkers*, first to the central European countries, and later to northern European countries. This movement was initiated by Germany in the 1960s, looking for a workforce to repair the damage the two World Wars had induced, and to rebuild and strengthen industry. However, the side-effects of the presence of these guest workers were not well calculated. As the Swiss author, Max Frisch, has wisely put it, the fallacy lay in the fact that '*We were looking for a work force, but human beings came.*'[12] Indeed, most of these people came from rural areas of Turkey to Europe, without having seen a city in their own country and without having a proper education at home, thus they had many social and cultural adaptation problems and were frustrated, as their social needs had not been fulfilled by the host country. The hosts, on the other hand, had difficulty in accepting these people as their 'equal neighbours', as they were not ready to live with the 'other/s'. They had considered these migrants as 'guest' workers who would serve their host country and one day go back to their own countries, whereas these people had no intention of doing this. So they had to live together with a minimum of interaction that led eventually to a lack of communication and disappointment on both sides. The lack of trust between the hosts and the migrants enhanced the cultural alienation on both sides. This, in turn, created ghettos in which the migrants shut themselves in and refused to integrate to the culture and social life of the country they had been living in. This vicious cycle ended in animosity between the groups.

By the time three generations had grown and a great generation gap came into existence between the uneducated parent generation and their children, and the grandchildren who had grown up in the host culture. Conflicts in the family, the generation gap, and identity problems of the young people, as well as of their elders, who did not feel at home in either Turkey or the host country, were also reflected in their relationships with their hosts. The hosts, on the other hand, have also faced problems because of miscommunication, misinterpretation and lack of understanding of the feelings of the others. However, there have also been cases of positive communication, the development of good impressions and friendships, but these were not sufficient to transform the mutually formed images in a positive direction. This coexistence also had its effects on the general image of the Turk in Europe, which was a prototype of the image of migrant workers in Europe, and has become a stereotype that is almost impossible to change. With the recent rise of 'Islamophobia', as mentioned above, a new aspect has been added to the unfavourable image of the Turks in Europe, which might well lead to violence.

The role of representations of Turks in Europe

Stuart Hall defines representation as the production of the meaning of the concepts in our minds through language.[13] He states that representation is the link between concepts and language that enables us to refer either to the 'real' world of objects, people or events, or indeed to imaginary worlds of fictional objects, people and events (Hall, 1997, p. 17). He defines these as two processes; two 'systems of representation'. Using this 'system', all kinds of objects, people and events are correlated with a set of concepts or mental representations that we carry around in our heads (ibid.). These mental representations are then cast in the form of oral, written, visual and audio-visual representations, and circulate in the world. Once they start circulating, they began to shape ideas in other human minds. Because of this structuring capacity Hall describes them as 'systemic', as they consist not of individual concepts, but of different ways of organizing, clustering, arranging and classifying concepts, and of establishing complex relations between them (ibid.).

We can infer from this that representations are constructs created by human minds, and reflected through the eyes of their author, in oral, written, visual and audio-visual 'texts'.[14] In this way they can, in turn, be effective in creating 'images' in the minds of other people. Within this perspective, the representations of the Turks of various kinds, types and shapes, and the circulation of these in the European media, are of immense importance for the subject of this chapter as they play a shaping function on the image of the Turk in Europe.

In the early Middle Ages, preaching of the popes and the altar pictures depicting the 'cruel' Turk represented as a 'heretic' comprised the oral and visual media through which the representations were spread throughout Europe (Kocadoru, 1990; Kuran-Burçoğlu, 2005a, 2003; Soykut, 2003). Memoirs of the captives of war, as well as the travel accounts and diaries of travellers and merchants, starting with the Crusades and extending to the present day, and the consulate reports of European envoys and consuls, occupy an important place among the media through which different characteristics of the Turks have been represented to the European audience. In the late Middle Ages and in the Early Modern Era, along with the preaching and writings of the clergy of different Christian sects (Protestants, Catholics and the Eastern Orthodox Church); European literature – Italian, Spanish and Portuguese epics, as well as the French Chansons de Geste, British plays of the Elizabethan Age, and German Baroque plays in which the Turks/Muslims/Saracens and Moroccans were presented as Europe's 'others', mainly in a negative light, as well as illustrations that appeared in flyers and similar handouts were the main sources of representation of the Turks in Europe. Representation of Turkish characters on the European stage lead to the creation of concrete images of these people that occupied European minds.

Folklore was another sphere of representation for the Turks in Europe especially during the Middle Ages, in which the Turks were presented in both a positive and a negative light according to the daily agenda of the time. Starting with the *Turquerie* in the eighteenth century and continuing in the nineteeth century, visual representations of the Turks gained importance. A new artistic genre emerged that was applied by the Orientalist painters. Dominated by romanticism and exoticism, the paintings by these artists reflected the fantasies of the West, showing the Turks as sensual people devoting their whole time to women in harems and hamams. As the architecture and decorative elements in these paintings were extremely detailed and based on reality, the scenes depicted in them created a deceiving impression to the Europeans that they were also real. The picturesque atmosphere created in these paintings, as if the time had stopped in the Orient, were considered by art critics of our time as a justification of the strategy of colonialism – that is, to dominate the 'others' who were inefficient and not capable of governing themselves because they were ignorant, backward and indulged in sensual activities (Nochlin, 1991). Turks were also represented through Oriental tales that appeared in European literature in the eighteenth century as a new genre, first in translation, then as imitation, and finally in original works of art. The mystery of the Orient and supernatural forces were foregrounded in these tales, that alluded to the dominance of the senses rather than the mind in the people of the Oriental world. The creation of the image of the Turks as the 'sick man of Europe' was largely achieved by the condescending representations of Turks in cartoons of the late nineteenth and early twentieth century that were printed in the newspapers and spread all over Europe. In the twentieth century, the invention of television and the development of the internet have provided vast opportunities for communication among people. They have been used effectively for producing representations and spreading them easily and rapidly all over the world. Thus their impact can be added to the use of the printed media to create and disseminate image of the Turk in Europe. The nature of these representations also varies according to the daily agenda of the time and the impact is immense. While summarizing various forms of representation in both the past and the present, we should not forget the impression that films and photographs can make on human beings. Finally, people's daily conversations are another medium, since they are more effective than any other representation in creating images and sustaining clichés about the 'others.'

Potential conflict areas in Turkey and in the EU on the cultural front

As has been explained so far, there are certain socio-cultural constraints that make the members of the EU, as well as the Turks, feel a little uneasy about Turkey's accession to the EU.

For the members of the EU, socio-cultural constraints can be presented as cultural differences; different mindsets; lack of sufficient motivation, and readiness to live together with a group of people who have been considered 'Europe's other' for many centuries, 'Islamophobia'; unwillingness and/or inefficiency in creating empathy for the other's feelings, and lack of efforts to understand the 'other'; difficulty in practising and sustaining peace with others; negative past experiences with Euro Turks being generalized to all Turks; difficulty in overcoming negative clichés about the Turks; considering them to be a social threat to European values and norms; considering them as rivals in the job market; evaluating the rapid increase in the Turkish population in Europe as a threatening risk for European stability and wealth; and psychological factors. These anxieties may lead to animosities, racism and xenophobia, as well as to a clash of civilizations between the Europeans and Euro Turks, in particular, and between the Europeans and the Turks in Turkey in general.

For the Turks these constraints can be presented as cultural differences; different mindsets; resentment of the discriminatory attitude of Europeans; fear of losing their national sovereignty; fear of losing one's national, religious and cultural identities; Euro-scepticism; difficulty in overcoming past experiences and existing clichés about the 'others'; loss of patience; loss of hope of being accepted as 'equals'; difficulties in objective self-assessment; unwillingness in accepting the other's norms and rules; fear of becoming a victim of 'Islamophobia'; and, finally, fear of becoming the 'scapegoat' of Europe.[15] These anxieties may lead to cultural conflicts, to the cleavage gap between Europe and Turkey, to alienation from Europe, and to a clash of civilizations. However, with mutual good intentions, efficient social governance and successful cultural management, these constraints can still be overcome.

Conclusion and perspectives

For a peaceful co-existence that would be for the benefit of both sides – that is, for the members of the EU as well as for the Turkish people, both parties have to try hard to built trust in the 'other', because without the existence of trust no collaboration can be achieved. After that, the four steps necessary for building and sustaining peace should be implemented, and 'common interests' should be specified. In this process 'inclusiveness' should be opted for.

With its talented and educated youth, its energetic, skilled and ambitious businesspeople, as well as with its natural resources and rich cultural heritage Turkey can make great contributions to the EU. In the course of their history, the Turks have gained a centuries-old cumulative experience in living with several other ethnic and religious groups in peace within the boundaries of the multicultural and multi-ethnic Ottoman Empire and later during the present Republic. For example, contrary to misperceptions of the concept, Turkish identity is not based on race, but on the common will to live within the geographical boundaries of the Republic. They have also developed certain human values, such as love for their neighbours, hospitality to their guests, affection for their children, and respect for their elderly. These values should be foregrounded and practised. Each party can learn from the other's experiences, life-styles and values (see Chapter 7 on the issue of governance of multiculturalism).

During the negotiation process between Turkey and the EU, the activities that would strengthen mutual co-operation and dialogue among groups of people should be fostered. There are several possibilities to that effect. These can be the mobility of students, people of various age groups and professions; educational exchange programmes and joint projects; cultural tourism programmes; travelling exhibitions, concerts and folk dances; joint sports activities; joint artistic activities and theatre performances, film, theatre and music festivals; women's and children's activities; as well as academic research and scholarly work focusing on the development and improvement of the socio-cultural aspects of the cohabitation that should be accomplished with a view to a much better future for the Turkish people as well as for the citizens of the EU.

Notes

1. Preamble to *Treaty Establishing the Coal and Steel Community*, Paris, 18 April 1951 (London: Her Majesty's Stationery Office, 1972) in T. H. Cohn (2005), *Global Political Economy*, London/New York: Longman, p. 4.
2. The author of this chapter participated in the second stage of this project, at the College of Europe, in Bruges, both as an expert in Imagology, and as the Vice Director (1991–7) of the Centre for Comparative European Studies, at Boğaziçi University.
3. Charles Taylor cited in İnsel, 2001, p. 102.
4. British author George Orwell coined this term in his political satire *Animal Farm*.
5. Reflections were produced by a group of international, but mainly Turkish, observers participating in an international workshop in Istanbul, September 2003.
6. The workshop was organized by the Turkish Society for Quality, September 2003. It provided data for the international congress that followed as the 12th National Quality Congress, which was convened with the main theme being 'The European Union for the World Leadership', in Istanbul November 2003. For further discussions in the series of workshops on the theme, see LaGro (2004).
7. That is, of the 'other country' – of groups of people with a different ethnic, religious, cultural, regional, national, political, etc. background.
8. For detailed information about 'Imagology', see Hugo Dyserinck (1981). See also Dyserinck (1995). The articles in are also examples of this discipline. *Colloquium Helveticum-Imagologie: Problemès de la représentation littéraire* (1988). For a comprehensive definition of the term in English, see Kuran-Burçoğlu, 2003, pp. 21–42.
9. For more information about the research that has been conducted by the author of this chapter, see Kuran-Burçoğlu 2000, 2002, 2003, 2005a, 2005b, 2006.
10. 'Vom Kriege wider den Türken' (1529); 'Heerpredikt wider den Türken' (1529); and 'Vermahnung zum Gebet wider den Türken' (1541).
11. The tax that was collected from those people who chose not to go to the Crusades during the Middle Ages was called 'Türkensold' (Turkish tribute).
12. The emphasis is mine here.
13. Language should be considered here not in its 'literal' meaning, in a narrow sense, but in its broader definition – that is, also covering visual, audio and audio-visual languages, mime and gestures (kinesics and paralanguage) that are used effectively in representation.
14. I am using the concept 'text' in its broader sense here.
15. The results of a recent poll carried out by the Centre for Turkey Studies (ZTS) in Essen on the Euro Turks show, as reported by the Director of the Centre, Professor Dr Faruk Şen, that the 2.7 million Turks living in Germany feel extremely disturbed by the association of 'Islamophobia' with

the Turks, and that 30 per cent of the interviewed Turks would like to return to Turkey (*Hürriyet*, 18 April 2006).

References

Anderson, B. (2003 [1983]) *Imagined Communities*, London: Verso.

Cohn, T. H. (2005) *Global Political Economy*, London: Longman.

Colloquium Helveticum-Imagologie: Problèmes de la représentation littéraire (1988) Schweizer Hefte für allgemeine und vergleichende Literaturwissenschaft, Berne, Frankfurt am Main, New York, Paris: Peter Lang Verlag, p. 7.

Delanty, G. (2004) *Avrupa'nın İcadı*, (trans.) Hüsametin İnaç, Ankara: Adres Yayınları.

Delanty, G. and Rumford, C. (2005) *Rethinking Europe: Social Theory and Implications of Europeanisation*, London: Routledge.

Dyserinck, H. (1981) *Komparatistik, Aachener Beiträge zur Komparatistik*, Bonn: Bouvier Verlag.

Dyserinck, H. (1995) 'The Comparative Study of Literature and the Problem of National and Cultural Identity. An Imagological Vision', in Léonce Bekemans (ed.), *Culture: Building Stone for Europe 2002 – Reflections and Perspectives* (The Brugges Conferences, College of Europe), Brussels: European Inter-university Press.

European Commission (2004) *Dialogue between Peoples and Cultures: Actors in the Dialogue*, Brussels: European Commission.

Habermas, J. (1999 [1996]) *'Öteki' olmak, 'Öteki'yle Yaşamak: Siyaset Kuramı Yazıları. (Die Einbeziehung des Anderen)'* (trans.) İlknur Aka, Istanbul: Yapı Kredi Yayınları.

Hall, S. (ed.) (1997) *Representation: Cultural Representations and Signifying Practices*. London: Sage.

Hall, S. (1998). 'Kültürel Kimlik ve Diaspora', *Kimlik: Topluluk – Kültür – Farklılık*, İrem Sağlamer (trans.) Istanbul: Sarmal Yayınevi, pp. 173–91.

İnsel, A. (2001) 'Çokkültürlülük, Çokkimliklilik, Çoğulculuk,' *Modernity and Multiculturalism*, Istanbul: Helsinki Citizens Assembly, pp. 100–4.

Kant, I. (1795) *Toward Perpetual Peace*, M. J. Gregor (trans.) in Mary J. Gregor (ed) 1996. Practical Philosophy, Cambridge University Press.

Kaya, A. and Kentel, F. (2005) *Euro-Turks – a Bridge or a Breach between Turkey and the European Union?* Brussels: Centre for European Policy Studies.

Kocadoru, Y. (1990) *Die Türken: Studien zu ihrem Bild und seiner Geschichte in Österreich*. PhD thesis, University of Klagenfurt.

Kula, O. B. (1992) *Alman Kültüründe Türk İmgesi I*. Ankara: Gündoğan Yayınları.

Kula, O. B. (1993) *Alman Kültüründe Türk İmgesi II*. Ankara: Gündoğan Yayınları.

Kuran-Burçoğlu, N. (1994) '2000'li Yıllarda Avrupa: Endişe ve Umutlar...', *Cumhuriyet Gazetesi*, December 6th, p. 2.

Kuran-Burçoğlu, N. (ed.) (1997) *Multiculturalism: Identity and Otherness*, Istanbul: Boğaziçi University Press.

Kuran-Burçoğlu, N. (ed.) (2000) *The Image of the Turk in Europe from the Declaration of the Republic in 1923 to 1990s*, Istanbul: The Isis Press.

Kuran-Burçoğlu, N. (2002) 'L'Image des Turcs en Europe', *Les chemins de la Turquie vers l'Europe*, Études réunites par Pierre Chaball et Arnaud de Raulin, Artois Presses Université, Le Havre, pp. 67–81.

Kuran-Burçoğlu, N. (2003) 'A Glimpse at Various Stages of the Evolution of the Image of the Turk in Europe: 15th to 21st Centuries', in *Historical Image of the Turk in Europe: 15th Century to the Present – Political and Civilisational Aspects*. Mustafa Soykut (ed.), Istanbul: The Isis Press, pp. 21–43.

Kuran-Burçoğlu, N. (2004a) 'Avrupa ve Avrupalılık', *Akademik Araştırmalar Dergisi*, Büşra Ersanlı (ed.), Istanbul, vol. 6, No. 23, November 2004–January 2005.

Kuran-Burçoğlu, N. (2004b) 'Perceptions and Representations of a Unified Europe: From the Idea of a Unified Europe to Common European Values', in *Shaping the Future – The European Union for the World Leadership: Towards new Global Governance?*,Esra LaGro (ed.), Istanbul: KalDer, pp. 145–151.

Kuran-Burçoğlu, N. (2005a) *Die Wandlungen des Türkenbildes in Europa*, Zurich: Spur Verlag.

Kuran-Burçoğlu, N. (ed.) (2005b) *Representations of the 'Other/s' in the Mediterranean World and Their Impact on the Region*, Istanbul: The Isis Press.

LaGro, E. (ed.) (2004) *Shaping the Future – The European Union for the World Leadership: Towards New Global Governance?* Istanbul: KalDer.

Nochlin, L. (1991) *Politics of Vision*, London: Thames & Hudson.

Parmar, P. (1998) 'Temsil Stratejileri', *Kimlik: Topluluk – Kültür – Farklılık*, İrem Sağlamer (trans.) Istanbul: Sarmal Yayınevi, pp. 119–30.

Soykut, M. (2003) 'The Turk as the "Great Enemy of European Civilization" and the Changing Image in the Aftermath of the Second Siege of Vienna (In the Light of Italian Political Literature)', in Mustafa Soykut (ed.), *Historical Image of the Turk in Europe: 15th Century to the Present – Political and Civilisational Aspects*. Istanbul: The Isis Press.

9
Euro-sceptic Concerns about National Identity in the European Union and Turkey

Menno Spiering

It is obvious that the European Union as it exists today differs greatly from the European Communities founded in the 1950s. The wish for an 'ever-closer union', formulated in the Treaty of Rome, has not been left unanswered. There is now free movement of capital, goods and labour, there is a European Parliament (albeit with limited powers) and, of course, an economic and monetary union is now in place. But it is equally obvious that the ever-closer union has run parallel with ever greater doubts. As the integration process has deepened, so critical voices have grown louder. In recent decades, Euro-scepticism has increased and has manifested itself in a great variety of pressure groups, political parties and other organizations (Harmsen and Spiering, 2004).

The term 'Euro-scepticism' was first coined in the 1980s in Britain. It was used to describe the policies of the then British prime minister, Margaret Thatcher, who was intent on defending national sovereignty and slowing down – and even reversing – the process of European federation (Spiering, 2004). Though initially cultivated on English soil, the term Euro-scepticism has progressively taken root elsewhere. The growth of a more critical European discourse, as in the debates on the ratification of the Maastricht Treaty in the early 1990s, has resulted in increasingly frequent references to 'Euro-scepticism' in many countries.

'Euro-scepticism' can be (and is) used to label different points of view. Following the work of Taggart and Szczerbiak (2002), it is now common practice to distinguish between 'hard' and 'soft' Euro-sceptics. Hard Euro-scepticism is a principled opposition to the EU and European integration. It can be seen in parties which argue that their countries should withdraw completely from membership. In the UK, an example is the UK Independence Party or the Campaign for an Independent Britain. Soft Euro-scepticism does not entail a principled objection to European integration or EU membership, but expresses qualified opposition to aspects of the EU because of concerns about one (or more) policy areas. Staying with the UK, an example of soft Euro-scepticism would be the New Europe Group led by the former Foreign Secretary, Lord Owen. It does not totally reject the EU or Britain's membership of it, but is critical mainly of monetary union. The United Kingdom, in their opinion, should stay in the EU, but keep the pound sterling. The rejection of the European Constitution in France and the Netherlands, surprising as the outcome of the referenda might have been, should also be classified as expressions of soft Euro-scepticism.

Different as the various Euro-sceptic parties and pressure groups might be, one phrase occurs frequently in their arguments: 'national identity'. This chapter first seeks to examine this aspect of Euro-sceptic discourse within, but also outside, the EU, as both member states and prospective members – such as Turkey – appear to be concerned about their identities in an 'ever-closer union'. Second, the response of the EU to these Euro-sceptic concerns is charted and evaluated.

Euro-scepticism and national identity in the EU

Euro-sceptics (whether 'soft' or 'hard') habitually claim that the EU threatens the viability of existing national identities. The abolition of borders; the free movement of capital, goods and labour; the creation of scores of directives aimed at harmonizing various national practices – in short, the ongoing process of Europeanization – is eroding the specific characteristics of individual European nations. These concerns are particularly strong in the UK and the Scandinavian countries, where there is a long tradition of feeling different from 'the Europeans', but similar voices can also be heard in other member states. Even in the Netherlands, commonly perceived as being utterly loyal to the European idea, national identity is an important political issue, as witnessed in the strong campaign of the 'antis' in the run-up to the referendum on the European Constitution in June 2005. Dutch identity, according to the manifesto of one of the parties, has been 'put up for sale' in Europe (Groep Wilders, 2005).

This Euro-scepticism – that is, the kind that wishes to protect existing national identities – might be labelled 'patriotic Euro-scepticism'. A patriotic Euro-sceptic is concerned about national identity because s/he sees his/her own nation as being distinct from, and often superior to, other nations. On the one hand, these sceptics argue that participation in the EU, or any union, by definition implies the loss of individuality, and thus of identity. On the other hand, they fear that the EU is a union of unequals, providing some nations with the opportunity to force their identity on others. An example may illustrate the point. Lord Tebbit, the former leader of the British Conservative Party and an outspoken Euro-sceptic, once compared the EU to a kitchen mixer blending all nations into a drab union soup. This imagery is common in much Euro-sceptic discourse. A variant is likening the Union to a meat-grinding machine, pulping the member states into 'Euro mince'. At the same time, however, Tebbit fears that Britain will not just be mixed with, but dominated by other nations. He is particularly fearful of the Germans and predicted that, in a few decades, the UK will be nothing but a German province (Tebbit, 1990). In a similar vein, Scandinavian Euro-sceptics fear that domination not by the Germans, but by the French and other 'Southern Europeans' will jeopardize their Nordic identity.

Patriotic Euro-sceptics tend to regard modern Europe as an abominable and perverse experiment. Nations, they argue, differ profoundly. The Germans are not like the Spanish; the British not like the French; the Greeks not like the Turks. Trying to unite them is as unnatural as mating dogs with cats. In the words of Alan Sked, the founder of the UK Independence Party: 'Making one's own laws and shaping one's own destiny is the normal thing for nations to do. Trying to merge different cultures within an artificial, corporate state is distinctly abnormal. Peoples like to run themselves, which is perfectly natural' (Sked, 1992).

Using words such as 'natural' and 'abnormal', Sked clearly draws on the ideas of the famous nineteenth-century patriots and cultural nationalists, such as Johann Gottfried von Herder, who once claimed:

> Nature brings forth families; the most natural state therefore is also one people, with a national character of its own. A people is as much a plant of nature as is a family. Nothing therefore seems more contradictory to the true end of governments than the endless expansion of states, the wild confusion of races and nations under one sceptre. An empire made up of a hundred peoples and 120 provinces which have been forced together is a monstrosity, not a state-body. (Herder, 1784)

The European Union offers plenty of scope for patriotic Euro-scepticism because, as anybody can see, rather than providing a platform for reconciliation, the union often functions as an arena for national rivalry.

One only has to think of the strife between the UK, Germany and France in the run-up to the Iraq war in 2003. This was not just a question of differing political positions. It was also a patriotic battle between nations. Elements of the British press, for example, accused not only the German and French governments, but the entire German and French nations, of cowardice and ingratitude. These characteristics, it was implied, were typical of German and French national identity. In the EU the British should be careful not to be contaminated by such foreign manners. Another, and continuous, patriotic battle between France and the UK concerns the status of their respective languages. This competition flared up again when the British commissioner, Neil Kinnock, proposed that fewer EU documents be translated into the EU languages. Reactions in France were swift and fierce. Speaking on BBC radio, a correspondent of *Le Monde* declared that such a measure would favour the English language and was therefore tantamount to an Anglo-Saxon plot to take control of Europe. Concerned French officials who declared that language and identity are inextricably linked, backed him. If the EU were to adopt English as its language, its very structure would be affected, for speaking and writing in English would stimulate thinking in English, and this in turn would impose Anglo-Saxon manners on the entire union. In other words, you are what you speak (BBC, 2001; see Bellier, 1999).[1]

That the EU may in fact amplify oppositions between the various national identities is also illustrated by the ideas of the historian Paul Johnson. According to him, modern Europe is a battlefield between the nations of the North (whose identity is determined by rationality, honesty and Protestantism) and the nations of the South (whom Johnson sees as being emotional, dishonest and Catholic). If there must be a European Union, this Euro-sceptic argues, it would be better to have two separate ones: a Northern Union and a Southern Union (Johnson, 1991).

What unites patriotic Euro-sceptics is a dislike not just of each other's nations, but, obviously, also of the entire EU. The bureaucrats of the Union are often described as 'Eurocrats', which in Euro-sceptic jargon denotes a clique of officials who are not only out to enrich themselves, but who also identify unnaturally with 'Europe' rather than with their own nations. In his book *Building Europe*, Chris Shore argues that EU officials increasingly see themselves as de-territorialized civil servants, whose identity is European rather than national. The aim of the Eurocrat, whom Shore dubs '*Homo Europaeus*' (Shore, 2000, p. 138) is to serve Europe rather than to defend the national interest of his or her mother country. Pro-Europeans see *Homo Europaeus* as the positive end-result of human evolution. He is an evolved, modern human being who has left the primitive stages of racism and nationalism behind, thinking instead in supranational, pan-European terms. Being a Euro-sceptic, Chris Shore does not agree with this picture of progress. He, too, reverts to the arguments of Herder and other cultural nationalists, and portrays *Homo Europaeus* as something abnormal; as a degenerate betraying his national and natural origins (Shore, 2000, p. 139).

This situation is comparable to what happened 200–300 years ago, when national identities began to be asserted in Europe. The Eurocrats of those days were the cosmopolitan upper classes, who forged strong connections regardless of national borders or linguistic differences. The whole of Europe was their playground. Language barriers presented no problem (they usually conversed in French) and they pursued – or thought they pursued – common transnational goals in the arts and science. The Euro-sceptics were the middle-class nationalists who argued that these cosmopolitan Europeans were a self-serving elite out of touch with the common people, who were proud of their national identities. These nationalists of the eighteenth, nineteenth and twentieth centuries presented cosmopolitanism as something of a disease. It was seen as unnatural, even unhealthy, to mix freely with outsiders. As was the case in this nationalist discourse, the terms cosmopolitanism and 'elite' are always used disparagingly by present-day Euro-sceptics, who argue that the European Commission in Brussels is controlled by a ruling class who wilfully and at their peril ignore the wishes of the common people (Bellier, 2000).

Patriotic Euro-sceptics, then, are anxious to defend existing national identities, because they are proud of their own nations and because they fear the European blending machine, the domination of other nations and the unnatural intentions of the ruling elite. Another group of Euro-sceptics is equally concerned about national identity in the EU, but not because of feelings of pride or xenophobia. A significant number of Euro-sceptics argue that, for better or worse, the EU members are nation-states – that is, states in which cultural and political identities coincide. Or are generally *perceived* to coincide, because pure nation-states do not, of course, exist in practice. The nation-state, as most of these Euro-sceptics would readily admit, is not necessarily the best model for human coexistence. Nor is it a natural condition that the common people instinctively desire, but which is threatened by a perverse cosmopolitan elite. Such romantic anxieties are not usually the concern of this group of Euro-sceptics. They simply conclude that the nation-state appears to function reasonably well because on the whole it has no legitimation problems. The people of nation states may disagree frequently and strongly with their rulers, but they identify with them nevertheless. The rulers of the nation-state are co-nationals; hence their authority is accepted. The British socialist, Tony Benn, for example, argues that a properly elected, fully empowered European Parliament would not be the answer to Europe's democratic deficit, because the authority of such a parliament would simply not be recognized by the voters. From their national perspectives, these voters would always see this multinational European Parliament as being dominated by foreigners (Tromp, 1995; Helmer, 2002). Tony Benn, and with him many other Euro-sceptics, may be called pragmatic Euro-sceptics.

Unlike patriotic Euro-sceptics, pragmatic Euro-sceptics' concerns about national identity are of a practical nature. What they appear to be saying is: leave well alone. Europe's nation states have evolved over a long period and most are now democracies where the *demos* feel a bond between themselves and their rulers. In many ways, the EU can be considered unique. It is not a federation, it is not a confederation, and it is not just an intergovernmental talking shop. But whatever it is, most would agree that over the years it has increasingly assumed some of the characteristics of a state, or, as many Euro-sceptics would have it, a 'super state'. It has, for example, evolved a centralized structure of authority and is in the process of producing a constitution and an army. Most, however, would also agree that this state does not serve a single, homogenized European nation. According to pragmatic Euro-sceptics this invariably results in all sorts of complications. Lack of identification between the rulers and the ruled allows the authority of the Union to be perceived readily as illegal. Therefore, it is assumed that the Union can never function as a democracy in the sense of yielding power for the people and by the people.

Pragmatic Euro-sceptics do not object to Europeanization because they glorify or venerate existing identities. These are not flag-waving enthusiasts. They object to Europeanization because they see it as an unnecessary and dangerous experiment: 'Don't play with fire' is what Tony Benn and others appear to be saying. A supranational EU, going beyond simple economic co-operation, might yield some benefits, but we cannot be sure. The possible benefits of a 'United States of Europe' do not outweigh the hazard of great civil unrest and a potentially explosive breach of trust between the rulers and the ruled. Referring to recent events in the Balkans or the Soviet Union, these pragmatic Euro-sceptics warn that a violent break-up of the EU is a serious possibility (Sked, 1992).

Summing up, Euro-sceptics who are concerned about national identity may be classified as patriotic or pragmatic. Patriotic Euro-sceptics are concerned about national identity mainly because they are proud of their nations, and the EU, as they see it, threatens their sense of national belonging. Their protests against the Union are often couched in emotive language. Europe is portrayed as a monster devouring their countries. Pragmatic Euro-sceptics aim to conserve the principle of national identity because it forms the basis of a tried and tested system of sovereign nation-states. Patriotic Euro-sceptics seem driven by emotion, while the pragmatic Euro-sceptic appears more rational. Both groups, however, are conservative in nature. Patriotic and pragmatic Euro-sceptics alike wish to maintain the European status quo; preservation is preferred to experimentation and change.

Being concerned with the effects of EU membership, Euro-scepticism is not expressed only in the EU itself, but can also be found in prospective member states, as seen in the situation in Turkey, where the term is used increasingly as the membership negotiations prove to be more and more difficult. Some expect 'a dramatic rise in Euro-scepticism in Turkey in the coming years' (Civitas Research, 2005), but, according to others, the phenomenon has in fact always been there. Only, because of the 'apparent consent among political elites, many Turkish Euro-sceptics were probably hesitant to deplore EU membership'. Consequently 'one could argue that past polling data on EU membership support in Turkey may have overstated the real levels of public support' (Avcı, 2005, p. 133). Having conducted his own poll, Yılmaz concludes that Turks are no strangers to Euro-scepticism, arguing that 'Euro-scepticism in Turkey tends to increase as we move along from modern to traditional life styles, or to put it in more precise terms, from modernized to modernizing strata of the society' (Yılmaz, 2003). And Güneş-Ayata contends that 'since the country signed a treaty with the European Common Market in 1963, there has been no political tendency (right, left, centre, Islamist, nationalist) that has not gone to some degree through a state of Euro-scepticism' (Güneş-Ayata, 2003, p. 205). Concern about national identity, moreover, is an important aspect of Turkish Euro-scepticism, as it is indeed of many debates in 'a country that has particularly high levels of patriotism (Civitas Research, 2005) and can be 'ultra-sensitive about its national identity' (Avcı, 2005), as witness Article 301 of the Turkish Penal Code, which

makes punishable by imprisonment any 'public denigration of Turkishness, the Republic or the Grand National Assembly of Turkey'.

Euro-scepticism and national identity in Turkey

The exact meaning and implications of Euro-scepticism differ according to the national context (Harmsen and Spiering, 2004). As was
argued in the preceding paragraphs, however, certain broad classifica-
tions may be formulated, such as a general distinction between 'hard'
and 'soft', and 'patriotic' and 'pragmatic' Euro-scepticism. Turkey, it
would seem, is no exception to this rule.

Soft Euro-sceptics in the existing member states insist that their
nations should not withdraw, but rather significantly loosen their ties
with the EU. Similar wishes may be heard in Turkey, where it is argued
that a permanent form of 'association status' or 'special relationship'
should be considered as an alternative to full membership (Civitas
Research, 2005). Interestingly, the non-member Turkey may thus
create a precedent that Euro-sceptic member states, such as the UK,
might one day want to follow.

Instances of 'hard Euro-scepticism' are not difficult to find in Turkey.
Public opinion traditionally shows a large majority of Turks favouring
EU membership, but these figures do not tell the whole story. Turkey
may be one of the most Euro-enthusiast countries, but it is also the
country showing the least knowledge about the EU (Güneş-Ayata,
2003, p. 206). This 'shallow consensus' on EU membership (Avcı, 2005,
p. 133) is confirmed by polls showing that the same Turks who support
EU membership are in fact highly critical of many of the changes that
membership will bring (Yılmaz, 2003). As Güneş-Ayata shows, in politics, Turkey has a long and varied history of hard opposition to the
European idea. Some nationalist groups, for example, argue that
'Turkey should give up its blind eyed enthusiasm for Europe and seek
new alliances' (Güneş-Ayata, 2003, p. 212). The Turkish left is generally
positive about EU membership, but there are and have been important
exceptions: 'As early as 1963 the Turkish Labour Party published a
declaration with the heading of "No to the Common Market"' (Güneş-
Ayata, 2003, pp. 212–13). Important sections of the left also approved
of the government's decision to freeze relations with the EU in 1979.
Finally, many labour union leaders co-signed the nationwide advertise-
ment of 7 June 2002 in which it was suggested that Turkey would be
better off outside Europe, as the EU was pursuing the same imperialist
aims that broke up the Ottoman Empire. Turkish Islamists took a hard

Euro-sceptic stance from the start. The shift to a more welcoming attitude in the late 1990s was not so much inspired by Euro-enthusiasm, but by the opportunistic expectation that the liberal policies of the EU might assist devout Muslims to gain more religious rights in Turkey (Kılınç, 2005; Yavuz, 2000).

As in the EU member states, concerns about national identity form an important part of Turkish Euro-scepticism. Here too it is possible to distinguish between patriotic and pragmatic Euro-scepticism. Patriotic pride regarding one's own nation, coupled with a fear of domination by others, is apparent in public opinion, with 50 per cent of respondents fearing that EU membership would lead to a weakening of the national identity (Güneş-Ayata, 2003, p. 207). Moreover, large numbers feel that 'the Europeans' do not 'understand' or 'empathize with Turkey and the Turks' (Yılmaz, 2003, p. 3). In politics, patriotic pride can be found in nationalist, left-wing and Islamist circles. Nationalists have argued that the aim of the EU is not only to weaken Turkey by forcing them to pull out of Cyprus, stunting economic development through the customs union, and by breaking the nation through the ideology of unity in diversity, but also by 'undermining the self-confident Turkish identity and pride, through the false image that Turks are brutal' (Güneş-Ayata, 2003, p. 212). In general, nationalists regard the demands that the EU has imposed on the country, even before starting membership negotiations, as demeaning and an affront to Turkish pride.

In the past, the left frequently likened 'the Europeans' to old-style imperialists and colonialists; today these concerns about national identity are centred mainly on certain sections of 'the National Left', who argue that the customs union and liberalization of the economy will only enslave Turkey to Europe (Güneş-Ayata, 2003, p. 214).[2] Pride about identity, finally, lies at the heart of the Euro-scepticism of Turkish Islamist groups. The idea that Europe as 'a Christian club' is 'the Other', is traditionally strong in these circles, as indeed it is in Turkish public opinion (in 2003, 49 per cent of the population saw the EU as 'a Christian club – Yılmaz, 2003, p. 2). The EU, it is believed by fervent Islamists, was established to prove that the cross is superior to the crescent (Güneş-Ayata, 2003, p. 216), and membership will bring Turkey into an alien Christian–Zionist alliance. Erbakan, leader of the Islamist Welfare party outlawed in 1998, regards 'the application of Turkey for full membership in the EC as treason to our history, civilization, culture, and sovereignty' (Kılınç, 2005, p. 8). A more EU-receptive attitude adopted by certain Islamists since the 1990s is under strong pressure, as some of the 'Copenhagen criteria', through which the EU seeks to effect changes in Turkey, are seen as an affront to Turkish Islamist values. For example, many supporters of the Turkish government were deeply uneasy at the way in which the EU forced the government to back down over its proposals to criminalize adultery (Civitas Research, 2005). Ironically, some 'Europeans' have reminded Turkish Islamists strongly of the identity question, and why they were Euro-sceptics in the first place. The notorious remarks of the former French president, Valéry Giscard d'Estaing, to the effect that Muslim Turkey is not, and cannot, be part of Europe, has once again popularized the image of the EU as a Christian club.[3]

Alongside patriotic Euro-scepticism, pragmatic Euro-scepticism can also be found in Turkey, as in current member states. Sections of 'the National Left' appear to treasure Turkish national identity not in the first place because they are zealous patriots, but because they feel 'the Europeans' will be seen as outsiders, which will eventually hinder rather than help progress. The 'Copenhagen criteria' are not in themselves rejected, but coming from abroad it is feared they might not be accepted as legitimate by the Turkish nation. The solution for Turkey is to distance itself from the EU and to solve its problems within the confines of its own sovereign state (Güneş-Ayata, 2003, p. 214).

Creating a European identity

European institutions and politicians have countered Euro-sceptic concerns about national identity in various ways. First, it is often flatly denied that existing national identities will be affected, let alone threatened, by Europe's ever closer union. Europeanization, if it is taking place at all, only means that the peoples of Europe increasingly accept and celebrate the multicultural, multinational character of the continent. 'Unity in diversity' is the popular slogan that sums up this position of denial. However, next to denial there is defiance. Some Euro-enthusiasts see no harm in promoting a common sense of European identity. A 1992 European Parliament report, for example, states that 'Policies should be developed "to foster a union of the European peoples founded on the consciousness of sharing a common heritage of ideas and values"' (Shore, 2000, p. 25).

So how would one 'foster' this shared European consciousness? According to some, no particular strategy is necessary. They argue that cultural integration, and thus a European identity, will emerge as a by-product of economic integration. This idea is, of course, central to the 'neo-functionalist' theory of integration, which predicts that European unity will emerge through the steady, cumulative effect of small, incremental steps. Harmonization in one area will generate urgency for harmonization in others, and so on. In other words continuous measures of economic integration should inevitably lead towards the desired 'ever-closer union' of the European people. According to this supposition, a European identity will develop more or less automatically, and a continuous spill-over effect will gradually merge individual nation states into a supranational structure.

There is no doubt that the persistent drive towards economic union has helped to foster some sort of European identity. Many millions of Europeans have discarded their national currencies in favour of the euro. They are now handling the same colourful notes showing pictures of supranational symbols such as bridges and archways. A common currency might, indeed, contribute to a common identity. This was assumed by the rulers of the imperial Roman Empire and of the Holy Roman Empire. It was also assumed by the first president of the European Central Bank, who stated 'The euro is far more than a medium of exchange. It is part of the identity of a people. It reflects what they have in common now and in the future' (Duisenberg, 1998).

But what if one is not so sure that a European identity will automatically emerge as a by-product of economic integration? What can be done to carry out the European Parliament's wish to foster a union of European peoples? One way would be to draw attention to non-Europeans (or perceived non-Europeans), so as to highlight what it means to be European. The idea that a collective European identity becomes visible when contrasted with alien identities is, of course, old, going back at least to the Middle Ages when Europeanness was equated with Christendom and set against Islam (Hay, 1957). In the early twentieth century, the spectre of a 'Yellow Peril' was often conjured up in calls for European unity and the defence of a European identity. In a remarkable series of publications on *Panropa*, the German engineer, Herman Sörgel, argued that the 'yellow races' (or 'Asians') were hell-bent on wresting power from the Europeans. Sörgel, like Signor Settembrini in Thomas Mann's 1924 novel *The Magic Mountain*, was convinced that two principles are perpetually at war with one another in the world: the Asiatic principle, which represents tyranny, superstition and rigidity; and the European principle, which embodies freedom, knowledge and progress (Mann, 1967, p. 157). Such blunt instances of contrastive self-definition cannot be found in the history of the EU but a European sense of identity has nevertheless been promoted by contrasting 'us' with 'them'. During the Cold War, the 'East' clearly functioned as the counter-image of the 'real' Europe of the West (Shore, 2002; Bugge, 2000, p. 63), and the ongoing exclusion of Turkey from the EU is at least partly inspired by the fear that the presence of an Islamic member state may complicate the rise of a common European identity. Finally, America has at times been presented as a threat to Europeanness. Some EU reports have called for the protection and promotion of the European identity by heavily restricting the import of American films and television series (Shore, 2000, p. 52).

Another way to meet the European Parliament's wish for a 'union of the European peoples' would be to introduce concrete symbols and a positive ideology of Europeanness. As has often been pointed out, the European national identities that patriotic Euro-sceptics cherish so much are, in fact, comparatively recent 'inventions' (Hobsbawm and Ranger, 1983). If it can be done once, it can be done again. Over the years the EU has formulated various policies to transform nationals actively into Europeans. One is reminded of Rousseau's famous saying, formulated in 1771, that 'every people has, or must have, a character; if it lacks one, we must start by endowing it with one'. His advice to the newly independent Poles was to 'invent' national 'manners' and 'usages'. This would make them 'love their country and give them a natural repugnance to mingle with foreigners' (Rousseau, 1962). To achieve this aim, Rousseau recommended the invention of folk dances. The EU has wisely not explored this avenue. In the 1973 Copenhagen Declaration on European Identity, the then nine members of the European Communities 'decided to define the European Identity', declaring that:

> The attachment to common values and principles, the increasing convergence of attitudes to life, the awareness of having specific interests in common and the determination to take part in the construction of a united Europe, all give the European identity its originality and its own dynamism. (Declaration on European Identity, 1973)

Ten years later, in a 'Solemn Declaration', adopted at the Stuttgart meeting of the European Council, it was suggested that, in the future, cultural co-operation should be pursued 'to affirm the European identity'. Concretely, it was proposed to 'promote a European awareness' by 'intensifying exchanges of experience, particularly among young people' and by 'improving the level of knowledge about other Member States and of information on Europe's history and culture' ('Solemn Declaration on European Union', 1983). Soon afterwards, at their meeting in Fontainebleau, the same Council declared it was 'essential that the Community should respond to the expectations of the people of Europe by adopting measures to strengthen and promote its identity and its image both for its citizens and for the rest of the world' (European Council, 1984). An 'ad-hoc Committee on a People's Europe' was then installed to turn these plans into action. It proposed, among other things, the creation of a European Academy, a European lottery, voluntary work camps for young people ('for the preservation of the heritage, or the restoration of historic buildings'), the annual celebration at schools of 9 May as Europe Day, and, under the heading 'Strengthening of the Community's Image and Identity', the committee recommended that Europe be given an anthem and a flag 'to be used at national and international events' (Report submitted to the Milan European Council, 1985).

But will these or any other top-down policies to create a European identity be successful? The psychologist William Bloom argued that people tend to be extremely protective of their group identity as it provides essential security and psychological well being (Bloom, 1990). For this reason, people do not shift their group identity unless they are literally forced to do so. This is an interesting thought, and it seems to be borne out by the history of national identities. Rousseau's idea that people should be 'endowed' with a national character was in practice often carried out with great force. In the burgeoning European nation-states, minorities were cleansed away; local languages and cultures were stamped out; in programmes of compulsory national education children were (and still are) indoctrinated to accept one approved version of their nation's history and identity. This conclusion – that the changing of group identities is usually a violent affair – is also a major theme in the famous lecture on national identity delivered by the French scholar Ernest Renan in 1882. The peoples of Europe, he claims, did not just develop, but were coerced into nations. The French national identity, for example, by no means just grew over the centuries, nor was it simply 'invented'. It was forced upon the people by their rulers by means of many acts of violence: 'l'unité se fait toujours brutalement' (Renan, 1994).

Obviously, violence is not part of the EU's strategy to construct a common identity. As mentioned above, there have been some overt attempts to highlight differences from non-European out-groups

(Islamists, Asians and Americans) or to introduce nation-building measures, such as a flag or an anthem. These attempts have, however, been few and far between and can hardly be said to be part of a sustained policy or strategy to coerce the peoples of Europe to become one nation. The European flag, the anthem and so on have only symbolic value and people are in no way forced to use them in place of their established symbols of nationhood. In fact, it is quite obvious that very few people know the European anthem, nor do they know when to celebrate Europe Day.

This leads us to a paradox. On the one hand, the efforts of the EU to create a European identity are much too weak to achieve any real effect. As Renan and others have shown, considerable pressure is needed before people change their group identities. On the other hand, the efforts of the EU are just about strong enough to generate a considerable amount of Euro-sceptic reaction in member states and prospective member states alike. Instead of an effective policy instrument, the nation-building ventures of the EU provide cores that foment Euro-sceptic discontent. Just as too small a dose of antibiotics creates super-resistant bugs, so a bit of Europeanization may well strengthen rather than reduce the old European forces of nationalism, assisting the cause of patriotic Euro-sceptics in particular.

Notes

1. The idea that language and identity are closely connected was, of course, another idea popularized by the cultural nationalists mentioned earlier. In his *Addresses to the German Nation* (1806), Johann Fichte, for example, equates a nation with 'a tongue'.
2. 'The National left is a concept first used by Bülent Ecevit ... claiming sensitivity to national interests and the beliefs of the people. The components of the National left include the Confederation of Turkish Labour Unions and some NGOs ... The Democratic Left Party for a very long time was one of the spokespersons of this ideology' (Güneş-Ayata, 2003, p. 214).
3. In November 2002, former French president, Valéry Giscard d'Estaing, claimed in an interview with *Le Monde* that '95 percent of [Turkey's] population is outside Europe. It's a different culture, a different approach, and a different way of life. It is not a European country.' EU membership for Turkey, according to d'Estaing, would mean 'the end of Europe'.

References

Avcı, G. (2005) 'Turkey's EU Politics: What Justifies Reform?', in Helene Sjursen (ed.), *Enlargement in Perspective*, Oslo: Centre for European Studies.

BBC News (2001) ('EU Translation Plan Provokes Protest' (http://news.bbc.co.uk/hi/english/uk_politics/newsid_1490000/1490243.stm).

Bellier, I. (1999) 'European Institutions and Linguistic Diversity: A Problematic Unity', in H. S. Chopra (ed.) *National Identities and Regional Cooperation: Experiences of European Integration and South Asia Perceptions*, New Delhi: Manohar.

Bellier, I. (2000) 'A Europeanized Elite? An Anthropology of European Commission Officials', in Robert Harmsen and Thomas M. Wilson (eds), *Europeanization: Institutions, Identities and Citizenship*, Amsterdam/Atlanta: Rodopi.

Bloom, W. (1990) *Personal Identity, National Identity, and International Relations*, Cambridge University Press.

Bugge, P. (2002) 'Shatter Zones: The Postwar Creation and Re-creation of Europe's East', in Menno Spiering and Michael Wintle (eds), *Ideas of Europe since 1914 – The Legacy of the First World War*, London: Palgrave.

Civitas Research (2005) *Turkey: Growing Concerns about EU Membership* (www.civilitasresearch.org/publications/view_article.cfm?article_id=6, 22 April 2005).

'Declaration on European Identity' (1973) *Bulletin of the European Communities*, vol. 12, pp. 118–22, December.

Duisenberg, W. (1998) 'Statement at the Joint Press Conference Following the ECOFIN Meeting' (http://www.nationalplatform.org/theborg/euspeak.html.)

European Council (1984) 'Conclusions of the Fontainebleau European Council', *Bulletin of the European Communities*, vol. 6, pp. 11–12.

Güneş-Ayata, A. (2003) 'From Euro-scepticism to Turkey-scepticism: Changing Political Attitudes on the European Union in Turkey', *Journal of Southern Europe and the Balkans*, vol. 5, no. 2, pp. 205–22.

Harmsen, R. and Spiering, M. (2004) *Euro-scepticism*, Amsterdam/Atlanta: Rodopi.

Hay, D. (1957) *Europe: The Emergence of an Idea*, Edinburgh: Edinburgh University Press.

Helmer, R. (2002) 'An Evening with Tony Benn' (http://www.rogerhelmer.com/wedgewood.asp).

Herder, J. G. von (1784, 1968) *Materials for the Philosophy of the History of Mankind*, Chicago University Press.

Hobsbawm, E. and Ranger T. (1983) *The Invention of Tradition*, Cambridge University Press.

Johnson, P. (1991) 'Cleansing Europe's Augean Stables', *Sunday Telegraph*, 20 October.

Kılınç, R. (2005) 'Transformative Role of Liberalism in Turkey after 1990s: The Case of Turkish Islamic Groups', Paper delivered at the Seventh Annual Kokkalis Program Graduate Student Workshop, Harvard University, Cambridge, Mass, 3–4 February.

Mann, T. (1967) *The Magic Mountain*, Harmondsworth: Penguin.

Renan, E. (1994) *Qu'est-ce qu'une nation?*, Leiden: Academic Press.

Report submitted to the Milan European Council (1985) *Bulletin of the European Communities*, Supplement 7/85, pp. 18–30.

Rousseau, J.-J. (1962) 'Considérations sur le gouvernement de Pologne', in C. E. Vaughan (ed.), *The Political Writings of Jean-Jacques Rousseau*, Oxford: Basil Blackwell.

Shore, C. (2000) *Building Europe: The Cultural Politics of European Integration*, London: Routledge.

Sked, A. (1992) *Manifesto, UK Independence Party*, London, UKIP.

'Solemn Declaration on European Union' (1983) *Bulletin of the European Communities*, vol. 6, pp. 24–9.

Sörgel, H. (1932) *Atlantropa*, Munich: Piloty & Loehle.

Spiering, M. (2004) 'British Euro-scepticism', in Robert Harmsen and Menno Spiering (eds), *Euro-scepticism*, Amsterdam/Atlanta: Rodopi.

Taggart, P. and Szczerbiak, A. (2002) 'The Party Politics of Euroscepticism in EU Member and Candidate States', Opposing Europe Research Network Working Paper 6 (http://www.sussex.ac.uk/Units/SEI/pdfs wp51.pdf).

Tebbit, N. (1990) 'Fanfare on Being English', *The Field*, May.

Tromp, K. (1995) 'Tony Benn on Europe', unpublished MA thesis, University of Amsterdam.

Voigt, W. (1998) *Atlantropa: Weltbauen am Mittelmeer, ein Architektentraum der Moderne*, Hamburg: Döling & Galitz Verlag.

Wilders, G. (2005) *Nederland Onafhankelijk* (www.groepwilders.nl).

Yavuz, M. H. (2000) 'Cleansing Islam from the Public Sphere', *Journal of International Affairs*, vol. 54, no. 1, pp. 22–42.

Yılmaz, H. (2003) *Indicators of EuroSupportiveness and Euro-scepticism in the Turkish Public Opinion* (http://selene.uab.es/_cs_iuee/catala/obs/dossier_turquia/tk_analisis/eutr_12_2003Yılmaz.pdf).

10
Identity, Interests and Political Culture in Turkey's Accession Negotiations

Levent Kırval

This chapter analyses the potential impact of the political culture differences between Turkey and the EU on the ongoing accession negotiations. It also analyses the ways to include the Turkish model successfully within the embryonic post-national formulation emerging in Europe. To this end, as well as the necessary transformations Turkey has to go through, the steps for a further deepening of European integration, which will also allow the coexistence of different political cultures, is analysed in a comparative perspective.

Turkey is one of the most intriguing EU candidates, as historically it has been the 'other' of the European culture and civilization (see Chapter 8 further on this issue). However, modernization, and to this end westernization (although the two are not always synonymous), have been a major goal of the political elite both in the last centuries of the Ottoman Empire and during the evolution of the modern Turkish Republic. On the whole, creating a secular-democratic state from a predominantly Muslim society has been Turkey's main challenge. These experiences are particularly important, as Turkey is one of the few countries that were relatively successful in harmonizing an Oriental culture with the administrative structures and political culture of the West.

The steps that are gradually being taken in Turkey have led to the formation of an institutionally strong democracy; however, the democratic consolidation did not go far, as the civil society involvement in political life remained limited (Özbudun, 1994). Today, it is still relatively difficult to see a fully-fledged civil society involvement in Turkish political life, as the modernizing elite is still in control of most of the institutional structures. The number of active NGOs is very limited, and participation in political life is generally considered to consist solely of voting in the elections. Moreover, people usually vote for particular parties because of a tradition of doing so among their families, villages or neighbourhoods. Most of the people are generally unaware of the manifestos of the political parties they vote for, and the idea of influencing the political decisions via civil organizations is not satisfactorily developed either. Furthermore, the full participation of women, young people, elderly people, disabled citizens and the different ethnicities of the country to the political processes are also lacking. This inequality in the participation by sections of society in the political processes and involvement in the relevant civil organizations creates problems with regard to the civilization of politics in Turkey (Evin, 1994). Therefore political differences still exist between Turkey and the EU, and these can be considered as important challenges for the ongoing accession negotiations. Moreover, these challenges have not yet been addressed adequately by the West European countries that are interested in bringing Turkey into the family of Europe. Without doubt, this picture has begun to change gradually during the early 2000s. The speeding up of Turkey's European orientation has had a positive effect on the further democratization and civilization of the political regime in the country. However, Turkey is still in the phase of consolidating its democracy, and the ongoing accession negotiations will be an important opportunity for the successful conclusion of this process.

In fact, the different political cultures of the member states and candidate countries also impede the deepening of European integration. For example, for most of the recent members and current candidate countries, the long years of communist rule have resulted in a political culture divergent from that of Western Europe, emphasizing institutional control rather than popular participation. Decades of ethnic conflict and religious clashes in the Balkans encouraged different ideas about individual–state relations in south-eastern Europe. Given the plethora of challenges, the rapid inclusion of citizens in the supranational integration process is also difficult, as the different political cultures of member states, and member and candidate countries, allow for rapid integration at the level of elites. This in turn tends to alienate the masses from the supranational political processes. With the above ideas in mind, below we shall discuss the current state of European integration and the impact of political cultural differences on the further legitimization of the EU. Subsequently, Turkey's political culture and its compatibility with European integration will be examined.

Legitimizing the EU by means of inputs and outputs: flourishing of a European political culture resting on multiculturalism and social policies

A political culture is a distinctive and patterned form of political philosophy consisting of beliefs on how governmental, political and economic life should be pursued. Political cultures create a framework for political change and are generally unique to nations, states, other forms of political structures and societal groups. A political culture differs from political ideology in that people can disagree on an ideology (what the government should do) but still share a common political culture. Some ideologies, however, are so critical of the status quo that they require a fundamental change in the way government is operated, and therefore also embody a different political culture. In general, the political culture of a society is extremely important for the development of democratic governance forms. The compatibility of the existing political culture of a society with the participatory nature of democracy usually determines the success of political change and modernization. Furthermore, the political culture of a society plays an important role in the development of economic governance models. To a large extent, the political culture of a society is decisive for the improvement of a fully competitive market model or the deepening of a welfare state. Consequently, the legitimacy of a regime derives from the match between the political culture and political structures, whereas a mismatch leads to a legitimacy deficit.

By and large, the legitimacy of a political structure is explained under the two main headings within classical political theory. The first camp explains legitimacy with the concept of recognition. Here, the political institution is considered to be legitimate when the individuals living under its authority consider it to be a legitimate body. Hence, there is a belief in legitimacy, and both the individuals and the rulers believe in the legitimacy of the governance mechanisms. The key political thinker in this camp was Max Weber, and he set out a threefold typology distinguishing rational-legal, traditional and charismatic foundations of legitimate authority. Legitimacy, he maintained, could consist of the recognition of efficiency and the rule of law, of continuity with valued past practices, or of the personal qualities of individual leaders. This approach to legitimacy as an empirical, rather than a normative matter, informed much subsequent research. After the Second World War, for example, Gabriel Almond and Sidney Verba used newly developed survey techniques to measure legitimacy in terms of aggregate levels of support for and identification with particular institutions. They attempted to use 'civic propensities' to explain the stability of governments. Almond and Verba's method was groundbreaking for comparative political scientists, who were mainly employed in analysing constitutions at that time. But just reading these legal documents did not prove much explanation for social changes. This was the context in which Almond and Verba's work progressed. In the opening chapter of *The Civic Culture*, Almond and Verba define a civic culture as 'a pluralistic culture based on communication and persuasion, a culture of consensus and diversity, a culture that permitted change but moderated it' (Almond and Verba, 1989, p. 6). For them, Britain and the USA were prime examples of such cultures. Citizens of a civic culture are not actively involved or interested in politics, but they believe that 'the people' are politically powerful. There is just the right mixture of pragmatism and emotional commitment. For Almond and Verba, this type of culture can only develop in certain societies where there is a sufficient level of economic development. This explanation is still used as a general framework for describing political cultures within which democracies and the subsequent legitimate political authorities can flourish.

On the other hand, the second camp explains legitimacy not only as an empirical problem but also as a normative one. The importance of individuals' involvement in politics is underlined, and material conditions are not considered to be fundamental. For example, some centuries ago John Locke argued that the legitimacy of the political institutions derives from the representation of the will of society. Similarly, Rousseau underlined the individual will but argued that this can best be represented within a state structure. However, as the philosophers of classical liberal theory could not foresee a political structure beyond the nation-state and only considered a political model driven by the elites and the state institutions, their offers could not go beyond procedural democracies. With recent discussions about increasing civil society involvement in the political arena, the normative dimension of legitimacy started to become more important. As a result, when we speak of legitimacy today, we begin to mean democratic legitimacy that includes full participation and representation within the political processes.

Undeniably, there are still problems with regard to this type of a democratic transformation at both national and supranational levels in Europe. National identities are still very strong and nation-state institutions do still have some influence on political life, although their area of activity is gradually shrinking. Nevertheless, several recent developments in the EU further increased the discussions of such alternatives. For example, the existing discussions about Turkey's entry to the EU, and the eastern and south-eastern enlargements have forced European countries to consider such inclusive and elastic identity models in advance. Surely, any of these alternatives will not be established on cultural but on political rights. As Jean-Marie Domenach argues, 'European culture does not exist, but there is European cultural space, or being precise, spaces, the limits of which follow neither the common wealth nor any national borders' (Domenach, 1990, p. 7). And these cultural spaces, interwoven with the values of Enlightenment are surely crucial for such a transformation. This is why the continent of Europe can be the testing place of such a post-national alternative and renovation.

However, there are fairly limited discussions on the transformation towards such an inclusive model. With the exception of works by Jürgen Habermas, most of the existing literature is limited, offering participatory political models for both national and supranational levels. Only Habermas's 'communicative action' theory gives us a possibility of establishing bonds in society not with ethnic or cultural ties but through rational discourse between existing differences and without losing our faith in modern institutions.

Classical liberal theory largely follows an elitist conceptualization of democracy. Following more or less the arguments of Mosca, Pareto and Schumpeter, theorists in this tradition equate democracy with regular elections without analysing in detail the social conditions and the state of civil liberties (Grugel, 2002, pp. 72–86). Huntington, for example, sees a system as being democratic as long as the candidates for the political posts run in fair elections (Huntington, 1968, pp. 32–3). Following more or less a Schumpeterian tradition (Schumpeter, 1943), theorists in this camp give extreme importance to the institutions of procedural democracy and argue that going beyond these procedures and permitting more individual participation can even lead to chaos, as governance becomes impossible with a number of diverging voices. Obviously, as a result of this understanding, the civil society involvement in political processes remains an unnecessary and even problematic process.

As well as scholars in the liberal tradition who write on the individual–political structure axis, other liberal thinkers who equate democratization with capitalism also have difficulty in accepting the role of civil society in decision making structures. First, as stated above, here civil society is equated with the market, which makes the definition of a civil society with democracy in the political domains extremely difficult. Moreover, several of these scholars equate democracy with welfare and the basic institutions of capitalism. For example, Seymour Martin Lipset argues that stable democracies can survive only with the development of certain economic and social conditions (Lipset, 1961). For Lipset, various prerequisites must exist to establish a democratic regime, such as welfare, education and urbanization. Again, Almond and Verba argue that without the development of certain conditions that are mainly related to material well-being, democratization cannot take place (Almond and Verba, 1989). Overall, there is an exaggeration of structures for the development of democracy in this group. Democratization arrives as the result of material conditions.

On the other hand, one other group of scholars in the classical liberal theory exaggerates the role of various groups in the democratization processes. Hence the relations between the opponents and the supporters of the regime determine the path of the democratic processes for them. Here, the elites are generally given the most important role in guiding the society (Munck and Skalnik, 1999). For this group of scholars, democratization can take place with powerful groups supporting this transformation. Hence a democratic transformation can only take place from above.

A final group of scholars stresses the importance of legacies for democratization. In particular, the power of political institutions is underlined, and here it is argued that previous state structures can shape the following political developments. In this context, democratization is explained with historical experiences with state structures and the political cultures of societies (Skocpol, 1993).

Starting from the latter, one can say that more or less all the member states and candidate countries share the basic values of European enlightenment. This cannot be explained as a totally shared European culture. In this context, the existence of different legacies within the EU cannot be considered as a great threat to the development of a more inclusive democracy at the supranational level. On the other hand, if we look at the EU from an institutionalist perspective, we can see that most of the tools of procedural democracies are already there, and in this context this prerequisite also exists. Economic differences seem to be one of the most important problems in moving towards a more inclusive democratic model; however, regional policy and structural funds are still important tools to overcome these inequalities. Leaving aside democratization, even the Single Market cannot operate successfully in a totally unbalanced economic structure. Hence, economically speaking, homogenization is an inescapable fact of European integration, and this fulfils the classical liberal theory's prerequisite for democratization.

On the whole, the most important problem seems to be the diverging opinions between different groups in the EU about this type of a transformation. The change in the existing nation-states in the EU towards a more inclusive political model, which acts in harmony with the national civil societies, will hardly change the intergovernmental nature of the Union. Surely, this will still be a positive development for national level governance; however, without the development of a European-level civil society and politics, this type of democratic transformation will not take place at the supranational level. Surely, for such a supranational transformation, individuals should consider the EU also as a political identity. At this point, as long as an attractive citizenship formulation that goes beyond the national level is not offered, and the EU competences remain limited to the area of the Single Market, this transformation would not be possible in the short run. As the nation-states are still the implementers of the policies, increasing the power of the EU institutions will only bring them institutional power in their relations with the national level, but not legitimacy and public support. For the latter to be achieved, an inclusive supranational political identity defined by European civil society, with effective supranational institutions providing social and welfare policies, seem absolutely crucial.

Recently, in the ordinary life of the individuals, the European identity has come to be associated with various emblems and symbols by which the European Commission has sought to influence people with a view to persuade them of the appeal (and the inevitability) of a federal Europe. These include the European anthem, the European passport, the European driving licence, European citizenship, twinning, the European flag and the ubiquitous twelve stars displayed on every project part-funded by the EU: and, above all, the single currency. Yet, these symbols are not enough to increase the legitimacy of the supranational institutions. Besides these symbols, the individuals should also have a feeling of belongingness towards the supranational institutions for the solution of the general legitimacy problem. To this end, democratic participation and social policies seem to be the most important tools to hand.

To provide a genuine democracy, the EU has to balance the input and output legitimacy dimensions, and to this end civil society involvement in the political sphere and the post-national welfare state policies are of utmost importance (Scharpf, 1999). For healthy functioning, civil society should be independent of the state and also from the market. Therefore, this model should be supported by social policies, as the individuals involved cannot reach freedom solely by democratic participation. By combining both democracy and a welfare state, the EU can be a post-national alternative and attain higher levels of legitimacy (Habermas, 2001). Consequently, the different political cultures of Europe can coexist in harmony within such a supranational political model.

For many Europeans the EU is still an elite project that functions without the participation of the individuals and civil society in the decision-making processes. Moreover, the steps that are taken during the historical development of the EU are also considered as decisions of the elites. On the whole, the local and national elections are not run on EU policies today. The winning parties generally get most of the votes because of national or local considerations. Moreover, one cannot talk about EU political parties that aim to get votes in all the member states. This lack of Europe-wide politics hampers the deepening of the EU and keeps it as an intergovernmental structure. If the EU can succeed in increasing the masses' feelings of belonging to the supranational institutions this will increase the political significance of the supranational level. In this context, increasing individual participation in the supranational decision-making mechanisms is crucial. As long as the participation is existent and transparent, the legitimacy of a political regime will hardly be questioned. Here, a supranational political identity that is established on democracy and political rights is essential. Instead of a culture-based definition of Europe, a participatory political identity that is able to include all the ethnic, cultural and religious sub-identities can further the deepening of the EU. But this will not be enough. The EU should also be able to act decisively in the dimension of wealth distribution to become a more important political actor.

Without the development of stronger social and welfare policies at the supranational level, the EU will always lack popular support. Hence the EU's multicultural nature should be supported by a strong social dimension. This new supranational model may exist in harmony with the national and regional levels as long as these governance forms are not defined as conflictual sovereignties. Recent discussions on multilevel governance also support this type of understanding. Within these discussions, the EU is defined as a system in which public power is divided into layers of government, where each layer retains autonomous power and none can claim ultimate power over the others (Christiansen, 1997). Along the same line of thought, Wolfgang Wessels describes the EU as 'a system of complex, multitiered, geographically overlapping structures of governmental and non-governmental elites' (Wessels, 1997). The multilevel governance approach is based on a more pluralistic view of the state as an arena in which different agendas ideas and interests are contested. Similarly, the Hollow State arguments underline the importance of civil society in such new governance forms. Here, the state is presented as a collection of inter-organizational networks made up of governmental and societal actors with no sovereign actor able to steer or regulate them. Citizens can regain control of government through their participation in networks as users and governors (Rhodes, 1996, p. 666). As James Rosenau argues, this passage from centralized government to decentralized governance empowers citizens and makes political forms beyond the nation-state a possibility:

> Given a world where governance is increasingly operative without government, where lines of authority are increasingly more informal than formal, where legitimacy is increasingly marked by ambiguity, citizens are increasingly capable of holding their own by knowing when, where, and how to engage in collective action. (Rosenau, 1992, p. 291)

Hence one can at most say that today, in parallel with the influences of globalization (or glocalization[1]), regionalization and localization, the nation-states have to take into account a number of different political levels. Similarly, the European nation-states are forced to function at international, European, the national and local levels. The local or regional level became particularly important with the decentralization of the state structures and the increasing demands for participation by the masses in recent decades. As a result, unlike the Rousseauian tradition, today's nation-states are forced to look at societies not as indivisible units but as multi-linear mosaics. General will is not considered to be more valuable than individual wills. Today, the political structures are considered as the arenas where the wills of all individuals are represented and are treated equally. Similarly, the EU, being a product of nation-states, cannot escape from following more or less a similar path. Furthermore, the model can be revitalized at the supranational level. With the necessary reforms being undertaken, the EU can transform into a more progressive and elastic 'nation(s)-state'. This new term stands for a novel political model representing democratic participation and social rights; and makes it capable of including different political cultures within it.

With regard to the participation dimension, the existence of a hybrid supranational identity is crucial, as it makes the inclusion of all types of differences to the political model a possibility. To this end, the effects of Turkey's accession to the EU (with regards to the multicultural transformation of the model) will be discussed below. Subsequently, Turkey's future integration to the European social model (the output dimension of EU's legitimization) will be analysed.

Digesting a 'so-called' dissimilar political culture: Turkey's accession to the EU

Being one of the first nations to undertake rapid political, economic and social modernisation in the twentieth century, Turkey also undertook what is perhaps the most difficult transformation of all – the conversion of a traditional society into not only a 'modern' but also a democratic one (Weiker, 1973, p. 22). However, in most of the political surveys about Europe or the Middle East, Turkey tends to be treated generally as the odd man out, receiving only passing attention, or is even omitted entirely. While Turkey always claims the status of a European power, it is usually left out of regional studies of Southeastern or Eastern Europe. In fact, the reasons for this omission are not too hard to find. Since the foundation of the Republic in 1923, Turkey's internal political structures have tended to diverge fairly sharply from those of its Arab neighbours. Even today, the foreign news pages of Turkish newspapers report events in the 'Middle East', on the assumption that Turkey is not a part of it. At the same time, Turkey's political evolution has been clearly distinct from that of its Slav and even 'so-called' European neighbours to the north and west, especially during the long years of the Cold War. As a result, both academics and the practitioners tend to let Turkey fall between the two blocs (Kedourie, 1996, pp. 4–11).

In its attempts to modernize its traditional society following the 1923 Revolution, the new republic worked for converging existing understanding with western ways of governance. Focus was mainly on some symbolic examples from the Ottoman past, and these were eliminated first to show the long-run aims of the revolution. In 1924, both the Caliphate and the Ministry of Islamic Law and Pious Foundations were abolished, and schools and law courts were secularized. All dervish orders, which were widespread in Turkey, were made illegal. In 1926, the Ottoman codification of Islamic law, which was still in force for all personal matters, was replaced by a slightly amended translation of the Swiss Civil Code. At the same time, the French-based Ottoman codes of commercial and penal law were also replaced by composite codes based mainly on the German and Italian models. In 1928, the Arabic alphabet was replaced by Latin script. Nominally, in five years, Turkey had adopted a new constitution within a new set of frontiers; crushed the power of vested interests in established religion; changed completely the system of law, and introduced a new way of writing (Ahmad, 1993, pp. 5–9). With these steps, the revolution succeeded in establishing a set of formal political institutions providing a shell within which a democratic society could be built, and the government effectively created a situation in which most of the older, traditional Turkish political institutions were permanently a part of history (Weiker, 1973, pp. 33–4). The implementation of the new values was not a matter of overnight transformation, but of years of learning and adaptation. Over the course of time much has been learnt and soundly adopted by the masses, and a secular and pluralist culture has gradually been planted. Decades of experience with multi-party democracy has created a relatively responsible electorate, widespread values of pluralism and a distinct mass dislike of oligarchic rule to an unparalleled extent compared to any previous era in Turkish history. The masses have started to assign a positive value to multi-party pluralism, seeming to correlate it with their personal welfare (Özbudun, 2000).

However, historically, one should also accept the relative weakness of Turkish civil society, although it has been developing gradually in recent decades. For the masses, Mustafa Kemal Atatürk's movement in the 1920s was largely seen as an initiative that targeted the independence of the country. The declining Ottoman Empire was already suffering various social and economic problems, and its final defeat in the First World War brought it to a state of total collapse. In this context, Atatürk has been considered as a national hero fighting for the survival of the Turkish nation. Atatürk was also a strong believer in the necessity of modernization, and as the West was the main example at hand in those years, he initiated his reforms one after another with a view to replicating Western ways of governance in the country. This was generally a top-down process, as most of the society did not foresee such a radical transformation taking place immediately. This approach resulted in a modernist 'social engineering' project.

In fact, in the entire major revolution one can see social engineering as an important tool at the service of the centre. In this context, it would be unfair to criticize the Kemalist elite, especially in the years following the revolution, because they followed a similar path. Moreover,

Atatürk and his reformist group were also aware of the fact that a real transformation could only take place through education. This is why, in the first years of the republic, Public Houses (*Halkevleri*) were established all over Turkey, where the teachers and relatively well-educated Turkish intellectuals (army officers, doctors, lawyers and so on) taught on voluntary basis reading and writing using the Latin alphabet, and the basic social and natural sciences to the population at large.. It was expected that, over time, the increasing intellectual accumulation would lead to further civil society involvement in political life. As a result, all citizens would become the guardians of the modern institutions rather than a few elite groups.

However, this was a big challenge because of the long years of experience with the Islamic governance of the Ottoman Empire. For most people, the state was not considered to be an institution working for the good of the people, but rather as a sacred entity for the benefit of which individuals themselves should work. Moreover, various segments of society still considered religion as capable of ruling both the social and political life of the country. As a result of this background, the inclusion of the citizens in the reformation and modernization processes began to become extremely difficult. Moreover, following the death of Atatürk, the state institutions started to put less of an emphasis on education, which in turn began to push the overall transformation to the elite level once more. As stated above, this Rousseauian state understanding can hardly be criticised. At the end of the day, the modern Turkish Republic was the first example of such a transformation in the Oriental world, and moreover, even in the West, one could easily find similar examples in those years. However, this elite-driven process became more problematic in the following years, as new governments started to use the existing strong state institutions for their own political goals, which had nothing to do with the aims of modernization and the emancipation of individuals. Moreover, instead of considering this Rousseauian state as a transition period towards a more democratic and participatory form, following governments tried to strengthen it further against the diverging individual wills. Instead of supporting the flourishing of civil society as the backbone of modernization, various governments that followed opted for the strengthening of the modernist state institutions against the citizens. The Turkish army made a similar mistake, as they considered their main role to be solely protective of the Kemalist institutions, and mainly equated modernization with the existence of these institutional structures. As a result, the tensions between society and the administrative structures began to increase, as the the elites modernization project could not continue to include the masses. This problem began to become more acute, particularly after the 1960s.

Atatürk's reforms created the basic institutional structures for a democratic society to flourish in this direction. However, the social inclusion and civilianization of the regime could not be developed further in the decades that followed. One can find various reasons of this delay: the Second World War in the years after the death of Atatürk; the following Cold War years that led to left- and right-wing confrontation in the 1960s and 1970s; Turkey's more challenging international relations after the Cyprus intervention of 1974 (especially with Greece); the Kurdish problem of the 1980s and 1990s; and the problems of its neighbouring countries in the greater Middle East and Caucasus kept the country as a security-orientated state. This also hampered democratic consolidation, as developing civil society could not support the institutional structures. The increasing frustration caused by the delays in Turkey's integration with the EU also helped the conservative groups in the country to develop counter-arguments against the modernization steps. This also increased the criticisms against the Western ideal that the country followed after the proclamation of the Republic.

However, in recent years, Turkey has begun to experience the civilian transformation of its already existing parliamentary democracy, which has also been affected positively by the speeding up of the EU membership process. After the 1980 military coup, there was a return to a civilian government in 1983. This clearly did not constitute a significant step toward the 'civilianization' of politics, but it was the beginning of a process that would gain momentum later in the decade (Evin, 1994, p. 23). The political dynamics of the 1960s were based on the confrontation between leftist and rightist ideologies. This conflict resulted in armed clashes between the two camps during the 1970s. However, from the 1980s onwards, the political debate centred mainly on policy rather than political ideology. Because of this new political contest, the leftist and rightist movements of the 1970s, which rejected the existing order, left their places to moderate social democratic and centre-right parties (Göle, 1994, p. 213).

Changes in the political map were paralleled in the economic and cultural spheres, especially starting with the economic liberalization policies of Turgut Özal, who became prime minister in 1983. With the shift from the official import substitution policies of the 1960s and 1970s to the new export-orientated economic policy of the 1980s, economic issues started to substitute for classic political debates. The argument of the 'self-sufficiency' of the Turkish Republic was the main rhetoric of the elites for decades. However, this began to change towards a more foreign-orientated approach, and the country started to integrate with the world more speedily after the 1980s. With the relative autonomization of economic activities, political groups and cultural identities, an autonomous societal sphere began to develop, and the focus has shifted increasingly from the state to society. Consequently, the modernizing elites began to lose their power to transform the society from above, and increasingly were replaced by more representative elites (Göle, 1994, p. 178).

Economic diversification has also led to a diversification in cultural discourse and symbols (Davison, 1998). Thus, in addition to the increasing political power of provincial capital, the ideological basis of the Turkish Republic has been challenged by privatization in education and the media, with around 100 television stations supplementing the single state channel that had the monopoly until the mid-1980s. Newspapers and magazines representing a wide spectrum of views have proliferated. Civil society-based associations, including cultural foundations and trade unions, gradually used their votes and economic means to shape the political parties of the centre-right as well as the religious right. These changes have begun to have an important impact on the reformulation of politics in Turkey (Geyikdağı, 1984, p. 65).

At this point, it could seem paradoxical that several decades of economic expansion and political liberalization have provided the grounds for the construction of an Islamic political identity. Yet this form of Islamic identity was detached from its traditional rural environment and rooted in an urban, market-driven context (Meeker, 1997, p. 190). It should also be stressed that the various challenges to the old secular nationalist identity have not led to its disintegration, but rather to an intermingling and adaptation between Islamic and nationalist secular identities (Bilgin, 1997, p. 39). In this type of environment, a political force such as the Justice and Development Party (JDP) could gain more power (contrasting with its predecessor, Erbakan's hard-line Welfare Party) as it moved to the centre of the political spectrum by changing its tone to a broadly moderate right movement in recent years. With the diversification of the elite and the development of new identity discourses constituting a radical challenge to the traditional statist discourse in Turkey, the JDP was able to gain more power and influence the masses. Oddly enough, a diluted communitarian Islamist movement (JDP) started to play a key role in the civilianization of politics in Turkey.

For decades, Turkey saw numerous changes of government and every kind of democratic institutionalization, yet democratization did not go that far. The developments in Turkey suggest that there is a large grey area between the moment of completed democratic transition (institutionalization of democracy) and that of democratic consolidation (Özbudun, 1994). Also, Turkish experience shows how 'excessive institutionalization' may constrain the healthy formation of a liberal democracy (Heper, 1992). The Turkish Republic inherited from the Ottoman Empire a strong and highly bureaucratic state. Indeed, the 'service' structures of the state (the civil service, armed forces, police and law courts) have been so highly institutionalized that this over-development of the state machinery, coupled with the predominance of a 'strong-state tradition' in Turkish political culture, impeded the emerging of more balanced relations between the state and civil society. These developments led to the general de-politicization of Turkish society and increased the loyalty to the state without any critical questioning of its institutions.

But for a real democratic transformation to take place the powers and role of the state must be delineated, allowing an autonomous civil society to flourish. Parties and groups, independent of the state and accountable to the citizens, have to be allowed to represent different views and interests: civilian control has to be established over the military. Importantly, governments must be formed on the basis of a majority, and power should be allowed to alternate peacefully between government and opposition. Turkey started to move in this direction with the help of the accelerating EU membership process and the changes in the international environment in recent years. The Cold War years are now over, there is a rapprochement in Greece–Turkey relations and Turkey's foreign affairs are also in a better shape. As a result of all this, Turkey is no longer solely a security oriented state.

The civilianization of politics in Turkey is also discernable, with the declining role of the army. Although the army still shares its views with society about political issues, they clearly accept the final outcomes of the democratic process. The army will always remain vigilant about the Kemalist institutions in the future, but they also seem satisfied about the civilianization of politics in Turkey, as decades of experience to further strengthen the modernization project also showed them the necessity of this transformation. At the end of the day, it is not only the institutions, but also the people of a country that create a democratic outlook. Turkey is now at the stage of further developing its democratic culture in an already well institutionalized democracy. The individuals who were forced to be free by the elites in the past, are now forcing the institutions to democratize further, as they began to become more emancipated beings. This gradually makes the political culture of Turkey compatible with the flourishing supranational model in Europe.

Concluding remarks: Turkey needs Europe, Europe needs Turkey for politico-cultural transformation

Turkey's accession to the EU is crucial for the transformation of European integration into a healthier form. As a culturally different country, Turkey proves the universality of the Enlightenment values, the basis of the European integration project. Turkey, as an institutional and increasingly civilianized democracy, has a place in the European integration project, and Turkey's inclusion will add extra colour to the already colourful European picture. Moreover, it will be a symbolic example to the development of a hybrid supranational identity. Europeanness is defined on heterogeneity by means of a flexible political model, and a democratic Turkey that functions on pluralism will be the living proof of its success. As an unfinished adventure (Bauman, 2004), which has huge potential to further expand the Enlightenment and modernity, Europe is the only place to disprove Huntington's theses (Huntington, 1998).

Turkey's accession to the EU is crucial for the further multicultural transformation of the supranational political model (see also Chapter 7 on this). This multicultural transformation will contribute to the democratic participation at the EU level, and enhance the civilianization of the supranational political institutions. However, Turkey will surely benefit the most from the accession process, as the country is gradually consolidating its democracy during this journey. On the other hand, Turkey's communitarian and solidaristic system (largely stemming from Kemalist Republicanism and moderate Turkish Islam) will add greatly to the European social model, which this chapter has analysed as being crucial for the deepening of European integration. The different cultures will coexist in harmony within this democratic participation and the social-service-providing nature of the supranational level. This will also be crucial for the reduction of the legitimacy deficit of the European integration. In addition to Turkey transforming itself during this process, towards a fully civilian and institutionally social model, it will improve the input and output dimensions of the deepening European model as well. It is therefore claimed that, for an ideal transformation, Europe and Turkey need each other.

Note

1. 'Glocalization' is a new term that is used to analyse recent developments in international relations. It refers to twin processes whereby, first, institutional/regulatory arrangements shift from the national scale both upwards to a supranational or global scale, and downwards to the scale of the individual body or to local, urban or regional configurations, and, second, economic activities and inter-firm networks are becoming simultaneously more localized/regionalized and transnational (see Swyngedouw, 2004).

References

Ahmad, F. (1993) *The Making of Modern Turkey*, London: Routledge.
Almond, G. and Verba, S. (1989) *The Civic Culture: Political Attitudes and Democracy in Five Nations*, London: Sage.
Apap, J., Carrera, S. and Kirişçi, K. (2004) 'Turkey in the Area of Freedom, Security and Justice', *EU–Turkey Working Papers*; No. 3, Brussels: CEPS.
Bauman, Z. (2004) *Europe: An Unfinished Adventure*, Cambridge: Polity Press.
Bilgin, N. (ed.) (1997) *Republic, Democracy and Identity*, Istanbul: Baglam Press.
Christiansen, T. (1997) 'Reconstructing European Space: From Territorial Politics to Multilevel Governance', in K. E. Jorgensen (ed.), *Reflexive Approaches to European Governance*, London: Macmillan.
Davison, A. (1998) *Secularism and Revivalism in Turkey: A Hermeneutic Reconsideration*, New York, Conn.: Yale University Press.
Derviş, K., Gros, D., Emerson, M. and Ülgen, S. (eds) (2004), *European Transformation of Modern Turkey*, Brussels: CEPS Publications.
Devos, C. (1999) 'The Myth of Globalisation and its Strategic Consequences', *Demokritos*, vol. 1.
Domenach, J. M. (1990) *Europe: le défi culturel*, Paris: La Découverte.
Evin, A. (1994) 'Demilitarisation and Civilianisation of the Regime', in M. Heper and A. Evin (eds), *Politics in the Third Turkish Republic*, Oxford: Westview Press.
Geyikdağı, M. Y. (1984) *Political Parties in Turkey: The Role of Islam*, New York: Prager.
Göle, N. (1994) 'Toward an Autonomization of Politics and Civil Society in Turkey', in M. Heper and A. Evin (eds), *Politics in the Third Turkish Republic*, Oxford: Westview Press.
Grugel, J. (2002) *Democratization: A Critical Introduction*, New York: Palgrave.
Habermas, J. (2001) *The Post-National Constellation: Political Essays*, Cambridge, Mass.: MIT Press.
Heper, M. (1992) 'A Strong State as a Problem for the Consolidation of Democracy: Turkey and Germany Compared', *Comparative Political Studies*, vol. 25.
Huntington, S. (1968) *Political Order in Changing Societies*, New Haven, Conn.: Yale University Press.
Huntington, S. (1998) *The Clash of Civilisations and the Remaking of the World Order*, New York: Simon & Schuster.
Kedourie, S. (ed.) (1996) *Turkey: Identity, Democracy, Politics*, London: Frank Cass.
Leibfreid, S. (1993) 'Towards a European Welfare State?', in C. Jones (ed.), *New Perspectives on the Welfare State in Europe*, London: Routledge.

Lipset, S. M. (1961) *The Political Man*, New York: Anchor Books.

Meeker, M. E. (1997) 'The New Muslim Intellectuals in the Republic of Turkey', in S. Bozdogan and R. Kasaba (eds), *Rethinking Modernity and National Identity in Turkey*, University of Washington Press.

Moravcsik, A. (2002) 'In Defence of the Democratic Deficit: Reassessing Legitimacy in the European Union', *Journal of Common Market Studies*, vol. 40, no. 4, pp. 603–34.

Muller, W. C. and Wright, V. (eds) (1994) 'Reshaping the State in Western Europe: the Limits to Retreat', *West European Politics*, vol. 17, no. 3, pp. 1–11.

Munck, Gerardo L. and Skalnik Leff, Carol (1999) 'Modes of Transition and Democratisation: South America and Eastern Europe in Comparative Perspective' in Lisa Anderson (ed.), *Transitions to Democracy*, New York: Columbia University Press.

Özbudun, E. (1994) 'Constitution Making and Democratic Consolidation in Turkey', in M. Heper and A. Evin (eds), *Politics in the Third Turkish Republic*, Oxford: Westview Press.

Özbudun, E. (2000) *Contemporary Turkish Politics: Challenges to Democratic Consolidation*, London: Lynne Rienner.

Rhodes, R. A. W. (1996) 'The New Governance: Governing Without Government', *Political Studies*, XLIV.

Rosenau, J. N. (1992) 'Citizenship in a Changing Global Order', in J. N. Rosenau et al., *Governance without Government: Order and Change in World Politics*, Cambridge University Press.

Scharpf, F. (1999) *Governing in Europe: Effective and Democratic?*, New York: Oxford University Press.

Schumpeter, J. A. (1943) *Capitalism, Socialism and Democracy*, London: George Allen & Unwin.

Skocpol, Theda (1993) 'Bringing the State Back In: Strategies of Analysis in Current Research', in Peter Evans, Dietrich Rueschemeyer and Theda Skocpol (eds), *Bringing the State Back In*, Cambridge University Press.

Swyngedouw, E. (2004) 'Globalisation or 'Glocalisation'?' Networks, Territories and Rescaling', *Cambridge Review of International Affairs*, vol. 17, no. 1, pp. 25–48.

Wallace, W. (1997) 'The Nation-State: Rescue or Retreat?', in P. Gowan and P. Anderson (eds), *The Question of Europe*, London: Verso.

Weiker, W. F. (1973) *Political Tutelage and Democracy in Turkey: the Free Party and its Aftermath*, Leiden: Brill.

Wessels, W. (1997) 'An Ever Closer Fusion: A Dynamic Macro-political View on Integration Processes', *Journal of Common Market Studies*, vol. 35, no. 2, pp. 267–99.

11
The European Neighbourhood Policy and Turkey
Özgür Ünal Eriş

Designed for the European Union's neighbours with no perspective of full membership, the European Neighbourhood Policy (ENP) can be summarized briefly as a strategy formulated by the EU to promote a generous integration scheme motivating the participants to embark upon reforms with long-term consequences for the EU's own security and stability, and at the same time stave off new accessions. The main aim of this chapter is to explore similarities and differences between the ENP and the security-related arguments in favour of Turkey's membership of the EU. The chapter analyses the potential success or failure of the ENP, while examining factors explaining why Turkey was never considered to be included in the ENP in the first place, and took its shaky place in the future of Europe despite the challenges and problems it brings with it.

The decision to open negotiations with Turkey on 3 October 2005 is considered a historical moment in Turkey–EU relations. However, though the EU's enlargement process has been highly complicated, no previous candidate has had such a divisive impact among member states as Turkey. When the European Council decided to open accession negotiations with Turkey, several arguments began to flow regarding the pros and cons of Turkish EU membership. The following section describes the main feature of the ENP, including the reasons for its launch and its potential success in securing the EU's external stability. Its concentration on security and stability shares some similarities with perhaps the most important supportive argument for Turkey's EU membership. As Helene Sjursen (2002) argues after comparing and contrasting different cases in the EU's enlargement process – that is, Central and Eastern European Countries (CEECs) and Turkey, that,

LIVERPOOL JOHN MOORES UNIVERSITY
LEARNING SERVICES

The main reason for enlarging to Turkey is neither that Turkey must be returned to Europe nor that the EU has a particular duty toward Turkey, but that Turkey is strategically important. That is when a rationale for admitting Turkey is constructed; it is explicitly linked to utility defined in terms of security related geopolitical and geo-strategic arguments. (Sjursen, 2002, p. 504)

The second section deals with Turkey's accession process, concentrating on the main challenges as well as the opportunities it might bring with it.

The third section explores potential links between Turkey's challenges and problems as a potential member of the EU and the ENP as an alternative to full membership. This can also be considered as a brief analysis of an alternative plan for Turkey. It is now commonly argued that if Turkey ever accedes to the EU, it would have a radical impact on European integration, as it will affect the EU's institutions, its role as an international actor, European identity formulations and the future of Europe in a more drastic fashion than the new member states that joined the EU in 2004. Based on these concerns, more recent opposition to the prospect of Turkey's full EU membership has been translated into support for an *alternative* model of advanced EU–Turkey relations, called 'privileged partnership'.[1] This formula, put forward by the opponents of Turkey as an alternative to full EU membership shares some similarities with the main elements of the recently formulated ENP.

In summary, the main contribution of this chapter is the provision of a detailed analysis of the ENP, focusing on its main aims as well as its possible convergence with Turkey's foreign policy goals *vis-à-vis* its own neighbourhood. Furthermore, the chapter discusses how Turkey can help the EU to reach its ENP goals through the security-related assets it can offer. Finally, the chapter examines a scenario in which Turkey becomes a target of the ENP rather than contributing to its further development.

The European Neighbourhood Policy

The eastward enlargement was seen as being probably the principal mode of institutionalizing the process of expanding EU's characteristic of security community and producing security. In particular, the progressive institutionalization of interdependencies has led the EU to follow a *non-conventional* strategy for the creation of security. This was aimed at the promotion of democracy and civil values as 'shared values'; the EU inevitably acted as an anchor of stability and a standard of reference for the democratic reforms in the entire region of Eastern Europe. So enlargement became a mechanism for reducing instability outside the core by reducing the latter's exposure to external threats, and by projecting democratic values and political stability into its periphery.

However, EU integration cannot bring about the ultimate unification and stabilization of Europe, as its enlargement policy creates new divisions *vis-à-vis* non-members on the periphery. These divisions have major socio-political and security implications, and cause political and societal insecurity, within both the core and the periphery (Stefanova, 2005, p. 12). Hard experience since the mid-1990s has shown governments member states of how difficult it is to police the EU's extended land and sea borders. With each new effort to stem the routes of illegal entry, other weak points are discovered. Hence the EU has been confronted by a new challenge, namely the necessity to maintain and strengthen European order by securing the periphery, to extend its zone of peace and prosperity further east and south, and to find incentives to offer these states excluded from future enlargements.

Without an acceptable alternative to membership, the EU was likely to face an increasingly long queue of applications from governments resentful of their exclusion and envious of the privileges that members and potential members have gained. Thus, complementary to enlargement, the Union has developed a network of agreements with these countries. The strategy was named the European Neighbourhood Policy and it was made sure that the ENP provided a framework for the development of new relationships that would not include a perspective of membership. Known also as the Strategy for the Wider Europe, the ENP was launched as a major security-creating strategy, derived from the eastward enlargement of the EU, and an illustration of the security-orientated character of the process.

By opening the prospect of a level of association below the threshold of membership, the new initiative offered a privileged relationship with the EU's neighbours.[2] The EU's approach to its neighbours included seven major incentives (see Box 11.1).[3]

The ENP supplemented, though did not replace, other frameworks for relations with the EU's neighbours, such as the Euro-Mediterranean Partnership (EMP), Partnership and Co-operation Agreements (PCA),

---

Box 11.1   Seven major incentives to join the ENP

- Extension of the internal market and regulatory structures
- Preferential trading relations, market opening and enhanced assistance
- Perspectives for lawful migration and movement of persons
- Intensified co-operation to prevent and combat common security and greater EU political involvement in conflict prevention and crisis management
- Greater efforts to promote human rights, further cultural co-operation and enhance mutual understanding
- Integration into transport, energy and telecommunications networks and the European research area
- New instruments for investment promotion and protection, support for integration into the global trading system and new sources of finance

---

and the TACIS assistance programme. Latent and actual political crises, economic stagnation and rapid population growth have made it necessary for the EU to take a leadership role in the region, if it wants to avoid instability and migration spreading northwards. The ENP can simply be seen as the most recent attempt to do this (Holden, 2005, p. 21).

It remains to be seen how successful this policy will be for the Union. Any assessment of the prospects for a coherent and effective neighbourhood policy must start with reflections on the relative failure of Mediterranean policies. The former External Relations Commissioner, Chris Patten, has noted the wide gap between financial commitments and disbursements under the *mésures d'accompagnement financiers et techniques* (MEDA) programme, caused by both weaknesses in recipient state administrations and a shortage of Commission staff in this field. The presence of Israel and the Palestinian Authority within the Euro-Mediterranean Partnership has also been a major obstacle to progress and multilateral co-operation. Unfortunately, specifically in terms of the EU's Mediterranean partners, the scheduled Action Plans of the ENP are necessarily taking place against the sombre background of the hitherto scarce results of the Euro-Med agreements and the difficulty of moving ahead regionally because of obstacles in the Middle East peace process.

Despite the fact that the ENP is shaping up to be an ambitious cross-pillar and possibly well-funded foreign policy initiative, it is for many reasons difficult to say that it will provide its neighbours with clear benchmarks for reform, and thus enhance security and stability in its surroundings. One of the reasons is that, as this EU geo-political doctrine emerges, tensions caused by the simultaneous dynamics of inclusion and exclusion become very conspicuous, despite the fact that this was quite the opposite of what the EU intended. The fact that EU membership is not an option for these states, which consider themselves to be very close to the EU, becomes a serious problem for the success of the ENP. No matter how frequently EU officials reiterate that they have no intention of re-dividing Europe, irrespective of how many 'partnerships' they offer to non-members, the inevitable consequence of admitting some countries to membership and excluding others is that the prospective outsiders feel frustrated.

The second reason is that, by projecting its own values and standards as 'shared values', the EU goes further away from stabilizing and securitizing its surroundings, and only creates a buffer-zone that shields Core Europe from threats of political and economic destabilization (Scott, 2005, p. 434). Because the EU determines these standards, the process inevitably creates a system of hierarchical relationships, unilateral asymmetrical measures, and top-down communication structures (Schimmelfennig and Sedelmeier, 2004, p. 665). Unfortunately, when the EU follows a strategy geared towards stabilization and integration, with an attempt to bind third countries to the pursuit of internal policy goals without giving them the benefits of full membership, it does not extend its values and tries to enhance the reform processes in these countries, but they only benefit from the latter's political and material problem-solving resources. Thus, when Robert Cooper (2002) refers to Europe's contemporary order as a post-modern *imperial* configuration, in which the EU is the leading representative of a particular type of liberal imperialism, the imperialism of neighbours, he may not be for wrong.

Thus the ENP is, first of all, the result of a process in which the EU was concerned primarily with *itself* – not with the realities on its periphery. The strong dynamics within the EU, which spur the extension of parts of the Union's *acquis communautaire* beyond the circle of member states and towards its immediate neighbourhood, may be conceived of as a form of external governance that satisfies its *own* functional needs conditioned by the resurgence of its fundamental identity as a security community. Hence the ENP is framed unmistakably in terms of the 'interests' of the EU, and is far from providing security to the EU's surroundings. It provides security and welfare to its own citizens as well as contributing to an effective control of its borders.

The European Commission was aware of these deficiencies of the ENP, and its inability to prevent the future borders of the EU from becoming a dividing line between plenty and poverty in Europe, and contributing to the socio-economic development of the EU's neighbours. In this sense, the Commission is one of the architects within the EU that started to stress the impact that Turkey would have on the EU's external relations, especially with its role in improving the ENP, given that it is located in an important geo-political location between Europe, the Middle East and the Caucasus region, which include countries that are also targets of the ENP.

Is Turkish foreign policy compatible with the ENP?

The EU's main objectives in launching the ENP, namely 'developing a zone of prosperity and a friendly neighbourhood; a ring of friends', is largely compatible with Turkey's foreign policy goals regarding its neighbourhood. On the one hand, Turkey is generally active *vis-à-vis* its neighbourhood and, furthermore, increases its commercial, social and cultural links with the Middle East. Turkey strives to eschew the eruption of yet another war and does not find it fits with the country's national interests to have the events in Iraq repeated in Syria or Iran. Laciner (2004) argues that, regarding the Middle East, Turkey has a three-stage integration plan:

- *National integration.* To preserve the national integrity of the region's countries within the framework of democracy, human rights, minority rights, and free market principles.
- *Regional integration.* To improve relations and lines of communication between the region's countries, to be followed by co-operation and regional integration. At this stage, integration could be bilateral or trilateral, and might eventually cover sub-regions and the Middle East as a whole.
- *Global integration.* The Middle East's failure to integrate with the global system has an adverse effect on regional stability as much as on the world at large. Many problems in the post-Cold War era are the result of a lack of integration between the Middle East and the rest of the world. In this respect, one of Turkey's basic objectives is to integrate the Middle East fully with the global system.

On the other hand, Turkey has military links with Israel, and border disputes with Iraq and Syria, and has intervened repeatedly in Iraq's northern Kurdish regions. Furthermore, Turkey's interactions with these regions have so far proved to be insufficiently strong 'to bring the different complexes together into one coherent strategic arena' and thus remain somewhat limited in stabilizing its neighbourhood (Buzan and Wæver, 2003, p. 395).

This might change, as Turkey's approach to the Middle East generally is in line with the EU's ENP and Middle East policies. Thus, being a member of the EU, with a strong focus on 'co-operation to prevent and combat common security threats and involvement in conflict prevention and crisis management' (European Commission, 2003), would also help Turkey accomplish its foreign policy goals regarding these issues. In addition, after the mid-1980s, Turkey has become both a migration 'receiving' and a 'transit' country, and a major country for asylum seekers, for two main reasons. First, political turmoil and regime changes – such as the Iranian revolution in 1979, wars and civil wars, and the numerous conflicts in the Middle East such as the Gulf War and in several countries in Africa – have led to numerous flows of people away from these regions. In addition, since the collapse of the Soviet Union, Turkey has also become a country receiving an increasing number of illegal workers and immigrants from the Balkan countries and former Soviet republics. Conflicts in the Balkans and the Caucasus, such as in Chechnya, have forced refugees, transients and all types of migrants into the country. The fact that Turkey maintains cultural and political links with the Turkic-speaking countries of Central Asia is an additional factor explaining increased migration. Second, Turkey's geographical location between East and West, and South and North, has made the country a *transit zone* for many migrants aiming to reach Western Europe (İçduygu, 2005, p. 332). Thus co-operation with the EU within the area of the ENP, which includes several Central Asian countries with a focus on 'lawful migration and movement of persons and efforts to promote human rights' (European Commission, 2003), would be helpful to Turkey in confronting these problems.

To the extent that the reasoning underlying the establishment of the ENP and Turkish foreign policy motives for its neighbourhood regions converge, it becomes necessary to analyse in detail how Turkey can help the EU to secure its neighbouring regions. This is another way of saying that the Turkish accession to the EU would bring benefits, specifically from a security point of view, and assist in stabilizing the EU's periphery, and thus the EU overall.

Security-related benefits of Turkish accession

By examining the literature on Turkey–EU relations, one can conclude that geo-political and geo-strategic arguments are among the key issues on the agenda of professionals working in this field. Many politicians, policy-makers, academics and bureaucrats share the view that Turkey's geo-political/geo-strategic importance is working to Turkey's advantage. Despite the fact that Turkey's geo-political importance and its role as a security asset for the EU seem to have disappeared after the Cold War, there are three strong arguments that support Turkey's accession to the EU from a security-centric view.

First, with Turkish accession, the EU's borders will extend to Turkey's neighbours – that is, to the Southern Caucasus states of Armenia and Georgia – already included in the ENP – and to Syria, Iran and Iraq, who are very important for the EU as the Middle East has an effect on the EU through oil supply, terrorism, migration, human trafficking, narcotics and arms proliferation. Thus when these countries become *direct* neighbours of the EU, the Union's foreign policy concerns in these regions will inevitably become more pronounced. Because the EU lacks the means to tackle the problems originating in this region, and has been unable to play a role in the Middle East on a par with that of the USA, it will be necessary to improve the ENP so that it will not only be a means of strengthening the EU's internal security (see above) but will also become a strong framework aiming at extending security and stability to the EU's neighbourhood.[4] Unfortunately, it is a fact that, should the EU fail to play its part as a guide, the Middle East might be reshaped adversely, perhaps even in a way that could cause serious harm to the EU. As a country familiar with the region and having a significant role, Turkey could contribute to the EU's regional policies. Turkey's membership will not only strengthen the EU's Mediterranean policy and the ENP, but also increase the EU's potential role as an international actor; something it has always wanted but as yet never accomplished. In addition, the EU would then have to be involved in issues that previously would have been considered as either as essentially bilateral between Turkey and her neighbours, or not seen as a high priority for the EU because they were not related to its internal security. Such issues range from visa and border controls, to diplomatic recognition of Armenia, or disputes over resources such as water. New visa regimes may be unwelcome; not only in third countries but also in Turkey, just as new members such as Poland and Hungary were concerned at creating powerful divisions with neighbouring Ukraine. This is where the ENP will be tested again – whether it is able to create good relations in the region rather than new divisions and barriers. If it really wants to be influential in this region, the EU would inevitably have to adopt stronger positions on these than the ones taken in the ENP, and pay more attention to these countries' demands.

Furthermore, and related to the first argument, Turkey's accession could have an impact on the rest of the Muslim world. At a time when the war on terror is creating global tension and division, and where the 11 September attacks on the USA in 2001 created a backlash experienced by many Muslims worldwide, Turkey's relations with the EU take on a broad geo-political significance. In the highly turbulent security environment of post-11 September, as the only secular Muslim democracy anchored clearly to the West, Turkey represents an antithesis to religious fundamentalism movements in the Middle East, with the capacity to act as a bridge between the Western world and Islamic countries. This has several implications. Turkey could be presented as a 'model' for Islamic countries where, one can argue, it is possible to have a functioning democracy, liberal markets, Western outlook, an open civil society, and tolerance for diversity in a country that has a predominantly Muslim population. This would also have a positive effect on the ENP. If these countries transform themselves from authoritarian regimes to democracy, it will be easier and more productive to deal with them within a similar framework. In addition, after the 11 September attacks, terrorism started to be seen as the major international threat for the twenty-first century. The fact that many terrorists turn out to be of Middle Eastern origin has led to a new demarcation in international politics, as predicted by Samuel Huntington: Western versus Islamist civilization. Thus, inevitably, Turkey's inclusion within the EU would ease some of the tensions between these seemingly different worlds, and would be seen by many, both within the Union and globally, as a signal that the Union is *not* a Christian club but rather a multicultural entity. In this way, the EU can avoid some of the criticisms of the ENP and of its role as a dominant partner that in some way displays post-imperial attitudes *vis-à-vis* its neighbours (Müftüler, 2004, pp. 41–2).[5]

Finally, one of the underlying reasons for the formulation of the ENP in terms of expanding the EU's concept of a security community was to divert the spill-over of security threats coming from the south and south-eastern peripheries of the Europe. Given that Turkey is located at the centre of this turbulent neighbourhood, the effects of any domestic unrest and internal chaos in Turkey is also highly likely to spill over into areas adjacent to it and reach the EU in the end. Thus Turkey as a member of the EU, would be a much better guarantor of stability, especially if this were to be coupled with an effective European Neighbourhood Policy (Diez, 2004, p. 10).

In summary, Turkey's accession to the EU will in the long run help Brussels to realize its hard and soft security interests, in particular because Turkey would help to change the ENP, so that it becomes an instrument providing stability. Significantly, Turkey's membership would accelerate the transformation of the EU into a global security actor, adding to its capability of defining the security parameters in the Greater Middle Eastern region.[6] Therefore, in the current international climate, Turkey's place in the Europe of the future would depend not only upon its democratization and economic stability, but also on the decision that the new Europe will make about its power and role in the post-11 September world.[7]

This is not to suggest that Turkey's path towards full membership is likely to be a smooth and linear process, or that everyone agrees with the view, that Turkey – with its role in a problematic region of the world and the potential improvement of the ENP – is a security asset for the EU. If the future of Europe continues to be an essentially inward-looking integration project, insensitive to broader regional or global issues beyond the EU's immediate borders, and is satisfied with the already accomplished steps of economic integration, democratization and the establishment of peace within its boundaries, the incorporation of a country such as Turkey would come to mean more of a security liability than an asset. Thus the real meaning under the label of 'liability' requires a detailed analysis of the challenges that might arise with Turkey's accession.

Security-related challenges derived from Turkey's accession

In the context of strategic security thinking, Heinz Kramer (2000) has quite rightly argued that the EU

> is still unable to develop a genuine strategic relationship with non-member countries, because it lacks effective common foreign and security policies. This has meant that the EU has never developed a strategic place for Turkey within political conceptions about, for instance, relations with the Middle East, Central Asia, or the Caucasus. The Association Agreement relationship was never regarded as an element of European strategic foreign policy, although it came into existence for such a purpose during the Cold War. Because of its

poor performance in pursuing strategic political interests, the EU has been ambiguous in defining its relationship with Turkey. It was hesitant to declare Turkish membership in the EU as the long term goal of relations and shied away from developing a political strategy toward that end. (Kramer, 2000, p. 177)

The main reason for this would be the tendency of Brussels to view Turkey as more of a security liability than an asset. This has two major implications. First, an important challenge that would stem from Turkey's future inclusion in the EU is regarded as the management of the EU's new borders with Turkey. Turkey's eastern regions are quite poor, and its borders there are difficult to protect, especially in the mountainous regions. Turkey is a transit country to the EU for problem areas such as human trafficking, drugs, illegal immigration and other aspects of organized crime. Managing these security threats will have to be facilitated through closer co-operation both before and after accession, which would constitute an important policy challenge and require significant investment (Güney, 2004, p. 153).[8] In addition, it might be easier to hit European or American targets in Turkey, because of the country's geographical proximity to the troubled areas of the Middle East. This physical accessibility of Turkey to Middle Eastern terrorist groups might increase the security challenges brought by the Turkish accession (Müftüler, 2004, p. 37).[9] Second, Buzan and Wæver (2003) raise some doubts concerning Turkey's role as a bridge to the Middle East – that is, one of the strongest arguments in favour of Turkey's membership. They argue that Turkey has never been a particularly strong player in the Middle East. Furthermore, Turkish–Arab relations have not always been easy, not least given the strong connection between Turkey and Israel. Instead of functioning as a strong bridge, they conclude that Turkey to some extent can act as an interpreter for the EU with the Middle East, but that should not be exaggerated and will vary by country. Turkey has strong interests in the Caucasus, and further east through its relations with the Turkic Republics of Central Asia. Relations with Azerbaijan are particularly strong, which in turn has impacted negatively on Turkey's relations with Armenia. Relations with Georgia, particularly given the closed border with Armenia, are also important to Turkey. However, analysts suggest that Turkey has not been highly successful in developing a strong foreign policy towards this region. Furthermore, they point to the rather equivocal approach to the Caucasus, leading to a lack of a clear strategy. This would not be of much help to the EU in strengthening its position in this region (Hughes, 2004, p. 29).

At a deeper level, the question of Turkish membership has increasingly become the focal point of an internal European debate concerning the nature and trajectory of the European integration process, and raised some fundamental questions concerning the nature of European identity and the very meaning of Europeanization. This means specifically the discussions about the precise boundaries of Europe and the question of where Europe, or at least the EU, ends (Kubicek, 2004, pp. 55–6).

Privileged partnership or Turkey as a target of the ENP

When the European Commission, in its *Progress Report* of October 2004, declared that Turkey was able to meet the political aspects of the Copenhagen criteria and recommended that accession negotiations be opened with Turkey, it almost started a wave of panic among the EU's member states as well as among the European public. Consequently, the December 2004 European Council Summit witnessed heated debates among the EU members over the question of Turkey. The final decision made by the Council was to open accession negotiations on 3 October 2005, based on Article 49 of the Treaty on European Union. However, in its *Recommendation on Turkey* to the European Council, which was issued in October 2004, the Commission stated that 'the pace of the reforms will determine the progress in negotiations'. This validates the argument that negotiations will be particularly long and draining. In addition, there were a number of mechanisms in the form of safety clauses suggested by the Commission to address the fears expressed by the European public.

First, the Commission stated, if there is a standstill in Turkish political reforms it might recommend the suspension of negotiations, in which case the European Council was to decide by qualified majority, rather than unanimously.[10] Second, the Commission's recommendation that the negotiations are 'an open-ended process, the outcome of which cannot be guaranteed', signalled that the negotiations might not ultimately result in Turkey's accession. Related to this was the clause that stated, 'while having full regard to the Copenhagen criteria, including the absorption capacity of the Union, if Turkey is not in a position to assume all the obligations of membership, it must be ensured that Turkey is fully anchored in the European structures through the strongest possible bonds'.[11] Third, there were also recommendations for safety clauses; as the *Negotiation Framework* stated, 'long transitional periods, derogations, specific arrangements or permanent safeguard clauses, i.e., clauses, which are permanently available as a basis for safeguard measures, may be considered'. The most important was a permanent safeguard clause on the freedom of mobility of workers.[12]

The *Commission's Recommendation*, the *Negotiation Framework* and the Council conclusions on Turkey's accession set it apart from the new member states and the Balkan states, which are waiting to join. For example, even though transition periods are usual, a permanent safeguard clause has never appeared in the Commission's previous recommendations for other candidates. Similarly, the Commission's recommendations for other candidates did not refer to the open-ended character of the negotiations. Thus, one could deduce from these documents that the EU is trying to calm down the public and enable accession negotiations to proceed without the EU losing credibility.

These debates are interpreted as a cover-up for the idea of 'privileged partnership' found by European leaders, who do not necessarily want to include Turkey within the EU, but who do not want to lose it either (Öniş, 2006, p. 20). The 'privileged partnership' concept was supported very strongly by the German Christian Democrats under the leadership of Angela Merkel, who campaigned throughout the summer of 2005 as part of the German election campaign for a change in Turkey's membership prospects. She has claimed repeatedly that Turkey should not become a member of the EU, but should instead be offered only a 'privileged partnership'. France's position was affected by the rejection of the EU Constitutional Treaty in the referendum of 29 May 2005. Opponents used Turkey as one of their campaign issues, identifying the country's possible accession as an example of the false path that European enlargement had taken. President Chirac and the French government under Prime Minister Dominique de Villepin attempted to appease French public opinion by diluting French support for Turkey's full membership. Austria is also a staunch advocate of privileged partnership, as support for Turkey's accession in Austrian public opinion is the lowest among EU member states (Grigoriadis, 2006, p. 154).

As has already been stated, even the supporters of this concept cannot define the 'privileged partnership' very clearly. Basically, it is not full membership, but an alternative to full membership, being related to the EU through harmonization of several parts of the acquis with national laws. This is exactly what the EU had designed for the countries included in the ENP: neighbours of the EU closely bonded with the EU through harmonization of several laws, but without any prospect of EU membership. Thus it would not be wrong to say that, when some Europeans offer Turkey 'privileged partnership', they may in fact be offering it a place within the ENP.

Whether Turkey wants this or not is different matter. Turkey, as a country with a large Muslim population, that has aspired to become part of the European Union, has adopted the EU's Copenhagen criteria, and has undergone an extensive political reform process since 1999 with major constitutional changes and packages, which will transform Turkey into a liberal democracy. After the country has struggled for so long with political and economic reforms, and considering the progress it has made in emulating European norms and principles of liberal democracy, Turkey would not be willing to consider a 'privileged partnership' either within or outside the framework of the ENP.

There is already some evidence for the fact that the Turkish foreign policy elite may resent the EU's grouping of Turkey with other countries that have no prospect of EU membership. For example, regarding the inclusion of Turkey in the Euro-Mediterranean Partnership (EMP), the Turkish policy makers' perception was that the Euro-Mediterranean Partnership scheme 'reduces the status of Turkey in the EU into a neighbouring country', and that Turkey cannot be put in the same 'Mediterranean' basket with the Maghreb and Mashreq countries that do not aspire to join the EU. Turkish policy-makers also consider the EU's mid-1990s attempts to transfer funds to Turkey through the EMP not as a goodwill gesture, but as 'political behaviour that proves the EU's exclusionary policy toward Turkey' (Bilgin, 2004, p. 285).

Knowing this, it would not be wrong to conclude that, though it would be willing to work for the improvement of the ENP as a full member, Turkey would never accept a privileged partnership with the EU or any alternative to full EU membership. However, what if the most negative scenario comes about, and the EU halts enlargement: what will be the alternative plan for the Turkish government? It is too early to elaborate on something that might happen no earlier than ten years from now. However, statements so often made by Turkish Prime Minister Erdoğan already give some hints about the potential reaction of Turkey if faced with such behaviour by the EU, 'If the EU rejects Turkey, the Turkish government will rename the "Copenhagen Criteria" as the "Ankara Criteria" and continue with the political and economic reforms it has committed itself to. A government that fails to meet the democratic demands of its citizens, guarantee stability and the security of its country will never be deemed successful.'[13]

Conclusion

This chapter has argued that Turkey's membership of the European Union is one of the major challenges for the EU in the next decade. Turkey's accession will have an impact on the EU's security role, international role and its institutions, as well as on the future of Europe. The process certainly has the potential to cause serious problems on both sides. None the less, none of these problems is insurmountable; compromises can be made; and transition periods can be discussed and agreed upon. However, in reality, the capability and willingness of the EU to accommodate Turkey rests on connotations of Europeanization. If the EU is seriously interested in becoming a genuine global actor with a multicultural orientation, a common identity and coherent foreign policy, influential enough to affect the course of international relations under American unilateralism, then the incorporation of a genuinely democratic Turkey with its geo-political importance and its pivotal status in the Balkans, Caucasus and the Middle East makes sense. If, on the other hand, Europeanization essentially means an inward-orientated integration project, which is insensitive to broader regional or global issues beyond the EU's immediate borders, the incorporation of Turkey would constitute more of a liability (Keyman and Öniş, 2004, p. 28).

The foundation of the ENP is an important sign, showing that the EU is trying to become an influential actor in world politics, and trying to secure its neighbourhood. As already indicated, Turkey is an important asset for the dream of the ENP to come true. For reasons stated throughout this chapter, it is also important for Turkey itself that the ENP will be successful in stabilizing the outer regions of the EU, as these are also Turkey's neighbourhood. With its 'zero problems with neighbours' motto and enthusiasm for active policies to solve the problems in the regions, the current government's motion is the strategy that the EU is seeking. Hence, Turkey's full membership will both present the EU with the opportunity to pursue its strategy, and allow it to increase its leverage through a weighty actor such as Turkey. Furthermore, Turkey's full membership would contribute significantly to solving problems originating in the Middle East, such as terrorism, drug trafficking and illegal migration, which are harmful both for Turkey and the EU.

If the EU really wants to use the Turkish factor to reach the aims of the ENP, it needs to show its good faith in Turkey's accession negotiations. This is not to claim that the EU is obliged to accept Turkey as a member, but rather that Turkey's membership of the EU is advantageous for both Turkey and the EU. One thing is certain, though – Turkey will never accept anything like a 'privileged partnership' or a place in the ENP. It will only agree to help to improve the ENP as a full member, help the EU to become a truly great player in international politics, to unite the European continent once and for all, and to deal with the challenges of the twenty-first century.

Notes

1. What this means remains unclear, as none of its proponents have described it in detail. Instead, the implication is that it would entail a closer strategic, political and economic relationship between the EU and Turkey, which would, however, fall short of full membership in such fields as freedom of movement for Turkish citizens, Turkey's access to EU structural funds, and subsidies from the EU Common Agricultural Policy. This idea has become popular specifically among the leaders of the German Christian Democratic Party.
2. The ENP stretches over a very large geographical area, and encompasses a wide diversity of countries. These countries are Algeria, Armenia, Azerbaijan, Belarus, Egypt, Georgia, Israel, Jordan, Lebanon, Libya, Moldova, Morocco, Palestinian Authority, Tunisia and Ukraine.
3. For details, see the Communication from the Commission to the Council and the European Parliament, entitled *Wider Europe-Neighbourhood: A New Framework for Relations with Our Eastern and Southern Neighbours*, COM (2003) 104 Final, 11 March 2003, Brussels.
4. In a certain sense, the EU already is a neighbour to the Middle East and is affected adversely by problems emerging from that region, but it lacks the weight and decisive role that it wishes to have.
5. Making the case for Turkey's membership, *The Economist* has noted: 'An EU that is open to Turkey should send a message to the troubled Muslim world of today: the West does not consider Islam and democracy incompatible as long as Islam doesn't. Offering a provisional date for the start of negotiations is an historic chance for Europe but also for the Muslim world to show that their two great civilizations are not fated always to clash' (*The Economist*, 7 December 2002).
6. As Christopher Hill (2002) has argued: 'Ultimately the citizens of the European Union have to decide whether they need collectively to be a major actor in world politics like the US, or whether they are willing to settle for an EU near the centre of a network of international processes but without the ability to have a decisive impact on matters affecting security and the pattern of international order. The process of Turkish accession will bring this issue inevitably into the open' (Hill, 2002, p. 104).
7. In the US-led war against Iraq the EU has already realized that its exclusive focus on democracy and economic prosperity without internalizing the importance of security does not constitute a sufficient criterion for making Europe a powerful actor in world politics.

8. But at the same time, once Turkey is a member of the Union, the EU will have more influence over the solution to these issues, as they will then be regarded as internal problems.

9. For Turkey in the EU, one of the major implications of the war in Iraq was probably to illustrate that Turkey is indeed located in a neighbourhood of major instability and, if Turkey ever accedes to the EU as a full member, the European Union will find itself bordering a region of high unpredictability. Thus the war might paradoxically have emphasized the pitfalls of having Turkey as a member of the EU, and make the EU a party to conflicts that might arise in Turkey's neighbourhood (Müftüler, 2004, p. 38).

10. It is for this reason that the Commission was watching very closely all the political developments in Turkey, such as the Orhan Pamuk case and the conference on the Armenian issue.

11. See *Recommendation of the European Commission to the European Council*, October 2004.

12. See *Negotiation Framework for Turkey*, 2005, p. 7.

13. See the Turkish daily newspaper, *Zaman*, 18 June 2005.

References

Aydın, M. (2005) 'Europe's New Region: The Black Sea in the Wider Europe Neighbourhood', *Southeast European and Black Sea Studies*, vol. 5, no. 2, pp. 257–83.

Bilgin, P. (2004) 'A Return to "Civilisational Geopolitics" in the Mediterranean? Changing Geopolitical Images of the European Union and Turkey in the Post-Cold War Era', *Geopolitics*, vol. 9, no. 2, pp. 269–91.

Buzan, B. and Wæver, O. (2003) *Regions and Powers: The Structure of International Security*, Cambridge University Press.

Cooper, R. (2002) 'Why We Still Need Empires', *Observer*, 7 April.

Diez, T. (2004) *Turkey, the EU and Security Complexes Revisited*, Paper prepared for the second Pan-European Conference, 24–26 June, Bologna.

Economist, The (2002) 'Turkey Belongs in Europe', 7 December.

European Commission (2003) *Communication from the Commission to the Council and the European Parliament on European Neighbourhood Policy*, 11 March.

European Commission (2004) *Recommendation on Turkey from the European Commission to the European Council*, October.

European Commission (2005) *Negotiation Framework for Turkey*, June.

Grigoriadis, I. (2006) 'Turkey's Accession to the European Union: Debating the Most Difficult Enlargement Ever', *SAIS Review*, vol. 26, no. 1, pp. 147–160.

Güney, A. (2004) 'On Turkey's Inclusion in EU Enlargement: An Asset or a Liability?', *Perceptions*, vol. 9, no. 3, Autumn pp. 135–155.

Hill, C. (2002) 'The Geopolitical Implications of EU Enlargement', in Jan Zielonka (ed.), *Europe Unbound: Enlarging and Reshaping the Boundaries of the European Union*, London: Routledge.

Holden, P. (2005) 'Partnership Lost? The EU's Mediterranean Aid Programmes', *Mediterranean Politics*, vol. 10, no. 1, pp. 19–37.

Hughes, K. (2004) 'Turkey and the European Union: Just Another Enlargement?', A Friends of Europe working paper prepared on the occasion of 'Turkey's EU End-game?' for the European Policy Summit of 17 June.

İçduygu, A. (2005) 'Turkey: The Demographic and Economic Dimension of Migration', in Phillippe Fragues (ed.), *Mediterranean 2005 Report*, Florence: European University Institute.

Keyman, F. and Aydın, S. (2004) *European Integration and the Transformation of Turkish Democracy*, EU–Turkey Working Papers, Brussels: Centre for European Policy Studies.

Keyman, F. and Öniş, Z. (2004) 'Helsinki, Copenhagen and Beyond: Challenges to the New Europe and the Turkish State', in Mehmet Uğur and Nergis Canefe (eds), *Turkey and European Integration: Prospects and Issues in the Post-Helsinki Era*, London: Routledge.

Kramer, H. (2000) A *Changing Turkey: The Challenge to Europe and the United States*, Washington DC: Brookings Institution.

Kubicek, P. (2004) 'Turkey's Place in the "New Europe"', *Perceptions*, vol. 9, no. 3, Autumn pp. 45–56.

Laçiner, S. (2004) 'Turkey's EU Membership's Possible Impacts on the Middle East', *Journal of Turkish Weekly*, 15 December.

Müftüler Baç, M. (2004) 'Turkey's Accession to the European Union: Institutional and Security Challenges', *Perceptions*, vol. 9, no. 3, Autumn, pp. 29–44.

Müftüler Baç, M. (2005) 'Turkey's Political Reforms and the Impact of the European Union', *South European Society and Politics*, vol. 10, no. 1, pp. 17–31.

Müftüler Baç, M. (2006) *Turkey's Accession to the European Union: Bridging the Divide between the EU governments and the European Public*, Paper prepared for the ISA Annual Convention, 21–26 March, San Diego.

Öniş, Z. (2004) 'Turkish Modernisation and Challenges for the New Europe', *Perceptions*, vol. 9, no. 3, Autumn pp. 5–28.

Öniş, Z. (2006) *Turkey's Encounters with the New Europe: Multiple Transformation, Inherent Dilemmas and the Challenges Ahead*, Paper prepared for the Conference on Europeanization, 10 May, Athens.

Schimmelfennig, F. and Sedelmeier, U. (2004) 'Governance by conditionality: EU Rule Transfer to the Candidate Countries of Central and Eastern Europe', *Journal of European Public Policy*, vol. 11, no. 4, pp. 669–87.

Scott, J. W. (2005) 'The EU and "Wider Europe": Toward an Alternative Geopolitics of Regional Co-operation?', *Geopolitics*, vol. 10, pp. 429–54.

Sjursen, H. (2002) 'Why Expand? The Question of Legitimacy and Justification in the EU's Enlargement Policy', *Journal of Common Market Studies*, vol. 40, no. 3.

Stefanova, B. (2005) 'The European Union as a Security Actor: Security Provision through Enlargement', *World Affairs*, Fall, pp. 51–67.

Conclusion and Perspectives: Whither Turkey's Accession?

Knud Erik Jørgensen and Esra LaGro

Negotiations on Turkey's accession to the EU have begun in an obviously unfavourable environment. They have been launched at a time when more states have acceded than the EU can currently cope with. The present time is also characterized by EU citizens who have become alienated and therefore question the *raison d'être* of the EU. Politicians who prioritize domestic politics often use the EU project as a scapegoat. One outcome of this *domestic politics first* trend has been the negative results of referenda on the Constitutional Treaty in France and in the Netherlands. It is therefore uncontroversial to claim that the debate on the future of Europe is far from over, but rather has only just begun. In this fashion, the negotiations on Turkey's accession have been greeted by their share of the unfavourable environment. Thus, everything indicates that Turkey's accession will not be an easy process. Domestic political concerns on both sides will shadow negotiations on each and every chapter of the *acquis*, and political issues, interwoven with economic and socio-cultural factors, will create further complexity. Taking into account that the negotiations are based on unequal positions and the EU politics of conditionality, the accession process may go on for years. The outcome will remain unclear until the very end, possibly with referenda in some EU member states on Turkey's accession. On the other hand, after more than forty years of being an associate member of the EU, negotiations on Turkey's accession are at last under way.

When reflecting on the accession process, there are many issues to be taken into account. In this context, we outline the main issues. Negotiations will be influenced strongly by individual member states' governments, and their domestic political concerns will largely determine the member states' positions. For Turkey, this means fighting a

221

political and cultural rearguard battle on every imaginable platform within the EU member states. Thus Turkey's main priority will not only be alignment with the *acquis*, but also to enhance political dialogue with every member state while at the same time, of course, pursuing its own foreign policy interests. The negotiations will be highly political in the sense that no matter the subject matter being negotiated technically, the closing of all chapters will be a political decision. The rift over the closing of the Science and Research chapter of the *acquis* has indicated a possible future pattern as well as the recent suspension of eight chapters in December 2006. In order to stall the process, the EU or some of its member states will try to dwell on the Cyprus issue, and even if the Cyprus issue is resolved there will be other issues – for example, the Armenian genocide issue (see debates in the European Parliament). Presumably, other issues will also arise. Hence negotiations will be determined by the degree to which the Turkish government is ready to make political concessions. Consequently, it is potentially misleading to claim that negotiations will be purely technical among unequal parties. The Turkish government is not ready to surrender its principles, and is ready to cut off negotiations if pushed too far on what it regards as sensitive issues. Erdoğan's government got what it wanted in terms of initiating negotiations, and elections are planned. At the same time, public support for the EU process is decreasing day by day. This trend is significant, because the really crucial battle will be fought in domestic Turkish politics. Put differently, the entire accession process is characterized by multiple dimensions, and progress on each dimension depends on the political agendas of the EU member states. However, the most crucial dimension concerns intergovernmental relations between Turkey and the individual EU member states.

Socio-cultural dimensions

The dimension of socio-cultural issues is very important, and the core of the politics of accession negotiations is markedly influenced by the way Turkish key actors interpret the political culture of Western Europe. This concept is in turn influenced by Turkey's own political culture and derived foreign policy priorities. Hence political culture constitutes one of the most important obstacles in the accession process. Whenever a political issue is discussed, political reflections or understandings seem bound to be different in Turkey compared to Western Europe. This is one of the prime factors explaining the crisis-prone relationship. Political culture is thus very important at the intergovernmental level. In Chapter 7, Pulat Tacar discussed the cultural and socio-psychological effects of the EU accession process on Turkey, from a political perspective. He argued that governance of diversity is crucially important, and in this respect pointed to the relevance of Turkey's legacy to the EU. He also highlighted similarities and differences pertaining to political culture and policy priorities between Turkey and the EU member states, particularly France. Finally, he maintained that the accession process should be considered as a two-way learning process and emphasized that the EU also has a lot to learn from Turkey.

It has been Turkey's historical fate to function as Europe's unifying 'other', and it is still easy to target it as the 'other', thereby contributing to the self-definition of Europe. The issue of religion, as it is often debated, only allows the EU to contradict itself, as it claims to represent universal or European values and inclusiveness, among other things. In this framework, it should be remembered that Turkey is a secular state in which the majority of the population has Islam as their faith. Concerning secularism, Turkey is more like France than any neighbouring country in the Middle East. In Chapter 8, Nedret Kuran-Burçoğlu presented a socio-cultural critique of the accession process, emphasizing the evolution of the historical images of Turks in Europe with a view to providing a perspective for both the present and the future. She pointed out that while the Turks were almost always 'the other' of Europe, there were times in the course of history when they were seen as a role model in terms of lifestyle and other cultural aspects. In the context of the accession negotiations, one key question is how long the Turk will continue to be considered as 'the other' of Europe? A second question is how to overcome negative images, embedded down the centuries in Europe? A third question is whether Turkey's contributions to the formation of a European identity could be used in a positive sense for the future. According to Kuran-Burçoğlu, the answer lies in the cultivation of socio-cultural aspects of cohabitation as well as in the current transformation of the European identity. Moreover, if the *unity in diversity* discourse continues to be a key term in the EU's public philosophy, the EU should be able to accommodate different cultures within a single Europolity.

Euro-scepticism is a phenomenon known in both present and potentially new member states. For both Turkey and the EU, this issue seems to have the potential to become increasingly important in the years to come. For the present, the EU has responded by means of the Laeken agenda on legitimacy, and the issue of a democratic deficit has also been addressed. In order to sustain the future of the EU, policy-makers realize increasingly that younger generations should be able to identify themselves with the EU. For the Turkish government, Euro-scepticism is already a major concern, not least when recent opinion polls show that the initial overwhelming support for membership has decreased faster than was envisaged. This problem may be overcome through systematic information campaigns by both sides, but this is not enough. It should also be noted that the engagement between Turkey and the EU established through negotiations is not an unconditional devotion on the part of the Turkish public *per se*, which will eventually be clear to both EU and Turkish politicians who demand endless concessions or overdo domestic populism. In the case of some Turkish politicians, the EU process is used for internal legitimization of political power and existence, a strategy that might backfire. In Chapter 9, Menno Spiering discussed the significance of Euro-scepticism in the context of present attempts at identity formation within the EU, and claimed that Europeanization and Euro-scepticism represent a paradox for the EU. While the process of Europeanization can create an impetus towards sustaining a common European identity – currently only embedded in symbols such as the EU flag, its anthem and so on – an overdose of these efforts might prove to be counter-productive and give a strong boost to Euro-sceptics. Hence a prudent balance in terms of Europeanization should be the aim in both current and future EU member states.

Perhaps among the significant questions to ask in the context of socio-cultural factors is how processes of collective EU identity formation will influence the accession process? Answers to this question may provide some clues for the prospects for the accession negotiations. Levent Kırval argued in Chapter 10 that the accession of a culturally different country such as Turkey might in fact sustain the founding pillars of the EU, which are basically the Enlightenment values. Moreover, he claimed that the entry of Turkey as a full member would sustain the hybrid supranational identity formation in the EU, leading to a transformation of a multicultural EU model. Turkey's entry to the EU would be the most significant indication of disproving Huntington but it would also be a win–win case for both sides.

The dimension of economics

In order to catch up with the EU economically, Turkey has to resolve several crucially important issues. In Chapter 5, Esra LaGro argued that the accession process alone was not sufficient to solve the inherent structural problems of a middle-income developing country such as Turkey. She offered five conclusions. First, the stability of the Turkish economy should be sustained in order eventually to fully accommodate the Maastricht criteria. She stated that she believes the current IMF conditionality is likely to be replaced by an EU conditionality, therefore stability would not be a problem for the future of accession negotiations. Second, she suggested that Turkey should immediately begin to engage in the Lisbon criteria and make them an indispensable part of its economic reform process and overall governance. This, in turn, will require two important political priorities: (i) the making of a genuine industrial policy, and (ii) a national Lisbon programme – simulating the process already going on within the EU – with a view to enhancing the competitiveness of the Turkish economy. Third, she concluded that both Turkey and the EU should increase investment in the education and training of Turkey's young and dynamic population. Such initiatives should be taken in order to offset problems in the future caused by an ageing EU population and the free movement of the Turkish workforce in the single market. In this fashion, she claimed that economics could be turned into a window of opportunity for both sides. Fourth, she pointed out that much-debated issues, such as the agricultural policy, regional disparities and reforming economic governance in Turkey, are more likely to be Turkish rather than EU concerns. Finally, she concluded that the large part of the costs of the accession process will most probably be paid by Turkey. This implies that debates on the costs of Turkish membership are likely to be based on mere speculation, given the fact also that by the time Turkey becomes a member, the EU budget is unlikely to offer any significant financial contribution to Turkey. Thus the important issue will be to determine how the costs of accession can be divided evenly within Turkey. It is LaGro's overall conclusion that a sound industrial policy is a *sine quo non* for the future of accession negotiations, and it should therefore be among Turkey's political priorities.

In Chapter 6, Erol Katırcıoğlu challenged conventional liberal wisdom, particularly the notion of a free market economy in the context of developing countries. He argued that the unquestioned merits of globalization and free market economy by international organizations such as the IMF and the World Bank, as well as by the Turkish public, pose problems for a developing country such as Turkey. If Turkey wants to catch up with the developed countries, the country needs to solve its problems through a well-designed industrial policy, entailing the participation of all relevant actors, and cutting off the almost institutionalized rent-seeking behaviour between the state and the market, though also with more participation, transparency and democracy. He also suggested a model to that end.

Political dimensions

For the EU, the Turkish accession process means, among other things, that the EU institutions and governance structures will be under constant pressure from the member states, therefore there is an urgent need to optimize in this context. The EU evolves through learning-by-doing, and the cumulative experience of previous accessions will undoubtedly shape the methodology of the EU in the case of Turkey and other future candidate countries. Thus not only the adoption but also the implementation of the EU *acquis* will be imperative. This will take a lot of time and effort, which could stall the process endlessly.

Turkey may potentially learn from the experiences of new member states, particularly Poland. In Chapter 2, An Schrijvers discussed the experience of Poland with a special emphasis on problems that Turkey might face during the accession negotiations. Schrijvers pointed to certain similarities with Turkey, in particular concerning the economic structure. Furthermore, she outlined the negotiation strategies of the Polish team, and emphasized that the unequal nature of the negotiations makes it crucially important for candidate states to find allies, be they the European Commission or specific member states. In order to avoid problems arising from the negotiation process, the Turkish government should establish a well-functioning and accountable national EU-policy co-ordination structure.

The much-stretched EU conditionality as an EU foreign policy tool is also likely to be counter-productive in the case of Turkey. Although the fulfilment of requirements from the Copenhagen criteria and the related democratization process in Turkey as well as human rights reforms, are a remarkable success, there is still a great deal to be done in order to enhance these reforms. The European Council has emphasized that compliance with these criteria will be observed until the very end of the accession process, so continued efforts will be a constant during the years to come. However, even if Turkey complies fully with the Copenhagen criteria, other preconditions might be introduced – for example, Lisbon conditionality as emphasized by LaGro in Chapter 5, on the economic dimension of the accession process.

From a scholarly perspective, the meaning of the term 'Europeanization' is relatively clear and an entire literature has been created on
the basis of this meaning. In the context of enlargement, the term has
been invoked to describe processes of adjustment to EU standards by
candidate states. From a (Turkish) political perspective, the term
Europeanization has certain negative connotations and politically
undesirable implications. The accession process is often presented as an
uneven and unequal process. The image is that Turkey has to adopt the
entire *acquis* and comply with the Copenhagen criteria, while the EU is
the *demandeur*, defining the rules of the game and judging whether
preconditions have been met. Kenneth Dyson rejected this image vig-
orously, emphasizing that an accession process *de facto* is a process of
mutual adjustment. In other words, the EU cannot possibly include
Turkey as a member without changing itself significantly. The acceptance of Turkey as a candidate state implies automatically an acknow-
ledgment of a demanding and complex reform of the EU. However,
this mutual process of adjustment does not imply a negotiated
outcome. If Turkish observers believe otherwise, they are bound to be
surprised, and possibly disappointed and frustrated. From a Turkish
perspective, the EU accession process is perceived as merely a new
phase, or a continuation of the long-term modernization or Westernization process launched in the 1920s, constituting one of the founding pillars of the Turkish Republic. For Turkey, the EU anchor is not a
general alignment and it might be problematic to accept it as such. In
any case, the accession process will only survive if Turkish citizens continue to identify accession with this fundamental and constitutive
choice. Hence the employment of the scholarly, neutral term triggers,
in a Turkish context, for better or worse, a range of connotations. Some
regard the term as being superficial, and others prefer not to use it at
all, and coin alternatives terms such as Euro-transformation, and claim
that the EU process is only a sub-set of the total modernization/
Westernization process in Turkey. In Chapter 3, Kenneth Dyson discussed accession as a two-way process. On the one hand, it is asymmetrical – that is, directed towards the adoption of the EU *acquis*, while on
the other, the changing nature of the EU brings unpredictable developments and thus choices to be made for the accession process. The two-
way process is characterized by several challenges. The length of the
negotiations is bound to imply repeated problems domestically and at
the EU level. Finally, Europe is currently searching its own soul and

identity, and Turkey will undoubtedly face difficulties as a result of this process.

In Chapter 4, E. Fuat Keyman and Senem Aydın Düzgit argued that the problem of democratic consolidation continues to be a problem in Turkey–EU relations, despite the obviously accelerated reform process implemented to date. However, the deeper the relationship becomes the more likely it is that the democratic consolidation will turn out to be a success. The outcome of the accession negotiations should be based on the will and ability of Turkey to fulfil the necessary conditions, but not on the country geography or religion. The EU's search for an identity should not be imposed on Turkey, and to use vague benchmarks for a candidate state while disregarding them for existing member states is to stretch the Copenhagen conditionality too far. The norms of universality and impartiality, the understanding of the Copenhagen criteria as embedded in the idea of democratic consolidation, and the ways of thinking about the process of implementing the Copenhagen criteria, together constitute what can be called a principle of fairness and objectivity. In this respect, the EU also has a choice to make.

The European Neighbourhood Policy (ENP) is important in two fundamentally different ways. On the one hand, it is important to explore the compatibility between the objectives and means of the ENP and Turkish foreign policy, respectively. While in particular the means seem to be different, Chapter 11 argued that the ENP can only succeed with the inclusion of Turkey as a full member of the EU. In turn, this would help the EU to become a genuine global player, improve the future of Europe in terms of security, and enhance its role in international institutions. In general, the chapter argues that Turkish accession would have a great deal to offer. On the other hand, the idea of a possible future 'privileged partnership' as an alternative to membership does not make Turkey a part of the ENP but rather a target of the policy. The chapter argued that the idea of a privileged partnership pertains to turning a blind eye to the present situation within the EU itself, and is very much a product of populism and domestic politics in certain member states. Turkey is in some ways already a privileged partner of the EU and probably could not be privileged any further. This concept of partnership is therefore devoid of any serious meaning. Currently, Turkey does not take this idea seriously and will not do so in the foreseeable future. None the less, the evolution of this idea can be used as a kind of benchmark to measure the domestic political climate in the EU member states.

Prospects of a difficult encounter

Keeping the above-mentioned issues in mind, it is possible to think about the prospect of the difficult encounter between Turkey and the EU in terms of four scenarios.

In the first scenario, the negotiation process will end successfully, and Turkey will accede to the EU in fifteen to twenty years' time. Hence, Turkey and the EU will evolve in a way that overcomes existing difficulties and will be able to turn the process into a mutually beneficial and progressive encounter. This scenario finds support in several think tank studies and reports that summarized events between 1999 and 2007. Furthermore, several factors speak in favour of this scenario. Though the highly political nature of accession negotiations implies the encountering of obstacles in every chapter, these will eventually be overcome. The governance of the accession process by the Turkish governing elite will be crucially important for achieving such an outcome, and what has been learned from previous experiences would be helpful in this regard. Much hinges on choices made by the Turkish government with regard to the Copenhagen criteria, and economic development problems as a middle-income country. The scenario assumes that the principle of 'fairness and objectivity' will prevail when the EU makes its definitive decision concerning Turkey's membership. Finally, the scenario emphasizes that the interaction on both sides will be able to offset the negative cultural perceptions and socio-psychological constraints currently characterizing significant parts of both Turkish and EU civil society.

In this context, a balance sheet for gains and losses arising from Turkish full membership of the EU is put forward in detail in all the above-mentioned studies. According to the overall content of the discussions pertaining to the first scenario, it is possible to say that the potential benefits outweigh the losses. There are several points to be mentioned in this respect. First, Turkish membership will help to clarify what Europe really is or is not, at least socio-culturally if nothing else. Clearly the definition of Europe is a mental and social construct, and the century we live in demands a more progressive approach which passes beyond traditional outlook and discourse in this sense. The peoples of Europe need a more modern logic with which to identify themselves, since the past logic of the EU no longer provides pay-offs for the new generations of citizens. Moreover, if the EU wishes to assert itself as a system of values, then Turkey's membership will only enhance and consolidate these values, thus transforming the EU into a cultural global leader whose values and credibility are firmly followed rather than largely questioned.

Second, on the political front, Turkish full membership will be a kind of litmus test for the future political existence of the EU. Clearly, the EU needs to reshape its governance structures in order to sustain the proper functioning of the EU, and this will in fact be completed long before Turkey can become a member. If, on the contrary, the EU continues to be crisis-prone in the way it is at the time of writing, and if domestic populism prevails in individual member states, the Turkish membership will be the last problem the EU wants to think about. Therefore, 'othering' Turkey is clearly not a solution to the problems of the EU, and it never will be. The formation of a political identity in the EU, the differences in political culture among the member states, the adverse effects of globalization *vis-à-vis* different segments of societies, the foreign policy outlook, and the internal/external security issues are among some of the leading problems that the EU needs to resolve. In fact, viewed from this perspective, the accession process of Turkey could accelerate the speed of reforms in the EU, as it will in Turkey. In this sense, those who take the accession negotiations as a one-way 'given' process, and argue constantly about specific details of Turkey's 'to-do' list could perhaps reconsider their position. Consequently, the trade-off between Europeanization and Euro-scepticim can also be solved in this way on the part of the EU. Moreover, the EU's global and local security solutions are clearly linked to Turkish full membership, as well as the success and credibility of relevant EU policies. Last, but not least, on the economic front, the size and population of Turkey will not be as important as it seems within the EU, as is suggested by many in Europe. The free movement of workers would be an asset by the time of Turkish membership if the EU and Turkey alike invest in the education of young people in Turkey. It will be Turkey that has to pay the total bill for accession, and considering the way the EU budget deals are evolving, Turkey will probably be paying the EU by the time it becomes a full member, considering that membership will take fifteen to twenty years and perhaps more. Therefore, there is no need to have any fears about Turkey's share *vis-à-vis* EU funds. In terms of the energy needs of Europe, Turkey is an important strategic partner, and Turkey as an EU member will undoubtedly be more beneficial than a non-member Turkey. Finally, these outlined discussions provide a summary for the first scenario as to pros and cons discussions of Turkish membership. One thing is definite in all these discussions: there is always another side to the coin, as Kenneth Dyson put forward in his chapter. Moreover, at the time of writing (that is, one year after the start of negotiations) the outlook suggests that the more concessions the EU asks for outside the general framework of negotiations, the less they will gain politically in the end, not least because the current public support in Turkey is down to 32 per cent (from an initial 70 per cent) a year after the start of negotiations, and this aspect certainly speaks for itself. Thus a positive outcome is a possible scenario, given that both sides 'read' each other well, and that accession is taken as a two-way mutual adjustment process.

According to the second scenario, an unexpected major external shock, such as that of 11 September 2001, would change all the currently known balances. Political necessity would cause Turkey to become a member of the EU much sooner than expected, possibly with a temporary ban on the free movement of persons and so on. This scenario is in line with the often articulated possibility of disproving Huntington's famous *Clash of Civilizations* hypothesis through Turkish full membership.

In the third scenario, Turkey would be anchored successfully to the EU reform process, and therefore develop positively. However, the Turkish population eventually prove unwilling to join the EU. As demonstrated by recent opinion polls, Euro-scepticism has been rising in Turkey. In the absence of a prudent balance about the level of Europeanization, Euro-scepticism is likely to grow. Finally, the costs related to accession and inflicted on Turkey will also contribute towards making this a likely scenario.

Finally, the fourth scenario emphasizes problems on the EU side that essentially it is unable to solve. On the issue of Turkey's accession, domestic political concerns in the EU member states will prevail, and an alternative to membership will be sought, possibly in the form of a so-called privileged partnership. Though the concept is currently devoid of any meaning, it could perhaps be 'filled' with meaning corresponding to the political preferences of most EU member states. Such an outcome would be totally unacceptable for Turkey, and the EU has a great deal to lose. Basically, the scenario depends on how the EU will define itself as 'a genuinely global actor with a multi-cultural orientation, a common identity, and a coherent foreign policy influential enough in affecting the course of international relations under American unilateralism' as was argued in Chapter 11.

In summary, we have presented the main features of the accession negotiations, which provide a sound background for assessing the prospects of this difficult encounter. The encounter is already difficult and complex, encompassing political, economic and socio-cultural dimensions, and the four scenarios demonstrate that there are several possible outcomes. It remains to be seen whether Turkey and the EU will evolve in a way that overcomes existing difficulties, and thus turn the process into a mutually progressive and optimal encounter as well as a sustainable partnership.

Index